CW00687495

# The Essence of Scholasticism

# THE ESSENCE OF SCHOLASTICISM
## Abhidharmahṛdaya. T1550

*Revised edition with a completely new introduction*

Includes bibliographical references, concordances, index of Sanskrit terms, Chinese Sanskrit-English glossary.

Charles Willemen

MOTILAL BANARSIDASS PUBLISHERS
PRIVATE LIMITED • DELHI

*First Indian Edition: Delhi, 2006*
*Originally published as* ***The Essence of Metaphysics*** *from Brussels:*
*Institut Belge des Hautes Etudes Bouddhiques, Serie Etudes et Textes 4, 1975.*



ISBN: 81-208-3094-6

MOTILAL BANARSIDASS
41 U.A. Bungalow Road, Jawahar Nagar, Delhi 110 007
8 Mahalaxmi Chamber, 22 Bhulabhai Desai Road, Mumbai 400 026
203 Royapettah High Road, Mylapore, Chennai 600 004
236, 9th Main III Block, Jayanagar, Bangalore 560 011
Sanas Plaza, 1302 Baji Rao Road, Pune 411 002
8 Camac Street, Kolkata 700 017
Ashok Rajpath, Patna 800 004
Chowk, Varanasi 221 001

PRINTED IN INDIA
BY JAINENDRA PRAKASH JAIN AT SHRI JAINENDRA PRESS,
A-45 NARAINA, PHASE-I, NEW DELHI 110 028
AND PUBLISHED BY NARENDRA PRAKASH JAIN FOR
MOTILAL BANARSIDASS PUBLISHERS PRIVATE LIMITED,
BUNGALOW ROAD, DELHI 110 007

Ignarus homo ludens
Hoc dedico negotium
Abhidharmae Cor
Erasmi Desiderii memoriae
Stultitiae Laudis auctoris

# *Contents*

# ABBREVIATIONS

| | |
|---|---|
| AH | *Abhidharmahṛdaya* T. 1550. |
| AH2 | *Abhidharmahṛdaya* T. 1551. |
| MAH | *Miśrakābhidharmahṛdaya* T. 1552. |
| CH | *Chusanzangjiji* 出三藏记集 T. 2145, by Fajing 法经, 594 CE. |
| G | *Gaosengzhuan* 高僧传 T. 2059, by Huijiao 慧皎, ca.530 CE. |
| JA | *Journal Asiatique.* |
| JPTS | *Journal of the Pāli Text Society.* |
| | Kaiyuan *Kaiyuanshijiaolu*开元释教录 T. 2154, by Zhisheng 智升,730 CE. |
| L | *Lidaisanbaoji* 历代三宝 T. 2034, by Fei Changfang 费长房, 597 CE. |
| Ms. | Chinese manuscript of the *Abhidharmahṛdaya*, found in Dunhuang.<br>L.Giles, *Descriptive Catalogue* nr. 4336 (Stein 6659), p. 127.<br>E.g. Ms. XXVIII 12: Giles nr. 4336, p. 28 of the photographical reproduction (British Library), line 12. |
| N | *Datangneidianlu* 大唐内典录T. 2149, by Daoxuan 道宣 , 664 CE. |
| T. | *Taishō Shinshū Daizōkyō*大正新修大藏经, ed. J.Takakusu and K.Watanabe. |
| WZKS | *Wiener Zeitschrift für die Kunde Sűdasiens.* |
| WZKSO | *Wiener Zeitschrift für die Kunde Sűd-und Ostasiens.* |
| Xű | *Xűgaosengzhuan* 续高僧传 T. 2060, by Daoxuan 道宣 , ca. 660 CE. |

| | |
|---|---|
| Zh | *Zhongjinglu* 众经录 T. 2146, by Fajing 法经, 594 CE. |
| ZDMG | *Zeitschrift der Deutschen Morgenländischen Gesellschaft.* |
| Zhenyuan | *Zhenyuanxindingshijiaomulu* 贞元新定释教目录 T. 2157, by Yuanzhao 圆照, 799-800 CE. |

E.g. Kaiyuan 527c: T. 2154, Vol. 55, p. 527, third column.

# Preface

Since my study of the Chinese *Abhidharmahṛdaya* in 1975, our knowledge of Sarvāstivāda literature has significantly increased. We now know that the Gāndhāran cultural area is the area from where Buddhism traveled to China, and ultimately to Japan. Although I was fully aware of that fact in 1975, our knowledge has advanced, and many questions have been raised and solved. But much is still hypothetical. This nevertheless has the advantage of being able to explain seemingly unrelated events. The process of trial and error, action and reaction, will advance our knowledge.

A new edition of the *Hṛdaya* became increasingly necessary. Not my translation of the text itself has changed much, but the introduction had to be completely rewritten. The Chinese text is still based on the Japanese edition *TaishÙ* 1550, pp.809a-833b (numbers in the translation refer to these pages and columns), but the interpretation is new, and I have clearly identified the 250 stanzas. To do this, I have used a Dunhuang manuscript and I have paid more attention to the variant readings, especially of the so-called three editions, i.e. *Sixi* or *Huzhou* edition, *Puning* edition, and *Yongle* edition. As the work was prepared in Shanghai, simplified characters are used.

Charles Willemen
Numata Chair of Buddhist Studies
University of Calgary

Shanghai, February 19, 2004

# INTRODUCTION

In the *Taishō* edition we have three texts which may be called *Abhidharmahṛdaya*, Heart or Essence of Scholasticism:

1. T. 1550: 阿毘昙心 *Abhidharmahṛdaya* 论 *Śāstra*, *Epitanxinlun*, 4 vols., by Bhadanta Fasheng 法胜, Dharmaśreṣṭhin, translated in Taiyuan 太元 16, 391 CE, by Sengqietipo 僧伽提婆, Saṃghadeva and Huiyuan 慧远 on Mount Lu 庐, during the Eastern Jin 东晋.
2. T. 1551: 阿毘昙心 *Abhidharmahṛdaya* 论经, *Epitanxinlunjing*, 6 vols., a commentary by Bhadanta Youboshanduo 优波扇多, Upaśānta, on Dharmaśreṣṭhin's work, translated in 563 CE, i.e. Heqing 和清 2 of the Northern Qi 北齐, by Nuoliantiyeshe 那连提耶舍 Narendrayaśas.
3. T. 1552: 杂阿毘昙心 *Miśrakābhidharmahṛdaya* 论 *Śāstra*, *Zaepitanxinlun*, 11 vols., by Bhadanta Fajiu 法救, Dharmatrāta, translated in Yuanjia 元嘉 11-12, 434-435 CE, of the Liu Song 刘宋, by Sengqiebamo 僧伽跋摩 Saṃghavarman, and others.

At present, these three texts do not exist in any language other than Chinese.

### Dharmaśreṣṭhin and his Work

Bhadanta Fasheng, Dharmaśreṣṭhin, probably wrote his *Hṛdaya* in the first century BCE in Bactria. The language used was most probably a Gāndhārī Prākrit, written in Kharoṣṭhī script. The title of his work is given in Qing Jixiang's 庆吉祥 Catalogue *Zhiyuanlu* 至元录 (1285-1287) as *Epidaluomo* 阿毗达啰麻

*heluodaya* 诃啰怛牙 [1]. It is mentioned there that a Tibetan version existed at the time, but this text is unknown today. The name of the author, Dharmaśreṣṭhin[2], has often been given as Dharmaśrī[3], but the Japanese usually follow Ono Genmyō[4] and call him Dharmaśreṣṭhin. It is noteworthy that abhidharma may be interpreted as 'excellent', *śreṣṭha, sheng* 胜*, dharma, fa* 法. There is a Tanmoshili 昙摩尸梨 mentioned in the *Chuyao* 出曜 *Udāna*,经 *jing*[5], a work of Bhadanta Dharmatrāta, Dārṣṭāntika and one of the four masters of the *Mahāvibhāṣā* (second century CE). So, on the one hand Dharmaśreṣṭhin must have preceded the *Mahāvibhāṣā*, while on the other hand his life must be situated after the Yuezhi 月支 came to Bactria around 130 BCE[6], because he is a Tokharian from the area of the river Vakṣu, Fuzhu 缚蠋, as Puguang 普光 and Fabao 法宝 inform us[7].

---

[1] *Zhiyuan Fabaokantongzonglu* 至元法宝勘同总录, in *Taishō* edition *Shōwa Hōbō Sōmokuroku* 昭和法寶總目錄, Vol. 2, pp. 232a.

[2] Willemen 1998, pp. 83-84.

[3] T. Kimura, *Abidatsumaron no Kenkyū* 阿毘達摩論の研究, Tōkyō 1922, pp. 261 and p. 271, was the first to call him Dharmaśrī. However, when this study was re-edited in his complete works, *Zenshū* 全集 IV, Tōkyō 1974, pp. 222, we read Dharmaśreṣṭhin.
Also P. Pelliot, "Les stances d'introduction de l' Abhidharmahṛdayaśāstra de Dharmatrāta", *J.A.* 217, 1930, pp. 267 note 1, prefers Dharmaśrī. In books in western languages after P. Pelliot we usually read Dharmaśrī, e.g. Lin Li-kouang, 1949, pp. 49; Frauwallner 1971, pp.71.

[4] Ono Genmyō 1999, pp. 37.
Akanuma Chizen 1967, pp. 166, argues that the name should be Dharmaśreṣṭhin because of the final *di* 帝 in the transcription Damoshilidi 达摩尸利帝. He refers to CH 89b, the list of Sarvāstivāda patriarchs, where this is translated as Fasheng 法胜. See also G 345b.

[5] T. 212 pp. 643a. The stanzas of this text form the *Udānavarga*, Collection of *Udānas*, as we know it. See: Willemen 1978, pp. XV-XVIII

[6] Lamotte 1988, pp. 450 .

[7] Puguang's *Jüshelunji* 俱舍轮记, T. 1821 pp. 11c; Fabao's *Jüshelunshu* 俱舍论疏, T. 1822 pp. 469a.
Litvinsky B.A. 1999, pp. 121, 147, 178, 182, 432. The Vakṣu is a river upstream of the Oxus River. Tukhāra or Tokharistan is today's northern Afghanistan and southern Uzbekistan and Tajikistan. It is northern Bactria, with such centres as Balkh, Termez, and Qunduz. See also: Li Rongxi 1996,

Daoyan 道梴 in his preface to Buddhavarman's translation of the *Abhidharmavibhāṣā*, a commentary on Kātyāyanīputra's *Abhidharma* by the five hundred arhats[8], places Dharmaśreṣthin before the *Aṣṭagrantha*[9]. Erich Frauwallner finds this a distinct possibility, considering the contents of Dharmaśreṣthin's work[10]. So we can go back to a period before the *Mahāvibhāṣā*, before the *Aṣṭagrantha* (1st century BCE, most probably). In his preface to the *Miśrakābhidharmahṛdaya*, Jiaojing 焦镜 [11] says that Dharmaśreṣthin wrote his *Hṛdaya* during the Qin-Han period, i.e. between 221 BCE and 220 CE. In his *Gaosengzhuan* 高僧传 Huijiao 慧皎[12] informs us that the Central Asian (Xiyu 西 域) monk Dharmakāla[13], who arrived in Luoyang during the Jiaping 嘉平 era of the Wei 魏(249-253), had seen Dharmaśreṣthin's work when he was young, twenty-five years old. Jizang 吉藏 (549-623), of Parthian descent, places Dharmaśreṣthin later than the (*Mahā*)*vibhāṣā*[14]. The anonymous preface to the *Miśraka*°,

---

pp. 31. It is the area south of the Iron Gate, north of the Great Snow Mountains, west of the Pāmir Range, and east of Persia.

[8] T. 1546 pp. 1b and 41.5a. See also CH pp. 74a. This Chinese *Vibhāṣā* was completed in 439 CE. This may be a Gandhāran adaptation of the Kāśmīra *Vibhāṣā* views. See Cox C., in Willemen 1998b, pp. 173 note 107.

[9] Willemen 1998, pp. 86.

[10] Frauwallner 1971, pp. 72, pp. 102, etc.

[11] CH 74bc, for Jiaojing's preface.

[12] G 324c-325a. See also L56b.

[13] In 250 CE Dharmakāla introduced the Mahāsāṃghika *Prātimokṣa*, *Sengqijieben* 僧祇戒本, in Luoyang. Shortly afterwards, in 252, the Sogdian (Kang 康, Samarkand) Saṃghavarman translated the Dharmaguptaka *Karmavācanā*, *Tanwudebuzajiemo* 昙无德 部杂羯磨 T. 1432. The Parthian Dharmasatya, Tandi 昙谛, made another version of this same work in 254, i.e. 羯磨 *Jiemo* T. 1433. These are the earliest known vinaya texts in China. See E. Zürcher 1972, pp. 55-56 and pp. 338 note 168; Lü Cheng 1979, pp. 305. The versions of the *Karmavācanā* text as seen in the *Taishō* edition, most probably are later redactions, influenced by T. 1428, *Dharmaguptakavinaya*. See Hirakawa Akira, *Ritsuzō no Kenkyū* 律藏の研究, Tōkyō, 1970, Sankibō Busshorin, pp. 202-218, 252-253.

[14] In his *Bailunshu* 百论疏 T. 1827, pp. 233b, Jizang places Dharmaśreṣthin 800 years after Buddha's nirvāṇa. In his *Sanlunxuanyi* 三论玄义 T. 1852, p. 2b-c, he says that arhat Dharmaśreṣthin lived more than 700 years after the nirvāṇa, and that he selected 250 stanzas for his work from the *Vibhāṣā*, as

translated by Īśvara and Guṇavarman, completed in 431, but lost[15], places Dharmaśreṣṭhin several hundred years after the *nirvāṇa*. Taking into account that Dharmaśreṣṭhin is mentioned in the *Chuyaojing* of the *Dārṣṭāntika* Dharmatrāta, and according to the evidence produced by Erich Frauwallner in his studies of the Abhidharma, Dharmaśreṣṭhin may have lived in the first century BCE.

## The Chinese Hṛdaya T1550

Dharmaśreṣṭhin compiled 250 stanzas and called his work *Abhidharmahṛdaya.*[16] In Sengyou's 僧祐 catalogue there are two prefaces to a text called *Abhidharmahṛdaya.*[17] One is anonymous, written after the death of Dao'an 道安 (312-385),[18] and the other is by Huiyuan 慧远 (334-416). Huiyuan took part in the bringing out of the final version of Saṃghadeva's text in 391, made on Mount Lu. This text is T. 1550.

The anonymous preface informs us that Dao'an asked Kumārabuddhi[19] in Chang'an to bring out the *Hṛdaya*. But

---

this work was too extensive. These remarks, made by a very influential source in East Asia, are responsible for the erroneous late date of Dharmaśreṣṭhin as given by some authors, e.g. Ono Genmyō 1999, p. 37. Was Jizang counting back from his own time when he placed Dharmaśreṣṭhin? Jizang, T. 1852 pp.26, also says that Dharmatrāta, author of the *Miśraka*°, lived in a period up to 1.000 years after Buddha.

[15] CH 74b. The text itself was already lost early 6th century. See CH 12b.

[16] CH 72c (Huiyuan) and 74b (Jiaojing).

[17] CH, ed. in 515 CE, 72bc.

[18] The date 391 is mentioned. Ren Jiyu 1985, pp. 192, supposes this is a first preface by Huiyuan.

[19] Jiumoluoba (scil. fo) ti 鳩摩啰跋(佛)提. The name is translated as *Tongjue* 童觉. So the second part is °*buddhi*, not °*bhadra*. Kumārabuddhi was a man who had occupied an important clerical position, scil. *purohita*, in the anterior (*qianbu* 前部) area of Turfan, Jūshi 车师, i.e. in Gaochang 高昌. On the occasion of a visit to the temple of his late master Fo Tudeng 佛图澄 in Ye 邺 in 382, Dao'an had asked Kumārabuddhi to bring out a translation of Vasubhadra's (Posubatuo 婆素跋陀, translated *Shixian* 世贤) *Collection from the Four Āgamas*, *Si'ehanmuchao* 四阿含暮抄, T. 1505. It seems that

Kumārabuddhi was not up to the task. His knowledge of Chinese was insufficient. The preface also says that Saṃghadeva brought out the final translation in 391 in the Nanshan 南山 Monastery in Xűnyang 浔阳. Huiyuan took an active part in the bringing out of this text.

**Gautama Saṃghadeva.**

Saṃghadeva was a monk from Jibin 罽宾 [20], i.e. northwestern India. His work shows that he was from the Gandhāran cultural area of Jibin, maybe even from its westernmost part, Bactria, and not from Kāśmīra. He arrived in Chang'an during the reign of emperor Fu Jian 符坚 of the Former Qin 秦, in the year Jianyuan 建元 19, i.e. 383. The aged Dao'an was still alive and witnessed the arrival of many monks from the Gandhāran cultural area in Chang'an during the years 380-385. Among them there was Saṃghabhadra. He translated the *Vibhāṣā*, *Biposhalun* 鞞婆沙论, of Shituopanni 尸陀槃尼 Śītapāṇi (?), in 383, with the help of the Tokharian Dharmanandin, of Buddharakṣa, and others, i.e. T. 1547 [21]. This was a commentary on an *Aṣṭagrantha* of Kātyāyanīputra. Dao'an wrote a preface. Dao'an mentions that this text actually explains the four *āgamas*. One may remember that this Sarvāstivāda text belongs to the Sautrāntikas. Saṃghabhadra brought out the text known as *Āryavasumitrasaṃgītiśāstra* [22], *Zunpoxűmipusasuojilun* 尊婆须蜜菩薩所集论, T. 1549, in 384, with the collaboration of

---

the use of the unexpected character ba 跋 in °*buddhi* comes from the second part of Vasubhadra's name. A revised T. 1505 may be T. 1506. See Ren Jiyu 1985, pp. 192-193, pp. 615-616; Châo, Thích Thiên 1999, pp. 85-88; Zürcher 1972, pp. 202 and pp. 408 note 73.

[20] Willemen 2001, pp. 167.
For an outline of Saṃghadeva's life and work: You Xia 1982, pp. 29-31.

[21] Saṃghabhadra, Sengqiebadeng 僧伽跋澄. See Ren Jiyu 1985, pp. 185-188.

[22] Vasumitra is one of the four masters of the *Mahāvibhāṣā*, author of the *Prakaraṇapāda* (T. 1541), of the *Samayabhedoparacanacakra* (T. 2033). Hirakawa Akira 1993, pp. 136, distinguishes at least two different Vasumitras, but Lü Cheng 1979b, pp. 53, says there is just one Vasumitra. See also Lamotte 1988, pp. 529-530.

Dharmanandin, Saṃghadeva, Zhu Fonian 竺佛念, and others. Dao'an also witnessed the arrival of Dharmanandin[23] in 384. He was an *Āgama* specialist, and he was asked to bring out the *Madhyamāgama* and the *Ekottarikāgama*. He also started the translation of the *Sanfadulụn* 三法度论, sometimes Sanskritized as *Tridharmakaśāstra*. T.1506 is the version by Saṃghadeva. Dharmanandin's translations apparently needed to be revised. Saṃghadeva soon started translating the *Aṣṭagrantha* in 383, but this text was revised by himself in Luoyang, where he stayed for four or five years after the fall of Fu Jian in 385. The text was finally completed in 390, after Dharmapriya had arrived in China with a section about causes and conditions, which Saṃghadeva had forgotten[24]. This text is Kātyāyanīputra's *Aṣṭagrantha*, T. 1543 *Epitanbajiandulun* 阿毘昙八犍度论, the main text of the Gandhārans, probably written in Gāndhārī and Kharoṣṭhī, in the late first century BCE[25]. In the second century CE this text was rewritten in Sanskrit, and called *Jñānaprasthāna*. It was considered to be the corpus of the new Kāśmīra so-called orthodoxy, upon which the *Mahāvibhāṣā* was written[26]. While in Luoyang with Fahe 法和, the companion of the late Dao'an, Saṃghadeva revised earlier translations, such as the *Aṣṭagrantha* T. 1543, and the *Vibhāṣā* T. 1547 in fourteen volumes. This last text was also called *Zaepitanpiposha* 杂阿毘昙毘婆沙[27]. The western Sarvāstivādins, a very heterogeneous group, seem to

[23] Ren Jiyu 1985, pp. 188-189.

[24] Ren Jiyu 1985, p. 190; Cox C., in Willemen 1998b, pp. 222 note 250; Lü Cheng 1979, pp. 67.

[25] Willemen 1998, pp. 86. Kātyāyanīputra seems to have been the compiler, the transmitter, rather than the author.

[26] Xuanzang's 玄奘 T. 1544 *Epidamofazhilun* 阿毘达磨发智论, and T. 1545 *Epidamodapiposhalun* 阿毘达磨大毘婆沙论.

[27] Ren Jiyu 1985, pp. 185.
Sengyou, CH pp. 10b, seems to say that an alternative title may be *Zaepitanxin* 杂阿毘昙心, i.e. *Hṛdaya*. Huijiao, G pp.328c, mentions a *Hṛdaya* in the Life of Dharmanandin, translated at the request of Dao'an in Chang'an. Sengyou does not mention this. It may be remembered that Dharmanandin took part in Saṃghabhadra's *Vibhāṣā* T. 1547 in Chang'an. However, it is possible that Saṃghadeva took part in the translation of a *Hṛdaya*, already in Chang'an.

have had more than one *Vibhāṣā* on the *Aṣṭagrantha*. Even after the *Mahāvibhāṣā* they seem to have continued this tradition, but now adapting their views to the Kāśmīra so-called orthodoxy. This may be seen in Buddhavarman's *Abhidharmavibhāṣā* T. 1546, completed 437-439 CE.

In 391, Saṃghadeva was on Mount Lu with Huiyuan. In that year he gave the final version of the *Hṛdaya*, and also of the *Sanfadulun* 三法度[28] 论, T. 1506. This text is said to be the work of Vasubhadra and of Saṃghadeva, who may have given a commentary. Lű Cheng says that this text is a Vātsīputrīya text, even Bhadrāyaṇīya[29]. Saṃghadeva was very interested in bringing out basic texts, e.g. *Hṛdaya* and *Aṣṭagrantha*. Was this text a, or the basic Vātsīputrīya scholastic text? Saṃghadeva's teaching seems to have had considerable influence among the monks on Mount Lu. Huiyuan's *Sanbaolun* 三报论 on the three kinds of retribution, was partly inspired by Saṃghadeva's *Tridharmaka*[30].

In Long'an 隆安 1, i.e. 397, Saṃghadeva went to Jiankang 建康, i.e. Nanjing, capital of the Eastern Jin 晋, where he was held in high esteem. He lectured on the *Hṛdaya* and he drew a large audience. It was there, in 398, that he completed the final rendering of the *Madhyamāgama* and of the *Ekottarikāgama*[31].

---

[28] Ren Jiyu 1985, pp. 616, explains that *du* 度 is a phonetic rendering, *zhendu* 真度. This means *khaṇḍa*, says Ono Genmyō 1999, pp. 110. This reminds one of Saṃghadeva's word for *grantha* in *Aṣṭagrantha*. It also reminds one of the mahāyāna *pāramitā*.

[29] Lü Cheng 1979, pp. 73-74; Idem 1979b, pp. 157. He explains that Vasubhadra was a bhadrāyaṇīya patriarch,that the structure (three times three parts) is Vātsīputrīya (referring to Paramārtha's T. 2033), and that doctrinally the text professes Vātsīputrīya ideas. The text is related to Kumārabuddhi's T. 1505, earlier in Chang'an. Châo, Thích Thiên 1999, pp. 43-85, gives an overview of the contents. The same author, pp.33, sums up the Pudgalavāda literature: T. 1506 and 1505; T. 1649 *Sāṃmitīyanikāyaśāstra*; T. 1461 the vinaya. See also Lü Cheng 1979b, pp. 62-64.

[30] T. 2102, p. 34bc, *Hongmingji* 弘明集 by Sengyou (515-518CE). This is translated by W. Liebenthal in *Monumenta Nipponica* 8, 1952, pp. 327-397, esp. 362-365. See also Zürcher 1972, pp. 230, Lü Cheng 1979, pp. 75.

[31] I.e. T. 26 and 125.

The translation of these texts had been attempted earlier in Chang'an by Dharmanandin. We do not know when Saṃghadeva died.

Finally, it is important to know that we have a manuscript (Stein no 6659, Giles no 4336), found in Dunhuang, of Saṃghadeva's *Hṛdaya* (T. 1550, pp. 809a-832b). It gives the text from p. 822c onwards. L. Giles translates the remarks at the end of the text: " Scripture offered as an act of worship by the Master of the Law Zheng-p'u (政 普)." He says it is copied in a clumsy hand, counts nineteen sheets of paper, and can be dated in the fifth century[32].

Fujieda Akira says that the period of ca. 400-600 CE corresponds to the transitional stage from *li* 隶 to *kai* 楷 style[33]. The style of writing of the manuscript S. 6659 is very similar to the *li* style. The manuscript must have been written early in the fifth century, shortly after Saṃghadeva had completed the translation in 391. From scrutiny of this manuscript it is clear that the text contains 250 stanzas.

## Upaśānta's Abhidharmahṛdaya T. 1551.

At first, the text seems to have been called *Fasheng Epitanlun*, seven volumes, i.e. *Dharmaśreṣthin's Abhidharma*[34]. Later, the text came to be called *Fasheng Epitanxinlunjing,* adding *jing*, *sūtra:* Dharmaśreṣṭhin's *Abhidharmahṛdaya*, six volumes [35]. Today, the text is known as *Epitanxinlunjing* 阿毘昙心论经 *Abhidharmahṛdaya*, six volumes. The text of this Sautrāntika Abhidharma text contains the stanzas of Dharmaśreṣṭhin's text, but the commentary is more detailed.

---

Lü Cheng 1979b, pp. 74, sees Mahāsāṃghika influence in this *Ekottarikāgama*. This is nôt surprising in a western Sarvāstivāda text.

[32] See Giles 1957, pp.127.

[33] Fujieda Akira 1969, pp. 18-19.

[34] Zh pp. 142b; L 87c.

[35] N p. 312a; Kaiyuan pp. 543c, 621a, 695c, 720b; Zhenyuan pp. 1043c, 945b.

## Upaśānta

Upaśānta, the author, must have lived between the time of the five hundred *Arhats* in Kaśmīra (second century CE) and the time of Dharmatrāta, author of the *Miśrakābhidharmahṛdaya* (early fourth century), who knows Upaśānta's work. Upaśānta's text mentions the Abhidharma-masters of Kāśmīra[36], adapts the Gandhāran views to the views of the *Mahāvibhāṣā*. In a note added to Dharmatrāta's text there is mention of a commentary of an Upaśānta in eight thousand stanzas, i.e. a text of eight thousand stanzas in length[37]. An informed guess would place Upaśānta in the third century. Upaśānta speaks about the Kāśmīri as if he were not from Kāśmīra himself. He fits into the tradition of western, i.e. Gandhāran, Sarvāstivādins[38]. Upaśānta's text was translated by Bhadanta Narendrayaśas, with the help of Fazhi 法智 and others, in Heqing 河清 2, i.e. 563, in the Tianping 天平 Monastery in Ye 邺, capital of the Northern Qi 齐 [39]. Narendrayaśas[40] was a Kṣatriya of the Śākya clan, born in Uḍḍiyāna, northern India. He travelled through India, and when he was forty years old he arrived in Ye in Tianbao 天保 7, 556. There he stayed in the Tianping Monastery. There he started translating the Indian texts that were there, and Upaśānta's text

---

[36] In the third century the most important part of *Jibin* was Kāśmīra. This remained so until the middle of the seventh century. Upaśānta mentioning the masters from Kaśmīra: T. 1551, pp. 841c, 855a and c.

[37] T. 1552, pp. 869c. Here it is further mentioned that a Vasubandhu had a text of six thousand stanzas in length, and a, or the (i.e. Dharmatrāta) master, had a text of twelve thousand stanzas in length.

[38] Also belong to the western tradition: The Tokharian Ghoṣaka, author of the *Amṛtarasa* T. 1553. Van Den Broeck, José 1977, pp. 83, says that this text is a first revised and enlarged *Hṛdaya*. He says, pp. 11, that the Chinese may date from the Cao Wei 曹魏 period, 220-265, but that it seems revised at the end of the fourth century.
Also Skandhila's *Abhidharmāvatāra* T. 1554, of which there is a Tibetan version, belongs to this tradition. Skandhila seems to have lived in the early fifth century. See: Dhammajoti 1998, pp. 65-76.

[39] Zh pp. 142b; L pp. 87c; Kaiyuan pp. 543c; Zhenyuan pp. 954b; N pp. 301a; Xü pp. 433a.

[40] For details about Narendrayaśas (Zuncheng 尊称): Xü pp. 432a-433ab; L pp. 87a; Kaiyuan pp. 543c-544ab.

apparently was one of those. When the Northern Zhou 周, who were not favourable to Buddhism, had put an end to the Qi in 577, Narendrayaśas had some difficult years, but when the Sui 隋 was established in Chang'an in 581, he was invited to come to this city in Kaihuang 开皇 2, 582. There he stayed in the Daxingshan 大兴善 Temple, and continued his translation activities. He died in Kaihuang 9, 589.

**Dharmatrāta''s Miśrakābhidharmahṛdaya T. 1552[41].**

Lin Li-kouang has made a thorough investigation into the different people called Dharmatrāta. He comes to the conclusion that there are three Dharmatrātas[42]:

1. Bhadanta Dharmatrāta, a Dārṣṭāntika and one of the four masters of the *Mahāvibhāṣā*, author of the *Chuyao* (*Udāna*) *jing* T. 212. He lived in the second century, and the *Mahāvibhāṣā* calls him either Dharmatrāta or Bhadanta.
2. Dharmatrāta, author of the *Miśraka*° and commentator of Vasumitra's *Pañcavastuka* T. 1550. He lived at the beginning of the fourth century.
3. Dharmatrāta, a Dhyāna-master, whose name is linked with the *Damoduoluochanjing* 达摩多罗禅经 T. 618, who lived at the beginning of the fifth century.

Jiaojing wrote a preface to the *Miśraka*° in 435[43]. He probably had his information from Saṃghavarman , the translator. He says that Dharmatrāta lived when the Jin 晋 was restored, i.e. 317. He added three hundred and fifty stanzas to

---

[41] Willemen 1998b, pp. 260-269. English translation and study by B. Dessein 1998, *Saṃyuktābhidharmahṛdaya*. The text is called *Miśraka*°, according to Lalji Shravak 2001, pp. 71-84. See also Willemen 2001, pp. 167.
Ryose Wataru 1986, mentions that Kudara Kogi in 1982 has found that the title is indeed *Miśraka*°. This title is mentioned in the Uigur translation of the *Tattvārtha*, a commentary on the *Kośa*. Also: a *Miśrakakāra* is mentioned in the *Vyākhyā* of Yaśomitra.

[42] Lin Li-kouang 1949, pp. 324-351.

[43] CH pp. 74bc

Dharmaśreṣṭhin's text, but he did not change the titles of the chapters. Only the tenth chapter, called *Tse* 择 Pravicaya, is new. Xuanzang informs us that Dharmatrāta wrote his work in a Saṃghārāma about four or five *li* north of Puṣkarāvatī, in Gandhāra[44].

The *Miśraka*° was translated in the Changgan 长干 Monastery in Jiankang, capital of the Former Song 宋, in Yuanjia 元嘉 12, 435. The translation was made by Saṃghavarman, Baoyun 宝云, and others. Huiguan 慧观 noted down the translation. An old manuscript (Stein no 996, Giles no 4335), found in Dunhuang, dated 479, gives the text of T. 1552, p. 898bc- 899 abc, i.e. the end of the *Karmavarga*[45]. The translator, Saṃghavarman[46], came to Jiankang in 434, where he soon had several hundreds of disciples. His first translation was of the text in which he was well versed, the *Miśraka*°. In 442 he boarded a merchant vessel and left for the West. We do not know anything about his death. It has been said that this *Miśraka*° was the fourth translation, three of which had already been lost in the eighth century[47]. The first translation was made by Saṃghadeva in Luoyang. There is much uncertainty about this lost text. Is the *Vibhāṣā* T 1547 meant, revised in Luoyang between 385-391, by Saṃghadeva, the translator of the *Hṛdaya*?

The second translation was the work of Faxian 法显, who had obtained the text about 406 CE in Pāṭaliputra, and of the

---

[44] Li Rongxi 1996, pp. 77.

[45] The colophon says that the copy was donated by Feng Jinguo 馮晋国, governor of Luo 洛 Province during the Northern Wei, and that it is part of 10 sets of the *Tripiṭaka*. The colophon further contains a prayer for the Emperor and the Empress, and concludes with an eulogy on the work in verse. The date is Taihe 太和 3, 479, of the Northern Wei.
Fujieda Akira 1969, pp. 23-24, commenting on the colophon, says that this manuscript is the earliest extant example of the Chinese *Tripiṭaka*.

[46] For details about his life: G pp. 342bc; CH pp. 104a-105ab.

[47] Kaiyuan, pp. 527c, pp. 621a (3 translations are lost), pp. 649b; Zhenyuan pp. 954b. Already Zh pp. 142b mentions 4 translations.
For the 4 translations: Willemen 1998b, pp. 262-263.

Dhyāna-master Buddhabhadra in Jiankang[48]. Huiguan, who later took part in Saṃghavarman's translation, was a well-known collaborator of Buddhabhadra, ever since his early days in Chang'an. Paul Pelliot has suggested that Faxian and Buddhabhadra translated Vasubandhu's commentary on the *Hṛdaya*[49], but why can this text not be Dharmatrāta's text?

The third translation of a *Miśraka*° was undertaken by Īśvara and completed by Guṇavarman[50]. This was a translation of Dharmatrāta's text. The anonymous preface[51] to the translation informs us that Yiyeboluo 伊叶波罗, Īśvara, was asked in 426 in Pengcheng 彭城 (Jiangsu Province) to translate the text. As he met with some difficulties, he only translated the first half of chapter ten : *Pravicayavarga*. The Indian Guṇavarman,who had come to China by sea, completed the translation. Guṇavarman[52] had been invited by the Song Emperor Wen 文 and by some monks, one of whom was Huiguan, to come to Jiankang in 431. The Fourth translation of the *Miśraka*° was the work of Saṃghavarman in 435. From Buddhabhadra to Saṃghavarman, the Chinese monk Huiguan was always around.

## The Hṛdaya and the Kośa T. 1559.

The *Abhidharmakośabhāṣya* was the work of Vasubandhu (ca. 400-480), a man from Puruṣapura (Peshawar) in Gandhāra. It was translated by Paramārtha in 567, i.e. T. 1559, and a second time in 654 by Xuanzang, i.e. T. 1558. The plan of the *Kośa* was inspired by the *Miśraka*°, which in its turn goes back to the *Hṛdaya*. Kimura Taiken has shown that the *Kośa* is a re-worked

---

[48] Faxian worked in Jiankang in 416. Shih 1968, pp. 108-115, for a French translation of Faxian's biography (G pp. 337bc-338ab), and pp. 90-98, for a translation of Buddhabhadra's (359-429) biography (G pp. 334bc-335abc).

[49] Pelliot 1930, pp. 272. See also supra note 37.

[50] CH pp. 12b.

[51] CH pp. 74b.

[52] Shih 1968, pp. 125-137, translates his biography in G pp. 340a-342b. See also CH pp. 104bc.

*Miśraka*°[53]. Also Lű Cheng has said so in China[54], based on Kimura's work. Kimura Taiken demonstrated that the initial seven chapters of Dharmatrāta's text form the basis of the *Kośa*. He advanced the opinion that the *Kośa* was nothing but an enlarged re-edition of Dharmatrāta's work. Not only the titles and the chapter sequence indicate this, but also the contents of these chapters. He compared in detail the contents of the first chapters, and came to the conclusion that, although the Chinese texts may differ, the Sanskrit original underlying them must have been identical. Only the *Lokanirdeśa* and the so-called ninth chapter about the *pudgala*, are not directly related to the *Miśraka*°. There is no obvious relation between the structures of the *Aṣṭagrantha* and of the *Miśraka*°.

In his preface to the *Miśraka*°, Jiaojing informs us that the chapters of the *Hṛdaya* correspond to the four noble truths[55].

| Noble truth | Chapter |
|---|---|
| I. *Duḥkha*° | 1. *Dhātuvarga* |
| II. *Samudaya*° | 2. *Saṃskāra*°; 3. *Karma*°; 4. *Anuśaya*° |
| III. *Nirodha*° | 5. *Ārya*° |
| IV. *Mārga*° | 6. *Jñāna*°; 7. *Samādhi*° |

The remaining chapters are supplementary: i.e. *Sūtra*°; *Prakīrṇaka*°; *(Dharma)kathā*.

Erich Frauwallner[56] has established that chapters 4: *Anuśaya*° and 5: *Ārya*° are the central part of the *Hṛdaya*. Chapter 5 explains the way to salvation. The summary of his explanation has this to say: "...It appears that this theory is to be considered as an original creation (scil. by Dharmaśreṣthin)... Canonical materials have been utilized. The attempt to show the causal relation between the liberating cognition and the disappearing of the anuśayāḥ was decisive in the creation of this theory. And as

---

[53] Kimura Taiken in his *Abidatsumaron no Kenkyū*, Tokyo 1922, pp. 297 et seq. Reprinted in his complete works, Tokyo 1974, pp. 259.

[54] Lü Cheng 1979, pp. 304; Idem 1979b, pp. 135-137.

[55] CH pp. 74bc.

[56] Frauwallner 1971, pp. 73 et seq.

this theory in all its parts forms a coherent whole, we are justified in regarding it as a unique creation representing the most important step to the formation of the Sarvāstivāda-System"[57]. Dharmaśreṣṭhin replaces the impurities (*āsrava*) of the canonical way to salvation by urges (*anuśaya*). This agrees with the noble path (*āryamārga*) as it is explained by Dharmaśreṣṭhin. Erich Frauwallner concludes that one may say the way to salvation and the theory of the *anuśayāḥ* are parts of one concept. He considers the *Hṛdaya* to be the oldest systematical doctrinal exposition of the Sarvāstivādins, and Vasubandhu's *Kośa* its reworked version[58]. Chapters 8: *Prakīrṇaka*° and 9: *Sūtravarga* of the *Hṛdaya* are supplements. The final chapter 10: *Kathā*, is a catechetic section by way of ten questions and answers, which test the disciple's understanding of the abhidharma. Dharmaśreṣṭhin, of course, relied not only on the āgamas, but also on earlier works, such as the *Pañcavastuka*[59]. When in the fifth century the Gandhāran Vasubandhu forced the Vaibhāṣikas into a defensive position, he did so by going back to the *Hṛdaya*, going beyond the *Aṣṭagrantha-Jñānaprasthāna* lineage. The Kāśmīra so-called orthodoxy quasi disappeared around the middle of the seventh century, and the old, western sarvāstivādins, or rather a large part of them, became predominant, now also known as Mūla-sarvāstivādins[60]. Tibet becomes Buddhist when these Mūla-sarvāstivādins had gained their prominent position.

In China an Abhidharma doctrinal lineage appeared in the fifth century, known as *pitanzong* 毘曇宗, based on the *Aṣṭagrantha* and on the *Miśraka*°[61]. The Vaibhāṣikas were non-existent in China at the time. After Paramārtha's *Kośa* in 567, the doctrinal

[57] Frauwallner 1971, pp. 121.
[58] Frauwallner 1971b, pp. 124.
[59] Frauwallner 1971b, pp. 124.
The *Pañcavastuka* was one of the earliest Abhidharma Texts in China, translated by An Shigao 安世高, T. 1557. An Shigao, from Anxi (*Ashkani*?). This Chinese text adds a Buddhist version (*fa* 法) to the then popular considerations about the five modes or elements (*wuxing* 五行).
[60] Are these the Sautrāntikas who used the long vinaya, i.e. the Dārṣṭāntikas?
[61] Willemen 1998b, pp. 266-267.

lineage of this *Kośa* became the continuation of the Abhidharma lineage. Also in northwestern India the *Kośa* had continued the *Miśraka*°. Xuanzang, who is reputed to have adapted his translations to the views of the Sautrāntikas[62], replaced this old *Kośa* lineage with his new translation of the *Kośa* in 654. This *Kośa* lineage went to Nara Japan (710-784).

## The Hṛdaya in Abhidharma Literature.

It may be reasonable to assume that, while Sthāvirīya Abhidharma goes back to Śāriputra's teaching, Mahāsāṃghika Abhidharma goes back to Mahākātyāyana, Kātyāyana the Elder, the successful propagator from Ujjayinī in Avanti[63]. The area which is of paramount importance for East Asia is India's northwestern area, the Gandhāran cultural area[64]. Kāśmīra hardly had any impact in China before Kumārajīva (350-ca. 409), and even up to the seventh century the influence of Kāśmīra was very limited in East Asia. The Gandhāran cultural area was an area of mainly Sarvāstivādins. These were called Sautrāntikas after the *Mahāvibhāṣā* and the *Abhidharmapiṭaka* of Kāśmīra, said to be Buddha's word, in the second century CE. Those among the western Sarvāstivādins who followed the long Vinaya of Mathurā, which included numerous stories (*avadānas* and *jātakas*), seem to have been the Dārṣṭāntikas[65]. The Gandhāran or western Sarvāstivādins were very diverse. Some had Vātsīputrīya ideas, believing in a *pudgala* or existing person, and some adopted some Mahāsāṃghika ideas. The *Abhidharma-hṛdaya* (Bactria) and then the *Aṣṭagrantha* (Gandhāra) in eight parts were, in the first century BCE, the culmination of Sarvāstivāda scholastic work, which had started earlier in the Gandhāran cultural area. But not all Sthāvirīyas agreed with this scholastic tendency. Part of the Sthāvirīyas preferred to keep

[62] One must not forget that Xuanzang studied and taught in Nālandā.

[63] For Mahākātyāyana: Lamotte 1988, pp. 189; Hirakawa 1993, pp. 76-77.

[64] See Willemen's articles in the *Indian (International) Journal of Buddhist Studies* since 1998, and also in *Asiatische Studien* 55, 2001.

[65] Willemen 2001b, pp. 531.
T. 1435 *Shisonglü* 十诵律: *Daśabhāṇavāra*, most probably was the vinaya of Kāśmīra.

stressing the Āgamas. They withdrew and became known as Haimavatas. This does not mean that they did not have an Abhidharma. They had one in five parts, now lost[66]. Their scholasticism was closely linked with the text known as *Śāriputrābhidharmaśāstra*, only known in Chinese translation *Shelifu'epitanlun* 舍利弗阿毘昙论, T. 1548. This text is thought to be of dharmaguptaka affiliation, and contains four parts[67]. The contents are very close to the ideas of the Sthāvirīyas known as Theravādins. But, as is so often the case in northwestern India[68], the dharmaguptakas were not exclusive. They included Mahāsāṃghika ideas in their Abhidharma. The dharmaguptakas had five *Piṭakas*, adding a *Dhāraṇī*° and a *bodhisattvapiṭaka*[69]. They clearly paid a great deal of attention to devotional practice, and less to scholasticism. Their influence in China was and is considerable, especially in the field of vinaya. It is not impossible that the Chinese custom to call sages Bodhisattvas (e.g. An Shigao, Aśvaghoṣa) can be explained by Dharmaguptaka influence. Lü Cheng [70] supposed that the

---

[66] Lamotte 1988, pp. 180 and pp. 190; Idem 1966, pp. 112 note 2. He refers to T. 1463 *Pinimujing* 毘尼母经, *Vinayamātṛkā* (?), pp. 818a 28-29.
Lamotte 1988, pp. 180, lists the five parts and gives Sanskrit equivalents: *Sapraśnaka*, *apraśnaka*, *saṃgraha*, *saṃyoga*, *sthāna*.

[67] The text was translated by Dharmayaśas, Dharmagupta, a.o., in 414-415.
Lamotte 1988, pp. 190, sanskritizes the titles of its four parts: *Sapraśnaka*, *apraśnaka*, *saṃyukta-saṃgraha*, *nidāna*. Lü Cheng 1979b, pp. 42, says that the theravāda abhidhamma (minus *Kathāvatthu*) and the dharmaguptaka T. 1548, both sthāvirīya after all, are linked.
*Paṭṭhāna-chusuo* 处 所 , *āyatana*? *Prasthāna*; *Dhammasaṅgani* and *Puggalapaññatti-apraśnaka*; *Vibhaṅga-sapraśnaka*; *Dhātukathā-saṃyoga*, *saṃgraha*; *Yamaka-saṃgraha*. Research by Kimura Taiken in 1922 and by L. de La Vallée Poussin in his *Kośa* has shown that ideas of T. 1548 are very similar to ideas of the Pāli *Vibhaṅga* and *Puggalapaññatti*, and that T. 1548 supports the ideas of the vibhajyavādins in the *Kośa* and in the *Vibhāṣā*. See Lamotte 1988, pp. 190-191, and 1966, pp. 112 note 2. The structure of T. 1548 is very similar to that of the Haimavata abhidharma.

[68] For examples: see Charles Willemen. *From where did Zen come? Dhyāna in the early Buddhist Tradition*. Numata Lecture, Calgary 2004.

[69] Lamotte 1988, pp. 531; Demiéville 1932, pp. 61. Is there a link between *dhāraṇī* (mnemotechnic means) and *dharmabhāṇaka*, preacher, in the northwestern area? The dharmaguptaka environment may have contributed to the development of bodhisattvas.

[70] Lü Cheng 1979b, pp. 41.

*Śāriputrābhidharma* might be Mahīśāsaka[71] or Dharmaguptaka. The Dharmaguptakas are relative newcomers in the northwestern area, developing belief in Bodhisattvas. As Sthāvirīyas they still had their Abhidharma from Śāriputra, but, indicating their difference, they saw Maudgalyāyana as no less important. In his *Upadeśa*,which may be understood as an Abhidharma-like Mādhyamika response to the Kāśmīra Abhidharma, a kind of Mādhyamika *Mahāvibhāṣā*, Kumārajīva says that the Vātsīputrīya Abhidharma was initiated by Śāriputra [72]. The Vātsīputrīyas were a Sthāvirīya group which had been discussing scholastic problems from a very early period on. They may have come to the northwestern area from western Central India. They disagreed with the Sarvāstivādins, but both Sarvāstivādins and Pudgalavādins, i.e. Vātsīputrīyas and later their main sub-school, the Sāṃmitīyas, co-existed in the Gandhāran cultural area, probably in its westernmost region. The Chinese *Nāgasenabhikṣusūtra*, *Naxianbiqiujing* 那先比丘经, T. 1670, may well be an early Bactrian Sarvāstivāda text (first century BCE?) with Pudgalavāda influence[73]. Some western (Bactrian?) Sarvāstivādins and Pudgalavādins were connected. Even at the end of the fourth century CE, Saṃghadeva, a western Sarvāstivādin, was still interested in Pudgalavāda literature too. The heterogeneous western Sarvāstivādins, who were all interested in Abhidharma and its related meditational practices, apparently had groups with Pudgalavāda sympathies. Other

---

[71] Mahīśāsakas are said to have a brāhmaṇa founder, versed in the Vedas, who " regulated (*śās*°) or converted the land (*mahī*)", Chinese *huadi* 化地. They propagated that everything exists, but only in the present. They also said that a gift to the saṃgha is more meritorious than one to the Buddha. The dharmaguptakas disagreed on this point.

[72] Lamotte 1988, pp. 190, renders Kumārajīva's words as follows:"...Śāriputra made the Abhidharma...Later, the Vātsīputrīya monks recited that work...called Śāriputrābhidharma." However, why would this necessarily be the title of T. 1548? This passage might just explain that the vātsīputrīyas used Śāriputra's abhidharma, not referring to a specific T. 1548.

[73] Or vice versa? The Chinese text may have been rendered from Gāndhārī at the end of the Han dynasty (second century CE), not in An Shigao's Luoyang. Terminology, proper nouns, and administrative titles lead to this suggestion. The Chinese differs considerably from the Pāli *Milindapañha*, but still belongs to the Sthāvirīya family.

groups added Mahāsāṃghika ideas about *prajñā*, wisdom, and *śūnyatā*, emptiness, even though the Mahāsāṃghikas had been the rivals of the Sthāvirīyas ever since the first schism. The groups and ideas of the non-Vaibhāṣika Sarvāstivādins, called Sautrāntikas after Kaniṣka, whose scholasticism was not Buddha's word, were diverse and eclectic. In such an environment devotionalism could arise within the Sthāvirīya family. The Mahāsāṃghikas in turn added the belief in Bodhisattvas to their rational view about *prajñā* and emptiness. The Kāśmīra Abhidharma, said to be Buddha's word, could not bring lasting order in the Gandhāran area, or stop the new Mahāyāna ideas and beliefs. The Mahāsāṃghikas may be considered to have brought the rational reaction to the Sarvāstivāda views[74], but other schools also took part in the new developments in northwestern India. Meant are the Dharmaguptakas and the Vātsīputrīyas. The six destinations or *gatis*, adding asuras, the rule in Mahāyāna in East Asia, were both Vātsīputrīya and Sāṃmitīya[75]. The Pudgalavādins also had

[74] The *Aṣṭasāhasrikāprajñāpāramitā*, probably first century BCE in the Gandhāran cultural area, called *Yogācāraprajñāsūtra*, *Daoxingborejing* 道行般若经 (Scriptural Text about Wisdom and the Practice of Yoga) T. 224, in its first Chinese translation (end second century CE), seems linked with the Mahāsāṃghika school in that same area. It is no coincidence that the term Mahāyāna is first mentioned in Mahāsāṃghika circles. Madhyamaka is the organized reaction in the South to the establishing of the Kāśmīra sarvāstivāda so-called orthodoxy.

[75] Lü Cheng 1979b, pp. 64.
T. 721 *Zhengfanianchujing* 正法念处经 *Saddharmasmṛtyupasthānasūtra*, the work of Gautama Prajñāruci in 539, is said to be Sāṃmitīya. Lü Cheng says that, even though the asuras are explained in detail, it is not absolutely clear whether they are a separate *gati*. Based on an analysis of the contents, Lü Cheng prefers to ascribe the text to the Bhadrāyaṇīya 贤胄 *xianzhou* sub-school, which distinguishes five *gatis*. Demiéville 1932, pp. 59 note b, informs us that Xuanzang's translation *xianzhou* means "descendants des sages", while Paramārtha renders Bhadrayāṇīya "vehicule des sages". Lü Cheng 1979b, pp. 65, further mentions that doctrinal differences between Vātsīputrīyas and Sarvāstivādins are very small, while the Mahīśāsakas markedly differ from the Vātsīputrīyas. The difference between Sarvāstivādins and Sāṃmitīyas is greater. One should keep in mind that Lü Cheng actually talks about Vaibhāṣika Sarvāstivādins. The Vātsīputrīya sub-schools supposedly completed the Abhidharma of the Vātsīputrīyas.

connections with Mahāsāṃghikas, i.e. Prajñaptivādins [76]. Paramārtha says that Śāriputra had explained the Abhidharma in nine parts, the so-called Abhidharma of the dharma-characteristics, *Dharmalakṣaṇābhidharma* [77]. This may have been a Vātsīputrīya Abhidharma[78]. Another kind of Abhidharma is mentioned in a note of Kumārajīva's *Upadeśa*. There a *Peṭaka* is mentioned. Is it a work inspired by Mahākātyāyana, the propagator from Avanti[79]? The work explains the Āgamas. The Pāli *Peṭakopadesa* is ascribed to an author with the same name. Mahākātyāyana seems to have been the source for Mahāsāṃghika Abhidharma. Paramārtha and his disciple Jizang 吉藏, commenting on Vasumitra's *Samayabhedoparacanacakra*, T. 2033, say that someone called Mahākātyāyana is at the basis of Prajñaptivāda scholasticism[80]. This Mahāsāṃghika sub-school

---

[76] Lü Cheng 1979b, pp. 157.

[77] Demiéville 1932, pp. 57.

[78] The founder of the Vātsīputrīyas had points of disagreement in the Abhidharma as it was handed down by Rāhula, who had received it from Śāriputra. The four sub-schools (Dharmottarīya, Ṣaṇṇāgārika, Bhadrāyaṇīya, Sāṃmitīya) completed the Abhidharma.
See: Châo, Thích Thiên 1999, pp. 26-27; Lamotte 1966, pp. 113 note.
Just a suggestion: could there be a relation between the nine parts of the Vātsīputrīya Abhidharma and the nine (three times three) sections of T. 1506 *Sanfadulun* 三法度论, sometimes sanskritized as *Tridharmakaśāstra*? Saṃghadeva apparently brought out basic texts in China, such as the *Aṣṭagrantha* and the *Hṛdaya*. Also the *Tridharmaka*?

[79] Lamotte 1966, pp. 113; Idem 1988, pp. 189; Lü Cheng 1979, pp. 68-69; Hinüber 1996, pp. 80; Demiéville 1932, pp. 49-50.
The Chinese reads *bile:* 蜫勒: *Peṭaka*, in T.1509, vol. 25, pp. 70 a.

[80] Lamotte 1988, pp. 189-191.
Apparently there is a Prajñaptivāda treatise, said to be a work of Mahākātyāyana. Is this the Mahākātyāyana who is the source of Mahāsāṃghika Abhidharma, or is this rather another Kātyāyana? The text is called *lun* 论 in Chinese. This seems to mean *Upadeśa*, not *śāstra*, just as in the title of the *Dazhidulun* 大智度论, Kumārajīva's *Upadeśa*. Is this treatise an *Upadeśa* on Mahākātyāyana's *Peṭaka*? It is possible that the Pāli *Peṭakopadesa* has a Mahāsāṃghika origin. It is interesting to remark that Mahākātyāyana is a man from Avanti, an area with which the Pāli language is closely associated. The Theravāda (Śāriputra) orthodoxy would, of course, not include a Mahāsāṃghika text in its canon. The Burmese included the text in their *Khuddakanikāya*, along with the *Milindapañha*. See: Hinüber 1996, pp. 80-82; Lamotte 1988, pp. 189-189; Idem 1966, pp. 109 note 2a.

has also been called Bahuśrutīya-vibhajyavāda[81], different from such Sautrantika-Bahuśrutīyas as e.g. Harivarman and his Prodbhūtopadeśa, T. 1646 usually called Tattvasiddhi [82]. Lü Cheng says that the Mahāsāṃghika (Prajñaptivāda) Abhidharma, called *Peṭaka*, consists of nine parts, i.e. *Lokaprajñapti*, etc[83]. What, if any, may be the link with the Vātsīputrīyas? The *Kośabhāṣya*, which is ultimately based on the Bactrian *Abhidharmahṛdaya*, geographically going beyond the *Aṣṭagrantha–Jñānaprasthāna* lineage, adds an annex to its eighth and final chapter, known to us as chapter nine, about the refutation of the *pudgala* [84]. One may remember that Saṃghadeva was a Sautrāntika with Pudgalavāda interests. There is no reason to think, as Lü Cheng does, that the *Hṛdaya* is related to Mahākātyāyana's *Peṭaka*[85].

---

The *Peṭakopadesa* contains eight chapters. Buddhaghosa used it as a canonical authority for his *Visuddhimagga*.

[81] Demiéville 1932, pp. 49-50.

[82] Lü Cheng 1979b, pp. 76; Demiéville 1932, pp. 49. The title is usually given as *Satyasiddhi*, but L. de La Vallée Poussin in his French study: *Vijñaptimātratāsiddhi. La Siddhi de Huan-Tsang*, Paris 1928-1929, pp. 223, proposes *Tattvasiddhi*.

[83] Lü Cheng 1979b, pp. 71-75, says that the Prajñaptivādā *Peṭaka* consisted of nine parts: *Lokaprajñapti*, *Samādhi*°, *Prajñā*°, etc.

[84] La Vallée Poussin 1971, vol. 5, pp. 227-302. He quotes, p. 227, Yaśomitra's *Vyākhyā* as saying that the pudgalavādins are the Vātsīputrīyas, more precisely the Sāṃmitīyas. The Sāṃmitīyas had their own *Prātimokṣa*, different from the sarvāstivādins. The information can be found in T.1461 *Lüershiermingliaolun* 律二十二明了论. Paramārtha participated in the bringing out of this text. See Châo, Thích Thiên 1999, pp. 28.

[85] Lü Cheng 1979, pp. 303-304, says that the *Hṛdaya* is based on the nine parts of Mahākātyāyana's *Peṭaka* (*Upadeśa*?). He sees nine parts in the structure of the *Hṛdaya*. But it is clear that the *Hṛdaya* is not Mahāsāṃghika, but Sarvāstivāda.

[809a] Treatise on the Essence of Scholasticism. Vol. I, composed by Bhadanta Dharmaśreṣṭhin, translated on Mount Lu by Saṃghadeva of the Eastern Jin, with Huiyuan .

# Chapter I. The Elements[1].

1.[2] First, I prostrate myself for the Most Excellent One, for his compassionate countenance without vexation. I also follow with reverence the whole of the teaching, and the *saṃgha* of the ones in harmony with the truth and without attachment[3].

When saying: "The characteristics of the factors[4] must be known!" for what reason must one know the so-called characteristics of the factors? He who has constant certainty[5] knows the constantly certain characteristics.

Others say: "When certain knowledge has the characteristics of certain knowledge, then it is certain. Therefore they say that the characteristics of the factors must be known."

Question: The world also knows characteristics of the factors. It may be extremely foolish, yet it knows that that which is characterized by solidness is earth, that which is characterized by dampness is water, that which is characterized by heat is fire, that which is characterized by movement is wind, that which is

---

1 *Dhātuvarga*.
2 Introductory stanza of taking refuge to the precious things: the Buddha (ab), the *dharma* ( c), and the *saṃgha* (d).
3 One in harmony with the truth and without attachment: two old translations of arhat.
4 Characteristics (*lakṣaṇa*) of factors (*dharma*).
5 *niścita*. See also stanza 139 about *jñāna*.

characterized by being without obstruction is space, and that which is characterized by being formless is consciousness[6].
So everything, as it is already known, must not be known again. If, though already known, it ought to be known again, then it would be endless. These things are not endless.
In what way do they say that the characteristics of the factors must be known?

Answer: The world does not know the characteristics of the factors. If the world knew the characteristics of the factors, all that is worldly should also be certain. But it is not certain. The so-called characteristics of the factors are constantly certain. One cannot say that one knows the characteristics of the factors but yet is not certain. If it were thus, what is not certain should also be certain, but it is not so. Therefore the world does not know the characteristics of the factors.

Furthermore, earth, which is characterized by solidness, is characterized by impermanence, suffering, and by selflessness[7]. If this were not so, (then) that which is characterized by solidness ought to be characterized by permanence, happiness, and selfness, but it is not so.

Therefore, that which is characterized by solidness is characterized by impermanence, by suffering, and by selflessness. If in relation to earth the world knew that it is characterized by solidness, its characteristic of impermanence, its characteristic of suffering and its characteristic of selflessness should also be known, but they are not known. Therefore the world does not know that earth is characterized by solidness.

Question: Previously we said that the characteristics of the factors must be known. What about these factors?

---

6 The six *dhātus* or elements: *pṛthivī°*, ab°, tejo°, *vāyu°*, *ākāśa°*, *vijñānadhātu*. cf. Kośa I 49.

7 *anitya*, *duḥkha*, *anātmaka*.

Answer: (2) When he knew the characteristics of all factors, the Fully Awakened One[8] opened the eye of wisdom[9]. He also showed (these) to others. I[10] will now explain them.

Question: Which factors does Buddha know?

Answer: [809b] (3ab) That which has permanence, a self, happiness, and purity[11] is separate from all impure formations[12].

As all impure formations are mutually produced while in process, they are separate from permanence. As they are not self-existing they are separate from a self. As they go to ruin they are separate from happiness. As they are disliked by wisdom they are separate from purity.

Question: If that which has permanence, a self, happiness, and purity is separate from all impure factors, how is it that the beings here experience them as having permanence, a self, happiness, and purity?

Answer: (3cd) When one believes in permanence, and so forth, one has false views as to the impure[13].

When the beings do not know the characteristics of impure factors they experience them as permanent, with a self, pleasant

---

8 *samyaksaṃbuddha.*
9 *prajñācakṣus.*
10 Scil. *Dharmaśreṣṭhin.*
In the prose to this verse AH 2 834a quotes 升摄波林经, *Shengshebolinjing*, and MAH 870c 申恕林契经 *Shenshulinqijing*. *Siṃsapāvanasutta* of the *Saṃyutta-Nikāya* V pp. 437 (P.T.S. ed. L. Feer, London 1960).
11 1. *Nitya* 2. *ātmaka* 3. *sukha* 4. *śubha*. Seeing something impermanent as permanent, etc. are the 4 *viparyāsas* or perversities.
12 Impure (*sāsrava*) formation (*saṃskāra*).
13 *sāsrava*.

and pure[14]. They are just like someone who sees something while walking at night, and assumes it is a thief.

Question: What about these impure factors[15]?

Answer: (4ab) When one produces the afflictions[16], they are called impure by the noble[17].

When in relation to the factors one produces the afflictions: the view of individuality[18], etc. as explained in the chapter: Urges[19], these factors are called impure.

Question: Why?

Answer: (4cd) So-called afflictions and impurities are different terms used by the wise.

The afflictions are called impurities. Because they leak from the bases[20], because the mental efflux flows uninterruptedly, because they detain (beings) in birth and death, because they are like that which is grasped by the unhuman[21], therefore they are called impurities[22].

Question: Do they have more names?

Answer: (5ab) They are called aggregates of grasping[23], and also afflictions and strife[24],

---

[14] See note 11.
[15] *sāsrava* dharma.
[16] *kleśa.*
[17] *ārya.*
[18] *satkāyadṛṣṭi.*
[19] Chapter 4, *Anuśayavarga.*
[20] 入: entrance, old translation for *āyatana*, sense-field. Here, the internal bases or senses, faculties (*indriya*) are meant.
[21] *amānuṣa.*
[22] Scil. *āsravas*, impurities.
[23] *upādānaskandha.* The Chin. means: aggregate of experiencing.
[24] Strife, *raṇa.*

These factors are called aggregates of grasping[25], they are called troubles[26], and they are called strife.

Question: Why?

Answer: (5cd) because affliction, grasping[27], and strife arise. This they ought to know!

Because the afflictions, (i.e.) the view of individuality[28], etc., trouble the beings, they are called afflictions[29]. Because one takes hold of a body, they are called grasping[30]. Because of the angry thoughts, they are called strife.

All impure factors are produced by the view of individuality, etc. Because they produce trouble, they are called troubles. Because they produce grasping, they are called grasping. Because they produce strife, they are called strife.

We have mentioned the aggregates of grasping[31]. The characteristics of the aggregates will now be explained.

> (6) All the formed which is pure, free from afflictions, and all the various aggregates of grasping, are the aggregates, expounded by the noble.

i.e. the formed factors –because they are produced by causes-, which are free from the afflictions: the view of individuality, etc., and which are free from the impurities, all these and the previously mentioned aggregates of grasping are all called

---

[25] 盛 (to hold) 阴: *Upādānaskandha*.

[26] 尘劳 or 劳, another word for *kleśa*.

[27] *upādāna*.

[28] See note 18.

[29] We follow the reading of the 3 editions (Song, Yuan, Ming), and translate 恼 only once.

[30] See note 27.

[31] See note 25.

aggregates[32]. They are the five aggregates: form, feeling[33], perception, formation, and consciousness[34].

Question: What about the aggregate form[35]?

Answer: [809c] (7) The material bases are said to be tenfold. Also non-information is supposed to be material. The Muni has expounded that these are distinctly established in the aggregate form.

The material bases are said to be tenfold: eye, form, ear, sound, nose, smell, tongue, taste, body, and the tactile[36]. Also non-information[37] is supposed to be material: as explained in the chapter: Actions[38].

These forms are the aggregate form. When he distinguished the aggregate form, the World-Honored One expounded them.

> (8) What is called the aggregate consciousness is the basis mind, and in relation to the eighteen elements, it is furthermore said to be sevenfold.

That is to say, the aggregate consciousness[39] is the basis mind[40], and among the elements[41] seven kinds are distinctly established: eye-consciousness, ear-, nose-, tongue-, body-, mind-consciousness[42], and also mind.

---

32 The *anāsrava saṃskṛtas* and the *sāsrava saṃskṛtas* (*Upādānaskandhas*), i.e. all *Saṃskṛtas* are called *skandhas*, aggregates.

33 In the *Taishō* edition we read the additional remark: "one should say: awareness", made by a commentator.

34 The 5 characteristics: *rūpa, vedanā* ("aching" is an old Chinese translation), *saṃjñā*, *saṃskāra*, and *vijñāna*.

35 *rūpaskandha.*

36 *cakṣus* and *rūpa*, *śrotra* and *śabda*, *ghrāṇa* and *gandha*, *jihvā* and *rasa*, *kāya* and *sprastavya* ("the subtle" in Chinese).

37 *avijñapti.*

38 Chapter 3: *Karmavarga.* cf. infra stanza 35.

39 *vijñānaskandha.*

40 Manāyatana.

41 18 *dhātus.*

42 *cakṣur°*, *śrotra°*, *ghrāṇa°*, *jihvā°*, *kāya°* and *manovijñāna.*

> (9) For the rest then we have three aggregates, non-information, and the three unformed ones. They are said to be the basis factor, and they are also the element factor.

For the rest then we have three aggregates: the aggregate feeling, the aggregate perception, and the aggregate formation[43].

Non-information [44], and the three unformed ones: space, cessation as a result of careful consideration, and cessation not as a result of careful consideration[45]. All these are called the basis factor and furthermore they are the element factor[46].

So these factors are called aggregates, elements, or bases[47]. However, aggregates are only formed. Elements and bases are either formed or unformed.

We have explained aggregate, element [48], and basis. The characteristics of each one will now be explained.

> (10) Among the elements one is visible. Ten are said to possess resistance. Eight kinds are said to be indeterminate. The rest are wholesome or unwholesome.

Among the elements one is visible[49]: the element form[50]. This can be seen to be here or there. Therefore it is visible. One should know that seventeen are invisible.

Ten are said to possess resistance [51]: ten elements possess resistance: eye and form, ear and sound, nose and smell, tongue

---

[43] *Vedanāskandha*, *Saṃjñāskandha*, and *Saṃskāraskandha*.

[44] See note 37.

[45] The three *asaṃskṛtas*: *ākāśa*, *pratisaṃkhyānirodha*, and *apratisaṃkhyā-nirodha*. 数缘 seems to mean: the several conditions (*pratyaya*). 数 scil. *saṃkhyā*. Cf. stanza 225.

[46] *Dharmāyatana* and *dharmadhātu*.

[47] *skandha*, *dhātu*, *āyatana*.

[48] Explaining the 18 elements or *dhātus*, MAH 874a mentions the 多界经, *Duojiejing, Bahudhātukasutta,* of the *Majjhima-Nikāya* III pp. 61 ff. (P.T.S. ed. Chalmers, London 1951.)

[49] *sanidarśana*.

[50] *rūpadhātu*.

[51] *sapratigha*.

and taste, body and the tactile[52]. They all oppose each other and all obstruct[53] each other. If in a place there is one, (then) there are not two. Therefore they possess resistance. One should know that eight do not possess resistance.

Eight kinds are said to be indeterminate[54]: eye, ear, nose, smell, tongue, taste, body, and the tactile[55]. Because these cannot be determined by a pleasant retribution, and because they cannot be determined by an unpleasant retribution, they are called indeterminate.

The rest are wholesome or unwholesome[56]: form, sound, mind, factor, and the six consciousnesses[57]. A wholesome bodily movement means wholesome form and an unwholesome bodily movement means unwholesome form. The other form is indeterminate. In the same way sound is a verbal movement. The seven elements of consciousness[58] which are clean thoughts, are wholesome, but when associated with unwholesome afflictions they are unwholesome. For the rest they are indeterminate.
They say that[59] when the element factor is associated with thought, it is explained as the thoughts. But when not associated, it is as explained in the chapter: Miscellaneous[60].

> [810a] (11) Fifteen are impure. The rest are ambivalent. Three are of three existences. In the existence of desire we have four. We have eleven in two existences.

---

[52] *cakṣus* and *rūpa*, *śrotra* and *śabda*, *ghrāṇa* and *gandha*, *jihvā* and *rasa*, *kāya* and spraṣṭavya.
[53] *āvṛ°*.
[54] *avyākṛta*.
[55] *cakṣus*, *śrotra*, *ghrāṇa* , *gandha*, *jihvā*, *rasa*, *kāya*, *spraṣṭavya*.
[56] *kuśala* or *akuśala*.
[57] *rūpa*, *śabda*, *manas*, *dharma*, 6 *vijñānas*.
[58] i.e. 6 consciousnesses and *manas*: the 7 *cittadhātavaḥ*, elements of thought.
[59] We follow the reading of the 3 editions: 谓.
[60] Chapter 9: *Prakīrṇakavarga*. See stanzas 222-223.

Fifteen are iṃpure [61] : five internal elements, five external elements, and five consciousness-elements, because impurity dwells within them.

The rest are ambivalent: the element mind, the element mind-consciousness, and the element factor[62], these are either impure or pure. When impurity dwells in them they are impure. Otherwise they are pure.

There are of three existences[63]: the elements mind, factor, and (mind-) consciousness can be obtained in three existences: the existence of desire, the existence of form, and the existence of formlessness[64]

In the existence of desire we have four: smell, taste, nose-consciousness and tongue-consciousness[65] are comprised[66] only within the existence of desire, not within the existences of form and of formlessness, because they have renounced the desire for solid food[67]. All smells and tastes have the nature of solid food. We have eleven in two existences: in the existence of desire and in the existence of form there are eleven elements: the internal five, form, sound, the tactile, and the consciousnesses of which these (three) are the ranges[68]. These are not in formlessness, because it is free from form.

> (12) There are five with adjusted thinking and with discursive thinking. Of three aspects there are three, and the rest do not possess them. Let it be known that seven possess an object. Some take the basis factor as their basis.

---

[61] Impure, *sāsrva*; pure, *anāsrava*.
[62] i.e. *manodhātu*, *manovijñānadhātu*, and *dharmadhātu*.
[63] *Tribhava*.
[64] *kāma*°, *rūpa*°, *ārūpyabhava*.
[65] *gandha*, *rasa*, *ghrāṇavijñāna*, *jihvāvijñāna*.
[66] *saṃgṛhīta*.
[67] Renouncing desire: *vairāgya*.
Food in lumps: *kavaḍīkārāhāra*.
[68] The five internal (*ādhyātmika*) ones: the faculties or senses from *cakṣus*, eye, to *kāya*, body; *rūpa; śabda; spraṣṭavya; cakṣur*°, *śrotra*°, and *kāyavijñāna*.
Range: *viṣaya*.

There are five with adjusted thinking and with discursive thinking[69]: five consciousness-elements are accompanied by adjusted and discursive thinking. They are associated with adjusted and discursive thinking because of their coarseness[70].

Of three aspects[71] there are three: the elements mind, factor, and (mind-) consciousness, these are of three aspects. When in the realm of desire[72] and in the first trance[73], they possess adjusted thinking and discursive thinking[74]. When in the intermediate trance[75], they do not possess adjusted thinking, only discursive thinking[76]. On a higher level they do not possess adjusted thinking nor discursive thinking[77].
The rest do not possess them: i.e. the other elements are accompanied neither by adjusted thinking nor by discursive thinking, because they are not associated[78].

Let it be known that seven possess an object[79]: seven elements possess an object. They are said to possess an object because they have[80] an object, in the same way that we say of someone with a son that he has a son. Eye-consciousness takes form as its object. Ear-consciousness takes sound as its object. Nose-consciousness takes smell as its object. Tongue-consciousness takes taste as its object. Body-consciousness takes the tactile as its object. Mind-consciousness takes the factors as its object[81].

---

[69] *savitarka savicāra.* The Chinese means: with awareness and with contemplation.
[70] *audārikatā.*
[71] *ākāra.*
[72] *kāmadhātu.*
[73] *dhyāna.*
[74] See note 69.
[75] *dhyānāntara.*
[76] *avitarka* and *vicāramātra.* The Chinese reads: with little contemplation (*vicāra*).
[77] *avitarka* and *avicāra.*
[78] Scil. with thought.
[79] *sālambana*, with an objective support.
[80] The text has 有此..., which is probably 此有...
[81] i.e. the six *vijñānas* and their objects. The seventh element is a small part of the *dharmadhātu.* See infra notes 82 and 84.

Some[82] take the basic factor[83] as their basis: the factors which constitute thought's concomitants[84] possess an object. The others do not possess an object.

> (13) Nine are unappropriated. The rest are ambivalent. One is both formed and unformed. Let it be known that those which are only formed consist of seventeen elements.

Nine are unappropriated[85]: they are called appropriated when the factors which constitute thought and its concomitants[86] proceed within organic forms[87] and within the ones not separated from the faculties[88], because they dwell within them. In the other case they are unappropriated. Among them nine elements are unappropriated: the elements: sound, those of thought, and factor[89], because the factors which constitute thought and its concomitants[90] do not dwell in them.

The rest are ambivalent: when the five internal elements[91] are present, they are appropriated. The factors which constitute thought and its concomitants dwell in them. When past or future, they are unappropriated.

It is not so that the factors which constitute thought and its concomitants dwell in them. When not separated from the faculties[92] and when present, form, smell, taste, and the tactile[93] are appropriated. Just as the factors which constitute thought and its concomitants dwell in the faculties, [810b] so they (dwell)

---

[82] i.e. a small part of the *dharmadhātu.*
[83] dharmāyatana.
[84] Only the *caitasikadharmas* are *sālambana.* See AH2 836a, and MAH 875c. When our text has 心 (*citta*) 心数 (*caitasika*) 法, this is probably a mistake. The Chinese renders *caitasika* as: counted as thought.
[85] *anupātta.*
[86] *cittacaitasikā dharmāḥ.*
[87] 根 translates *indriya*, faculty. 根数: *aindriya,* organic.
[88] *indriyāvinirbhāga.*
[89] *śabda*, the 7 *cittadhātavaḥ* (6 *vijñānas* and *manas.* Cf. supra note 53), and *dharma.*
[90] See note 86.
[91] *cakṣus, śrotra, ghrāṇa, jihvā, kāya.*
[92] See note 88.
[93] *rūpa, gandha, rasa, spraṣṭavya.*

in them, because they[94] are not separated from the faculties. The rest are unappropriated.

One is both formed and unformed[95]: the single element factor[96] is formed and unformed. In it three kinds[97] cannot be formed, since they are permanent. As the rest of the element factor is impermanent, it is formed. Because formed and unformed are established by means of combination, (this) single (element) is both formed and unformed.

Let it be known that those which are only formed consist of seventeen elements: seventeen elements are all formed since they are impermanent. Therefore they are formed only.
Question: Thus we have distinctly established the characteristics of the factors. What about how factors are comprised[98]? Is it within something of their own nature or within something of another nature?

Answer: Within something of their own nature.

Question: Why?

Answer: (14) All factors are separated from factors of another nature. Everything dwells naturally on something of its own nature. Therefore they say that all factors are comprised within something of their own nature[99].

All factors are separated from factors of another nature: i.e. the eye is separated from the ear, and thus are all factors. One should not say that factors are comprised when they are separated. Therefore it is not the case that they are comprised within something of another nature.

---

[94] i.e. the 4 of note 93.
[95] *saṃskṛta* and *asaṃskṛta*.
[96] *dharmadhātu*.
[97] Supra note 45.
[98] 摄: *saṃgraha*.
[99] We translate the reading of the 3 editions: 之. See also the explanation of this verse infra.

Everything dwells naturally on something of its own nature: the eye naturally dwells on something of the nature of the eye, and all factors are thus. One should say that when they are dwelled in, they are comprised.

Therefore they say that all factors are comprised within something of their own nature: we have already established that they are comprised within something of their own nature. Here a visible factor is comprised within one element, one aggregate, and one basis[100]. All factors are thus. The meaning of this will be comprehensively explained later in the chapter: Scriptural Texts[101].

---

[100] 1 *dhātu*, 1 *skandha*, 1 *āyatana*.
[101] Chapter 8: *Sūtravarga*. Stanzas 210 et seq. may be meant.

**阿毗昙心论卷第一**

尊者法胜造
东晋僧伽提婆
共慧远于庐山译

**界品第一**

1 前顶礼最胜 离恼慈哀颜
亦敬顺教众 无著应真僧

说曰法相应当知。何故应知法相者。常定知常定相。彼曰定智有定智相则为决定。以是故说法相应当知。问。世间亦知法相此极愚亦知坚相地湿相水热相火动相风无碍相空非色相识。如是一切不应已知复知。若已知复知此则无穷。无穷者此事不然。云何说法相应当知。答。世间不知法相。若世间知法相者一切世间亦应决定而不决定。法相者常定。不可说知法相而不决定。若然者不决定亦应决定。但不尔。是以世间不知法相。复次坚相地无常相苦相非我相。若不尔者坚相应有常相乐相有我相而不尔。是故坚相即无常相苦相无我相。若世间于地知坚相者无常相苦相无我相亦应知而不知。是故世间不知地坚相。
问。前说法相应当知。此法云何。答。

2 若知诸法相 正觉开慧眼
亦为他显现 是今我当说

问。佛知何法。答。

3 有常我乐净 离诸有漏行

诸有漏行转相生故离常。不自在故离我。坏败故离乐。慧所恶故离净。
问。若有常我乐净离诸有漏法者云何众生于中受有常我乐净。答。

计常而为首 妄见有漏中

众生于有漏法不知相已。便受有常我乐净。如人夜行有见起贼相彼亦如是。
问。云何是有漏法。答。

4 若生诸烦恼 是圣说有漏

若于法生身见等诸烦恼如使品说是法说有漏。问。何故。答。

所谓烦恼漏 慧者之假名

烦恼者说漏。漏诸入故心漏连注故留住生死故如非人所持故是故说有漏。
问。此更有名耶。答。

5 是名为受阴 亦复烦恼诤

是法说盛阴说劳说诤。
问。何故。答。

烦受诤起故　　是彼应当知

身见等诸烦恼劳于众生故说烦恼。受身故说受。忿怒心故说诤。从身见等生诸有漏法。是生劳故说劳。生受故说受。生诤故说诤。
已说盛阴。阴相今当说。

6　若远离烦恼　　无漏诸有为
一切杂受阴　　是阴圣所说

谓法离身见等诸烦恼亦解脱诸漏有为从因生故是一切及前说盛阴此总说阴。是五阴色痛[应云觉也]想行识。
问。色阴云何。答。

7　十种谓色入　　亦无教假色
是分别色阴　　牟尼之所说

十种谓色入者眼色耳声鼻香舌味身细滑。亦无教假色者如业品说。此色是色阴。分别色阴时是世尊说。

8　所名曰识阴　　此即是意入
于十八界中　　亦复说七种

谓识阴即是意人亦界中七种分别眼识耳鼻舌身意识及意。

9　余则有三阴　　无教三无为
谓是说法入　　亦复是法界

余则有三阴者痛阴想阴行阴。无教三无为者虚空数缘灭亦非数缘灭。此总说法入亦复是法界。如是此法说阴界入。但阴一向有为界。及入有为无为。
已说阴界入。一一相今当说。

10　界中一可见　　十则说有对
无记谓八种　　余则善不善

界中一可见者色界。此可视在此在彼。是故可见。当知十七不可见。十则说有对者十界有对眼色耳声鼻香舌味身细滑。是各各相对各各相障碍。处所若有一则无二。是故有对。当知八无对。无记谓八种者眼耳鼻香舌味身细滑。此非乐报可记亦非苦报可记故曰无记。余则善不善者色声意法及六识。善身动是善色。不善身动是不善色。余色无记。如是声口动。净心七识界善不善烦恼相应是不善。余无记。法界谓心相应彼如心说。若不相应如杂品说。

11　有漏有十五　　余二三三有
欲有中有四　　十一在二有

有漏有十五者五内界五外界五识界漏止住故。余二者意界意识界法界此或有漏或无漏。若漏止住是有漏。异则无漏。三三有者意法识界是三有中可得欲有色有无色有。欲有中有四者香味鼻识舌识是一向欲有中摄非色无色有离欲揣食故。一切香味是性揣食。十一在二有者欲有色有十一界内五色声细滑及是境界识。此非无色中以离色故。

12 有觉有观五 三行三余无
有缘当知七 法入少所入

有觉有观五者五识界与觉观具。粗故觉观相应。三行三者意法识界此三行。若欲界及初禅是有觉有观。若中间禅是无觉少观。是上无觉无观。余无者谓余界非觉俱亦非观俱不相应故。有缘当知七者七界有缘此有缘故故曰有缘。如人有子谓之有子彼亦如是。眼识缘色耳识缘声鼻识缘香舌识缘味身识缘细滑意识缘诸法。法入少所入者若心心数法是有缘。余则无缘。

13 九不受余二 为无为共一
一向是有为 当知十七界

九不受者受名谓若色根数亦不离根是心心数法所行于中止住故。异则不受。于中九界不受。声心法界非于中心心数法止住。余二者五内界若现在是受。于中心心数法止住。过去未来不受。非彼心心数法止住。色香味细滑若不离根及现在是受。如心心数法根中止住彼中亦尔不离根故。余则不受。为无为共一者一法界有为及无为。于中三种有常故不可有为。余法界无常故有为。有为无为合施设故是以为无为共一。一向是有为当知十七界者十七界无常故一切有为。是故一向有为。
问。如是分别法相已。云何摄法为自性为他性。答。自性。问。何故。答。

14 诸法离他性 各自住己性
故说一切法 自性之所摄

诸法离他性者谓眼离耳如是一切法。不应说若离者是摄。以故非他性所摄。各自住己性
者眼自住眼性如是一切法。应当说若住者是摄。故说一切法自性之所摄。已施设自性所摄。于中可见法一界一阴一人所摄。如是一切法。复次此义契经品当广说。

# CHAPTER II. FORMATIONS[1]

We have already explained the particular characteristics of all factors. How factors come into existence will now be explained.

Question: When all factors are comprised within something of their own nature, will they also come into existence through their own power?

Answer: (15ab) Finally, none can come into existence because they are without a companion[2].

Nothing can come into existence of itself. Why? Because all formations are by nature weak and without strength, just as a weak sick person cannot rise up by his own strength.

Question: When he cannot rise up by his own strength, how will he rise up?

Answer: (15cd) Through the power of all conditions[3], then the factors can come into existence.

Just as a weak person rises up when supported by another, so too are they. How thoughts come into existence on the basis of companionship will now be explained.

> (16) When thoughts come into existence, these thoughts must have companions: the collection of factors which constitute thought's concomitants[4] and the non-associated formations[5].

Thought is mind, and mind is consciousness[6]. They are really the same thing, called by different names. When the thoughts are

---

1 *saṃskāravarga.*
2 *sahāya.*
3 *pratyaya.*
4 *caitasika dharma.*
5 (citta) *viprayuktasaṃskāra.*
6 *citta* is *manas*, and *manas* is *vijñāna*.

dependent on something, when they take an object, and when they arise at a particular moment[7], the collection of factors which constitute thought's concomitants[8] comes into existence together with these thoughts.

Question: [810c] What is the collection of factors which constitute thought's concomitants?

Answer: (17) Perception, desire-to-do, contact, wisdom, mindfulness, volition, and resolve, attention to an objective range, *samādhi*, and feeling.

Perception[9]: when something is established, it is experienced according to its appearance[10].

Desire-to-do[11]: the desire to experience when experiencing an object.

Contact[12]: when thought, its base, and its object[13] are combined, not separated from each other.

Wisdom[14]: when one is certain and sure about an object.

Mindfulness[15]: when one is mindful in relation to an object, not forgetful.
Volition[16]: when that which is meritorious or evil[17], or that which is different from both, is formed in relation to thought.

---

[7] To be dependent, to have a basis or *āśraya (indriya);* to take an object or *ālambana (viṣaya);* moment or *kṣaṇa.*
[8] See note 4.
[9] *saṃjñā.*
[10] *nimitta.*
[11] *Chandas.*
[12] 更： (mutual) *saṃ°;* 乐： (pleasure) *sparśa.* The Chinese seems to be mistaken in its interpretation of *phassa: sparśa* (contact) or *spṛśya* (pleasant).
[13] *citta* (vijñāna); its *āśraya*, (indriya); its *ālambana* (viṣaya).
[14] *prajñā, mati.*
[15] *smṛti.*
[16] *cetanā.* The Chinese means: reflection.
[17] *puṇya* or *pāpa.*

Resolve[18]: when one experiences a notion in relation to an object, that (notion) certainly has that (object).

Attention[19]: when one is active[20] in a resolute way in relation to an object.

Concentration[21]: when experiencing an object, the thoughts are not scattered.

Feeling[22]: when a pleasant or an unpleasant object, or one which is different from both, is experienced.

> (18) The noble explain that they come into existence whenever a thought comes into existence. They proceed together within one object, and they are furthermore associated in a permanent way.

The noble explain that they come into existence whenever a thought comes into existence: whenever a thought comes into existence, these ten factors come into existence together with it. Therefore they are called of great extent[23].

They proceed together within one object: they proceed within one and the same object together with every thought, not separately.

They are furthermore associated in a permanent way: together with and accompanied by thought, they all proceed in common, associated in a permanent way. Because they are free from increase or decrease, they are called associated[24].

---

[18] *adhimukti*. The Chinese 解脱 means "to free, to let go". This makes sense when we read AH2 836c. There one reads: "When thought proceeds within an object, because it is unobstructed (*āvṛ*°)".
[19] *manaskāra*.
[20] 发动 may translate *ābhoga*.
[21] *samādhi*.
[22] *vedanā*.
[23] *mahābhūmika*.
[24] Associating implies *samatā*, equality.

Of the factors which constitute thought's concomitants, we have explained the ones that are said to be connected with every thought.

The ones that are not (so) connected, will now be explained.

> (19) The roots, adjusted thinking and discursive thinking[25], faith, repose, heedfulness, vigorous pursuit, even-mindedness, and all afflictions are sometimes not associated.

The roots: i.e. the wholesome roots: absence of covetousness, of hatred, and of foolishness[26].

Adjusted thinking[27]: the series[28] of coarse thoughts.

Discursive thinking[29]: the series of subtle thoughts.

Faith: sincerity[30] and true purity.

Repose[31]: happiness at the moments of wholesome thoughts, because one has renounced evil in body and in thought.

Heedfulness[32]: application[33], no negligence at the moment of performing[34] goodness.

Vigorous pursuit[35]: special strenuousness when doing things.

Evenmindedness[36]: when doing things, acting with non-acting, seeking with non-seeking, guarding oneself and forming nothing.

---

[25] *vitarka* and *vicāra*. AH2 837a and MAH 811a have *hrī*, shame, and *apatrāpya*, moral dread.
[26] The three kuśalamūlas: *alobha*, *adveṣa*, and *amoha*.
[27] *vitarka*.
[28] *saṃtati*, series (of thoughts).
[29] *vicāra*.
[30] Faith, *śraddhā*, is sincerity, 诚实.
[31] *praśrabdhi*.
[32] *apramāda*.
[33] *prayoga*.
[34] We follow the reading of the 3 editions: 作.
[35] *vīrya*.
[36] *upekṣā*. The Chinese means: watchfulness.
AH2 837a and MAH 881b define *upekṣā* as *cittasamatā*, evenmindedness.

All afflictions: as explained in the chapter: Urges[37].

These factors cannot be obtained in every thought. Sometimes they are associated and sometimes they are not associated.

Question: Why are they said to constitute thought's concomitants[38]?

Answer: They call mind thought[39]. Because they are related to it, they are said to constitute thought's concomitants.

We have explained the characteristics of the factors which constitute thought's concomitants. How they are produced will now be explained.

> (20) Regarding the class of unwholesome thoughts, the (factors) constituting thought's concomitants are twenty-one. [811a] For the defiled ones, the ones that are not unwholesome of the realm of desire, two are subtracted.

Regarding the class of unwholesome[40] thoughts, the (factors) which constitute thought's concomitants are twenty-one: the term unwholesome is used when thoughts produce the afflictions in the realm of desire, except the view of individuality and the view of extremes[41] in the realm of desire. Because they bring about an unlovely fruition, they are called unwholesome. Let it be known that regarding this class of thoughts there are twenty-one factors which constitute thought's concomitants: the ten ones of great extent, adjusted thinking, discursive thinking, two afflictions, shamelessness, absence of moral dread, sloth, excitedness, disbelief, heedlessness, and indolence[42].

---

37 Chapter 4: *Anuśayavarga*.
38 *caitasika*.
39 Mind, *manas*; thought, *citta*.
40 *akuśala*.
41 *satkāyadṛṣṭi* and *antagrāhadṛṣṭi*.
42 i.e 10 *mahābhūmikas* (cfr. stanza 17); *vitarka* and *vicāra*;
2 *kleśas*; *āhrīkya* and *anapatrāpya*; *styāna*, *auddhatya*, *āśraddhya*, *pramāda*, and kausīdya.

For the defiled ones[43], the ones that are not unwholesome in the realm of desire, two are subtracted: a class of thoughts, such as the thoughts associated with the view of individuality and the view of extremes[44], is said to be the defiled ones in the realm desire. They are not unwholesome.

Let it be known that regarding this class there are nineteen factors which constitute thought's concomitants, subtracting shamelessness and absence of moral dread[45], because they are only unwholesome.

> (21) The wholesome ones and the special ones number twenty. There are twelve indeterminate ones. Remorse and the thoughts in relation to sleepiness can be considered to imply an increase.

The wholesome ones and the special ones[46] number twenty: special are called the ones that are produced by the affliction ignorance alone among thoughts. They number twenty (factors) constituting thought's concomitants, subtracting one affliction[47]. The rest are as explained before[48]. The term wholesome is used when clean thoughts bring about a lovely fruition. Let it be known that the companions of these thoughts number twenty: the ten ones of great extent, adjusted thinking, discursive thinking, faith, vigorous pursuit, repose, heedfulness, the wholesome roots, evenmindedness, shame, and moral dread[49].

---

2 *kleśas; saṃprayuktāvidyā,* the associated ignorance, and one of the 4: *rāga, pratigha, māna, vicikitsā.* Cfr. AH2 837b.

43 *kliṣṭā* (i.e. *nivṛtāvyākṛta*).

44 See note 41.

45 *āhrīkya* and *anapatrāpya*.

46 i.e. *kuśala* and *āveṇika*. The Chinese translates *āveṇika* as: not collective.

47 cf. note 42. The *āveṇikas* do not include one of the 4: *rāga, pratigha, māna, vicikitsā*.

48 See stanza 20ab.

49 i.e. 10 *mahābhūmikas* (cfr. stanza 17); *vitarka* and *vicāra*; *śraddhā*, *vīrya*, *praśrabdhi*, *apramāda*; the *kuśalamūlas*; *upekṣā*, *hrī*, and *apatrāpya*. There are three wholesome roots (cfr. note 26), which seem to be counted as 1.
Even if the root *amoha* were already included in the *prajñā* of the *mahā-*

There are twelve indeterminate ones[50]: regarding the class of undefiled[51] thoughts there are twelve factors which constitute thought's concomitants: the ten ones of great extent, adjusted thinking and discursive thinking[52].

Remorse[53] and the thoughts in relation to sleepiness[54] can be considered to imply an increase: as for the term remorse: remorse is disappointment that a matter is not accomplished. It is either wholesome or unwholesome. To those classes of associated thoughts one may add remorse. The other factors which constitute thought's concomitants are as explained before[55]. As for the term sleepiness[56]: sleepiness[57] is being quite composed with quiet thoughts, without any being sovereign[58]. It is produced in all five classes[59], and these all increase (with it). The other factors which constitute thought's concomitants are as explained before[60]. When remorse and sleepiness proceed[61] within three classes[62], these increase with two. The other factors which constitute thought's concomitants are as explained before[63].

---

*bhūmikas* , still we would count 21. The Japanese translation, *kokuyaku, bidonbu* XXI p.146, leaves out *vīrya*. This brings the number to 20. AH2 837b and MAH 882a count 22: 10 *mahābhūmikas* , 10 *kuśalamahābhūmikas, vitarka* and *vicāra*. See also *Kośa* II 166.

50 *avyākṛta*.

51 *akliṣṭa*.

52 i.e. 10 *mahābhūmikas*, *vitarka*, *vicāra*.

53 *kaukṛtya*.

54 *middha*.

55 *kuśala*: stanza 21a.
*akuśala*: stanza 20ab.

56 See note 54.

57 The explanation of *middha* here, is a view held by the Sarvāstivādins in Gandhāra. See *Kośa* VII 18 and 20-21.

58 Quite, *ekānta;* composed, *saṃkṣipta;* sovereignty, *vaśitā.*

59 i.e. *kuśala*, *akuśala*, *kliṣṭa*, *āveṇika*, *avyākṛta*.

60 Stanzas 20-21ab.

61 The text has 不行: "do not proceed". This is obviously impossible. 不 probably stands for 俱: both. AH2 837c 俱转: both proceed; MAH 882a 俱生: both are produced.

62 In AH2 837c and MAH 882a the 3 classes: *kuśala, akuśala*, and *nivṛtāvyākṛta* (*kliṣṭa*) are meant.

63 See stanzas 20-21a.

Question: This is the explanation of the series of thoughts of the realm of desire. What about the realm of form?

Answer: (22) The first trance is free from the unwholesome one.
The rest are known to be as in the existence of desire.
The intermediate trance has done away with adjusted thinking, and in a higher (stage) the same applies to discursive thinking.

The first trance is free from the unwholesome[64] one. The rest are known to be as in the existence of desire[65]: the first trance is without the unwholesome one. In it there are four classes: wholesome, defiled, special, and indeterminate[66]. They are as explained for the realm of desire[67]: for the wholesome one twenty, for the indeterminate one twelve, and for the defiled one nineteen. As it is free from the unwholesome one, let it be known that it is also free from shamelessness and absence of moral dread[68], because they are only unwholesome. There are eighteen special ones[69].

[811b] The intermediate trance[70] has done away with adjusted thinking[71]: in the intermediate trance there is no adjusted thinking. It has completely done away with adjusted thinking. The rest are explained for the first trance.

In a higher (stage) the same applies to discursive thinking[72]: in the second, the third, and the fourth trances there is no discursive thinking either. In the realm of formlessness, there also one has completely done away with discursive thinking. Adjusted thinking had already been eliminated.

---

64 Scil. class.
65 *kāmabhava*.
66 In the first *dhyāna*: *kuśala*, *kliṣṭa*, *āveṇika*, *avyākṛta*.
67 Stanzas 20-21.
68 See stanza 21a. *āhrīkya* and *anapatrāpya* are to be subtracted from the 20.
69 *dhyānāntara*.
70 *vitarka*.
71 *vicāra*.
72 stanzas 20-21.

We have explained that the factors which constitute thought's concomitants are produced on the basis of companionship. Form will now be explained.

> (23) For the molecules in four faculties, ten seeds must be understood. In the faculty body there are nine seeds. In the remaining there are eight seeds, namely in the case of smell.

For the molecules[73] in four faculties[74], ten seeds[75] must be understood: i.e. one should know that there are ten seeds for the molecules in the faculty eye[76]: the seed earth, the seeds water, fire, and wind, the seed form, the seeds smell, taste, and the tactile, the seed which is the faculty eye and the seed which is the faculty body[77]. The same applies to the molecules of ear, nose, and tongue[78].

In the faculty body[79] there are nine seeds: i.e. for the molecules of the remaining faculty body there are nine seeds. Among them there is one seed which is a faculty[80], and the rest are as explained above.

In the remaining there are eight seeds: in this respect, regarding the remaining form which is not organic, the molecules have eight seeds[81].

Question: In which realm are these molecules mentioned?

Answer: Namely in the case of smell[82]: in the realm of desire there is smell, but the realm of form is free from smell. It has

---

[73] *paramāṇu*. The Chinese means: extremely small.
[74] indriya.
[75] *bīja*.
[76] *cakṣurindriya*.
[77] *pṛthivī*, *āpas*, *tejas*, *vāyu*, *rūpa*, *gandha*, *rasa*, *spraṣṭavya*, *cakṣurindriya*, *kāyendriya*.
[78] *śrotra*, *ghrāṇa*, *jihvā*.
[79] *kāyendriya*, the last of the 5 material faculties.
[80] Scil. *kāyendriya*.
[81] i.e. the 10 minus the faculties.
[82] *gandha*. I.e. in the *kāmadhātu*.

completely done away with the seeds smell and taste[83]. The other seeds are as explained for the realm of desire.

Question: Previously we mentioned that, when a thought is produced, factors which constitute thought's concomitants are necessarily produced relating to it, and also formations which are not associated with thought[84]. Among these we have already explained the factors which constitute thought's concomitants. What about the formations which are not associated with thought?

Answer: (24ab) All formed factors know birth, abiding, changing, and passing away.

All formed factors[85] have four characteristics[86] each: birth, abiding, changing, and passing away[87]. Because they arise in the world, they come into existence. Because, having arisen, the entities themselves are established, they abide. Because, when dwelling, their condition declines, they change. Because, having changed, they are extinguished, they pass away. These characteristics are called formations not associated with thought.

Question: When each of the formed factors has the four characteristics, do they also have the characteristics as characteristics?

Answer: (24c) These also have four characteristics.

Together with these characteristics, four other characteristics[88] are produced. A birth forms birth. An abiding forms abiding. A changing forms changing. A passing away forms passing away.

Question: If so, then it is endless.

---

[83] *gandha* and *rasa*.
[84] *cittaviprayuktasaṃskārāḥ*. See stanza 16.
[85] *saṃskṛtadharma*.
[86] *lakṣaṇa*.
[87] *jāti*, *sthiti*, *anyathātva*, *vyaya*. See also stanza 221b.
[88] i.e. the 4 so-called *anulakṣaṇas*, secondary characteristics: *jātijāti*, etc.

Answer: (24d) In the course of their process they form one another.

These characteristics all form one another. Just as the births[89] each produce one another[90], thus the abidings each produce[91] one another, the changings each cause one another to change, and the passings away each cause one another to pass away. For this reason it is not endless. Each one of the later four characteristics proceeds within one factor[92]. Each one of the first four characteristics proceeds within eight factors. Birth produces eight factors: three of the first ones, the four of the later ones, and the factor[93]. The same applies to the others[94].

We have already mentioned the companionship of the formations. We will now explain how they come into existence on the basis of companionship.

> [811c] (25) From these six kinds of causes: the reason of being, the concomitant (cause), the similar (cause), the universal (cause), the associated (cause), and the (cause of) retribution, one produces the formed factors.

Absolutely all causes are among the six causes[95]. These causes produce all formed formations.

Among them the cause which is the reason of being[96]: when it produces factors, it neither obstructs nor detains[97], and therefore it produces dissimilar factors, as is the case with the ten thousand things which are produced from earth.

---

89 生生, plural of 生: *jāti*, not *jātijāti*.
90 *jātijāti* produces *jāti*, and *jāti* produces *jātijāti*.
91 生: *jan°*, when 住: "to cause to abide" is expected.
92 e.g. *jātijāti* only in *jāti*.
93 *jāti* proceeds within the other 3 *lakṣaṇas: sthiti, anyathātva,* and *vyaya;* within the 4 *anulakṣaṇas;* and within the *dharma* it produces.
94 i.e. *sthiti*, *anyathātva*, and *vyaya*.
95 i.e. the 6 *hetus*.
96 *kāraṇahetu*. The Chinese 所作 seems to mean *karaṇīya,* which should be effected.
97 障碍: may translate *vighna*, and 留住: the causative of *sthā°* or a compound with *sthā°*.

The concomitant cause[98] : when the formations all accompany one another and are produced for this reason, as is the case with the factors which are thought and which constitute thought's concomitants, and the formations which are not associated with thought, and also as is the case with the molecules and the seeds[99].

The similar cause[100]: namely when the other thing and the thing itself are similar, as producing the wholesome when practicing the wholesome, producing the unwholesome when practicing the unwholesome and producing the indeterminate when practicing the indeterminate, and as the mutual causation of the kinds of things in accord with their particular kind.

The universal cause[101]: namely when the afflictions in their process are produced in a series[102], as when seeing a self one considers entering it[103] and plans to grasp it[104]. Because of this view[105] one considers entering and plans to grasp the permanence or the impermanence of a self[106]. Denying[107] the characteristics of the aggregates, one considers entering them and plans to grasp them [108]. Having doubts [109] about the characteristics of the aggregates, one experiences them as permanent, pleasant, and pure[110]. Thus one produces the afflictions. The explanation of all universal ones is as explained in the chapter: Urges[111].

---

[98] *sahabhūhetu.*
[99] *paramāṇu* and *bīja.* cf. stanza 23.
[100] *sabhāgahetu.*
[101] *sarvatragahetu.*
[102] 相续: *saṃtati, saṃtāna.*
[103] 审入: not in AH2 838b. MAH 884b: 审爾.
[104] 计著: also in MAH 884b. AH2 838b: 执著.
[105] i.e. *satkāyadṛṣṭi*: view of individuality.
[106] i.e. *antagrāhadṛṣṭi,* the view of extremes (*śāśvatadṛṣṭi,* view of eternity, and *ucchedadṛṣṭi,* view of annihilation).
[107] apavad°.
[108] i.e *mithyādṛṣṭi,* wrong view.
[109] i.e. *vicikitsā*, doubt.
[110] *nitya, sukha, śubha.*
i.e. *dṛṣṭiparāmarśa,* evil adherence to wrong views.
[111] Chapter 4: *Anuśayavarga.* See stanza 74 about the *sarvatragas.*

The associated cause[112]: the thoughts and the factors which constitute thought's concomitants, when the power of each one proceeds within one object and at one moment[113]. When separated from each other they are not produced.

The cause of retribution[114]: namely when a formation produces among the births and brings about a fruition. The lovely fruition of the wholesome and the unlovely fruition of the unwholesome is produced for this reason[115].

We have explained the causes. We will now explain that all factors are produced through causes.

> (26) Let it be known that, when they are produced by retribution, the thoughts, that which constitutes thought's concomitants, and also the afflictions, arise through five causes.

The factors which constitute thought and its concomitants, produced by retribution, and also the afflictions are produced by five causes. That which is produced by the cause of retribution is produced by the cause which is the reason of being[116]. At the moment of their production, similar or dissimilar things do not obstruct them, and so they are produced[117]. They are produced by the concomitant cause[118]. They are produced by the power of companionship. Each one of them is in reciprocal companionship, and collectively they are accompanied by the formations which are not associated with thought. They are produced by the similar cause[119]. They have the similar indeterminate factors of the former birth. They are produced by the associated cause[120], proceeding together at one moment within one object. They are

---

[112] *saṃprayuktakahetu.*
[113] *ekālambana* and *ekakṣaṇa.*
[114] *vipākahetu.*
[115] The *phala* of that which is *kuśala* and of that which is *akuśala.*
[116] Scil. *vipākahetuja* and *kāraṇahetuja.*
[117] For the confusion between 生 and 住, see supra note 91.
[118] *sabhabhūhetu.*
[119] *sabhāgahetu.*
[120] *saṃprayuktakahetu.*

produced by the cause of retribution[121]. When (the actions) are wholesome or unwholesome, they call them their fruitions. For the defiled factors which constitute thought and its concomitants one must subtract the cause of retribution[122], because they are indeterminate, but they are produced by the universal cause[123]. They are produced because of it. The other four causes are as explained before.

> (27) It is the case that the non-associated ones, and the remaining associated factors minus their first pure ones, are produced by four causes.

It is the case that the non-associated ones: i.e. the form produced by retribution [124], and also the formations which are not associated with thought [812a] are produced by four causes: the cause which is the reason of being, the concomitant cause, the cause of retribution, and the similar cause[125]. Defiled form and formations which are not associated with thought are also produced by four causes: the cause which is the reason of being, the concomitant cause, the similar cause, and the universal cause[126].

The remaining associated factors minus their first pure ones[127], are produced by four causes: the remaining factors which constitute thought and its concomitants minus their first pure ones are also produced by four causes: the cause which is the reason of being, the concomitant cause, the similar cause, and the associated cause[128].

---

[121] See note 114.
[122] See note 114.
[123] *sarvatragahetu.*
[124] i.e. *vipākaja.*
[125] *kāraṇa*°, *sahabhū*°, *vipāka*°, *sabhāgahetu.*
[126] *kāraṇa*°, *sahabhū*°, *sabhāga*°, *sarvatragahetu.*
[127] *duḥkhe dharmakṣānti,* patient acceptance of the law in relation to suffering, is the first moment of the *darśanamārga,* the path of vision, and the first moment which is *anāsrava,* pure. Cfr. infra stanza 104.
[128] *kāraṇa*°, *sahabhū*°, *sabhāga*°, *saṃprayuktakahetu.*

> (28) Let it be known that the causal production of the remaining non-associated ones is threefold, as is that of the remaining associated ones, the pure factors which are produced for the first time.

The factors which are not associated were mentioned before[129]. When the remaining ones among them minus that which is pure for the first time, have the similar cause, they are produced by three causes: the cause which is the reason of being, the similar cause, and the concomitant cause[130].

The associated ones which are pure for the first time are also produced by three causes: the cause which is the reason of being, the concomitant cause, and the associated cause[131]. Previously they were not similar.

> (29) There the ones not associated must be produced by two causes. One (only) produced by one cause, does not exist at all.

There the ones not associated must be produced by two causes: in the class of that which is pure for the first time, form and formations not associated with thought are produced by two causes: the cause which is the reason of being and the concomitant cause[132].

We have explained all that is formed. One among them (only) produced by one cause, does not exist at all.

We have explained all the causes. Such causes were explained by the Tathāgata in order to make conversions by teaching with his power of awakenment, knowing the characteristics of all factors with certainty.

---

[129] i.e. the ones which are *vipākaja* and the *kliṣṭa* ones. See stanza 27a.

[130] *kāraṇa°*, *sabhāga°*, *sahabhūhetu.*

[131] *kāraṇa°*, *sahabhū°*, *saṃprayuktakahetu.*

[132] *kāraṇa°*, *sahabhūhetu.*

The conditions[133] will now be explained.

> (30) The Wise One has explained that the factors are produced by four conditions: the one as immediate antecedent and the condition as object, the one as dominant factor and also the one as cause.

Condition as immediate antecedent[134]: when each of the thoughts is produced in a series and without interval.

Condition as object[135]: the ranges of the factors which constitute thought and its concomitants. The factors which constitute thought and its concomitants are produced because they take them as objects.

Condition as dominant factor[136]: this is the cause which is the reason of being[137], all ten thousand things. When the ten thousand things are produced, they do not bring about obstruction. That which only considers what it should effect[138] as essential, is called condition as dominant factor.
Condition as cause: the concomitant cause, the associated cause, the similar cause, the cause of retribution, and the universal cause[139].

We have explained all the conditions. We will now explain the production of all factors in accordance with the conditions.

> (31) The thoughts and that which constitutes thought's concomitants are produced by the four conditions, and the two right sensations by three (conditions). The rest must namely be explained in relation to two.

---

[133] *pratyaya.*
[134] *samanantarapratyaya.* The Chinese translates *samanantara* as subsequent.
[135] *ālambanapratyaya.*
[136] *adhipatipratyaya.*
[137] *kāraṇahetu.* See stanza 25a.
[138] cfr. supra note 96.
[139] *hetupratyaya*: *sahabhū°*, *saṃprayuktaka°*, *sabhāga°*, *vipāka°*, *sarvatragahetu.*

The thoughts and that which constitutes thought's concomitants are produced by the four conditions: the factors which constitute thought and its concomitants are produced by the four conditions. [812b] Produced because induced by the previous one, stands for the condition as immediate antecedent. Their ranges are the conditions as object. All factors except the particular one itself, are conditions as dominant factor[140].

The two right sensations[141] by three (conditions): the attainment without perception and the attainment of cessation [142] are produced by three conditions. Among them, the thought when engaging in the concentration, is the condition as immediate antecedent[143]. Here the previously produced qualities[144] of their particular stage, are the conditions as cause[145], and also the[146] birth, abiding, changing, and passing away [147] which arise together, are the conditions as cause[148]. The condition as dominant factor is as explained above[149].

The rest must namely be explained in relation to two: the other formations not associated with thought apart from these[150], in addition to form, are produced by two conditions: the condition as cause and the condition as dominant factor[151].

Question: Why do they call these factors formations?

---

[140] AH explains the three *pratyayas*: *amanantara*°, *ālambana*°, *adhipati*°. AH2 839 adds *hetupratyaya*, i.e. *sahabhū*°, *sabhāga*°, and *saṃprayuktakahetu*.

[141] A translation for *samāpatti*, attainment, or *samādhi*, concentration. Here *samāpatti* is meant.

[142] *asaṃjñisamāpatti* and *nirodhasamāpatti*.

[143] *samanantarapratyaya*.

[144] *guṇāḥ*.

[145] *hetupratyaya*, i.e. *sabhāgahetu*. See AH2 839a. As for the *bhūmis* or stages mentioned: for the *asaṃjñisamāpatti*: the fourth *dhyāna* (stanza 220a), and for the *nirodhasamāpatti*: the *bhavāgra* (stanza 106c).

[146] We follow the reading of the 3 editions: 彼.

[147] The four *lakṣaṇas*. See stanza 24ab.

[148] *hetupratyaya*. I.e. *sahabhūhetu*. See AH2 839a.

[149] See explanation of this stanza ab.

[150] i.e. the 2 *samāpattis* just mentioned.

[151] *hetu*°, *adhipatipratyaya*.

Answer: (32) Many factors produce one factor, and one can produce many. As formations formed by conditions and made by them, they must be understood thus.

Many factors produce one factor, and one can produce many: no factor can be produced by its own power, but a factor is produced by many factors. Many factors may yet be produced by one factor. Therefore they say: as formations formed by conditions and made by them, they must be understood thus.

**行品第二**

已说诸法自相。如法生今当说。
问：若诸法自性所摄者亦当以自力故生。答。

15 至竟无能生 用离等侣故
一切法不能自生。所以者何。诸行性劣无势力故如羸病人不能自力起。问若不自力起。当云何起。答。

一切众缘力 诸法乃得生
如羸病人由他扶起彼亦如是。如心由伴生今当说。

16 若心有所起 是心必有俱
心数法等聚 及不相应行
心者意。意者识。实同而异名。此心若依若缘若时起彼心共俱心数法等聚生。
问。何者心数法等聚。答。

17 想欲更乐慧 念思及解脱
作意于境界 三摩提与痛
想者事立时随其像貌受。欲者受缘时欲受。更乐者心依缘和合不相离。慧者与缘决定审谛。念者于缘忆不忘。思者功德恶俱相违于心造作。解脱者于缘中受想时彼必有是。作意者于缘中勇猛发动。定者受缘时心不散。痛者乐不乐俱相违缘受。

18 一切心生时 是生圣所说
同共一缘行 亦复常相应
一切心生时是生圣所说者此十法一切心生时共生。是故说名大地。同共一缘行者一切心共俱同一缘行不相离。亦复常相应者各各共俱及与心俱常相应共行。离增减故故曰相应。
已说心数法谓通一切心中。不通今当说。

19 诸根及觉观 信猗不放逸
进护众烦恼 或时不相应
诸根者善根无贪无恚无愚痴。觉者于心粗相续。观者于心细相续。信者成实真净。猗者善心时于身心离恶故快乐。不放逸者作善时方便不舍。进者作事专著。护者作事行以不行求以不求自守无为。众烦恼者如使品说。此法非一切心中可得。或时相应或时不相应。问。何故说心数。答。意谓之心。彼眷属故说心数。
已说诸心数法相。如所生今当说。

20 不善心品中 心数二十一
秽污二损减 欲界非不善

不善心品中心数二十一者不善名若心生欲界诸烦恼除欲界身见边见。是转成不爱果故谓不善。此心品中当知有二十一心数法十大地觉观二烦恼无惭无愧睡掉不信放逸懈怠。秽污二损减欲界非不善者谓心品是欲界秽污非是不善如身见边见相应心。此品中当知有十九心数法除无惭无愧一向不善故。

21 善不共二十 无记有十二
悔及于眠心 是能以为增

善不共二十者不共名谓心独一无明烦恼生。是二十心数除一烦恼。余如前说。善名谓净心能转成爱果。此心共俱当知有二十十大地觉观信进猗不放逸善根护惭愧。无记有十二者不秽污心品中有十二心数法十大地觉观。悔及于眠心是能以为增者悔名事不成恨为悔是善不善。彼相应心品中增悔。余心数法如前说。眠名灭心一向合不自在为眠。是一切五品中生彼尽增益。余心数法如前说。若悔眠不行三品中是增二。余心数法如前说。

问。此欲界心相续说。色界云何。答。

22 初禅离不善 余知如欲有
禅中间除觉 于上观亦然

初禅离不善余知如欲有者初禅无不善。彼中有四品善秽污不共无记。是如欲界说。善中二十无记十二秽污十九。已离不善当知亦离无惭无愧一向不善故。不共有十八。禅中间除觉者中间禅无觉。彼一向除觉。余如初禅说。于上观亦然者第二第三第四禅亦复无观。及无色界于中一切除观。觉前已除。

已说心数法由伴生。色今当说。

23 极微在四根 十种应当知
身根有九种 余八种谓香

极微在四根十种应当知者谓极微在眼中是知有十种地种水火风种色种香味细滑种眼根种身根种。耳鼻舌极微亦如是。身根有九种者谓余身根极微九种。彼有一根种余如上说。余八种者于中余非根色中极微有八种。问。此极微何界说。答。谓香欲界中有香色界中离香。彼一切除香味种。余种如欲界说。

问。前已说若心生彼中必心数法生及心不相应行。于中已说心数法。心不相应行云何。答。

24 一切有为法 生住变异坏

一切有为法各各有四相生住异坏。世中起故生。已起自事立故住。已住势衰故异。已异灭故坏。此相说心不相应行。问。若一切有为法各有四相者是为相复有相。答。

是亦有四相

彼相中余四相俱生。生为生住为住异为异坏为坏。
问。若尔者便无穷。答。

展转更相为

此相各各相为。如生生各各相生如是住住各各相生异异各各相异坏坏各各相坏。是以非无穷。后四相各行一法。前四相各行八法。生者生八法前三后四及彼法。余亦如是。
已说诸行伴。如由伴生今当说。

25 所作共自然 普遍相应报
从事六种因 转生有为法

一切因尽在六因中。此因生一切有为行。于中所作因者生法时不障碍不留住由此故生不相似法如由地万物得生。共因者诸行各各相伴由此而生如心心数法心不相应行及极微种。自然因者谓彼自己相似如习善生善习不善生不善习无记生无记如物种随类相因。一切遍因者谓诸烦恼转相续生如见我审入计著。由此见故于我有常无常审入计著。谤阴相审入计著。于阴相犹豫受有常乐净。等生诸烦恼如是。说诸一切遍如使品说。相应因者心及心数法各各力于一缘中一时行。相离则不生。报因者谓行生于生中转成果。如善爱果不善不爱果由此故生。
已说诸因。诸法随因中生今当说。

26 若心因报生 心数及烦恼
是从于五因 兴起应当知

若心心数法因报生及诸烦恼是从五因生。报因生者从所作因生。彼生时相似不相似物不障碍故生从共因生。伴力故生。彼各各相伴及心不相应行共伴。从自然因生。彼有相似前生无记法。从相应因生。俱一时一缘中行。从报因生。彼善不善谓此果。秽污心心数法除报因无记故是从一切遍因生。由此故生。余四因如前说。

27 是彼不相应 诸余相应法
除共初无漏 是从四因生

是彼不相应者若色从报生及心不相应行是从四因生所作因共因报因自然因。秽污色及心不相应行亦从四因生所作因共因自然因一切遍因。诸余相应法除其初无漏是从四因生者余心心数法除其初无漏亦从四因生所作因共因自然因相应因。

28 谓余不相应 因生当知三
及诸余相应 初生无漏法

谓不相应法前所说。于中余若有自然因除初无漏是从三因生所作因自然因共因。初无漏相应亦从三因生所作因共因相应因。是前无自然。

29 于中不相应 应从二因生
若从一因中 生者必无有

于中不相应应从二因生者初无漏品中色心不相应行从二因生所作因共因。已说一切有为。于中若从一因生者必无有。

已说诸因。如此因如来定知诸法相觉力教化故说。缘今当说。

30 次第亦缘缘 增上及与因
法从四缘生 明智之所说

次第缘者一一心生相续无间。缘缘者心心数法境界。缘彼故心心数法生。增上缘者是所作因一切万物。万物生时不作挂碍。但自所作为要是说增上缘。因缘者共因相应因自然因报因一切遍因。

已说诸缘。诸法随缘生今当说。

31 心及诸心数 是从四缘生
二正受从三 谓余说于二

心及诸心数是从四缘生者心心数法从四缘生。前开导故生是彼次第缘。境界是彼缘缘。除其自已余一切诸法是彼增上缘。二正受从三者无想定灭尽定是从三缘生。于中入定心是彼次第缘。于中自地前生功德是彼因缘及彼俱生生住异坏亦彼因缘。彼增上缘如前说。谓余说于二者离彼余心不相应行及色从二缘生因缘及增上缘。

问。以何故此诸法谓之行。答。

32 多法生一法 一亦能生多
缘行所作行 如是应当知

多法生一法一亦能生多者无有一法能自力生。但一法由多法生。多法亦由一法生。以是故谓缘行所作行如是应当知。

# CHAPTER III. ACTIONS[1]

We have explained the particular nature of the formations, and also that they are produced by the causes and the conditions[2]. We will now explain that, when these (factors) with a cause[3], mentioned previously, bear fruition[4], different kinds of birth can be arrived at.

> (33) Actions fashion the worlds with the courses everywhere. Reflect therefore on action and seek deliverance from the world!

Actions fashion the worlds with the courses[5] everywhere: the three worlds[6] are fashioned with the different kinds of bodies in the five courses[7]. The things by which the worlds are fashioned are actions indeed. Reflect therefore on action and seek deliverance from the world!

> (34) Bodily actions and verbal and mental ones are performed by those who exist. By them the formations are produced, bearing the kinds of bodies (as fruitions).

Bodily actions and verbal and mental ones[8] are performed by those who exist[9]: i.e. bodily, verbal, and mental actions are performed by those born[10]. By them the formations are produced, bearing the kinds of bodies (as fruition).

The characteristics of these actions will now be explained briefly.

---

1 *Karmavarga*.
2 The particular nature of the formations: Chapter 1: *Dhātuvarga*. Their production: Chapter 2: *Saṃskāravarga*.
3 *sahetuka*.
4 Fruition: *phala;* to bear (fruition), i.e. to fashion *alaṃkṛ*°.
5 *gati*.
6 i.e. past, present, and future: *atīta, pratyutpanna,* and *anāgata*.
7 The five *gatis* are: hell, hungry ghost (*preta),* animal, man, heaven.
8 i.e. kāya°, vāk°, *manaskarman*.
9 有有, and also 生生 are plural.
10 See note 9.

> (35) Let it be known that information and non-information of bodily action both exist. The same applies to verbal action. Mental action is only non-information.

Let it be known that information and non-information[11] of bodily action both exist: the nature of bodily action is twofold. [812c] It is by nature either information or non-information. In this case, information: a movement of the body is wholesome, unwholesome, or indeterminate. The wholesome one is produced by a wholesome thought, the unwholesome one is produced by an unwholesome thought, and an indeterminate one arises from an indeterminate thought.

Non-information: when the actions one performs are firm[12]. This element arises even though it takes place among thoughts which are different, e.g. even among unwholesome and indeterminate thoughts someone who is well ordained[13] follows (the precepts). Someone of evil actions follows his bad restraint[14].

The same applies to verbal action: the nature of verbal action is also twofold.

Mental action is only non-information: the nature of mental action is nothing but non-information. Why? Because it does not show[15], as it is a subtle series of volitions[16].

Question: How many of these five actions[17] are wholesome, how many are unwholesome, and how many indeterminate?

---

[11] i.e. *vijñapti* and *avijñapti*.
[12] *avijñapti* may be understood to be a latent force of habit.
[13] *sūpasaṃpanna*.
[14] *saṃvara,* restraint.
[15] In our text *manaskarman* is *avijñapti* only because it does not show, is not visible. The later sarvāstivādins reserve *avijñapti* only for *kāya*° and *vākkarman*. See *Kośa* IV 3f.; MAH 888bc.
[16] *cetanā*.
[17] *kāyakarman* (2), *vākkarman* (2), *manaskarman* (1).

Answer: (36) Let it be known that information is threefold: wholesome, unwholesome, and indeterminate. The same applies to the mental non-information. The rest are not said to be indeterminate.

Let it be known that information is threefold: wholesome, unwholesome, and indeterminate[18]: bodily and verbal information are said to be threefold: wholesome, unwholesome, and indeterminate. Among them, wholesome bodily information: practicing giving, morality[19], and so forth, are bodily movements caused by wholesome thoughts. Unwholesome bodily information: taking life, taking what is not given, impure conduct[20] are bodily movements caused by unwholesome thoughts. Indeterminate bodily information: bodily movements caused by indeterminate thoughts, such as the ones relating to deportment and to craftsmanship and expertise[21]. Likewise the wholesome ones of the verbal movements, such as no false speech[22] and timely words associated with ample advantages[23], are verbal actions produced by wholesome thoughts. The unwholesome ones, such as false speech, slander, harsh words, frivolous talk[24] are verbal actions produced by unwholesome thoughts. The indeterminate ones are verbal actions produced by indeterminate thoughts.

The same applies to the mental non-information: the non-information of mental action is also threefold: wholesome, unwholesome, and indeterminate. Volition[25] associated with wholesome thoughts is wholesome. Volition associated with unwholesome thoughts is unwholesome. Volition associated with indeterminate thoughts is indeterminate.

---

[18] *kuśala, akuśala, avyākṛta.*
[19] *dāna*; *śīla* (Chinese: keeping the precepts).
[20] i.e. *prāṇātipāta, adattādāna, abrahmacarya.*
[21] i.e. *airyāpathika* and *śailpasthānika.*
[22] *mṛṣāvādavirati.*
[23] Ample advantage, 饶益: *artha.*
[24] i.e. *mṛṣāvāda, paiśūnya, paruṣavacana, saṃbhinnapralāpa.*
[25] *cetanā.*

The rest are not said to be indeterminate: two remain: bodily non-information and verbal non-information. These are twofold: wholesome or unwholesome, never indeterminate. Why? An indeterminate thought is weak and cannot produce a forceful[26] action, i.e. one which, even though occurring among thoughts which are different, goes on in its selfsame fashion. Therefore there is no indeterminate bodily non-information or verbal non-information.

Question: What kind of nature does indeterminate action possess, and into what places is it linked?

Answer: (37) In the existence of form, that which is indeterminate is ambivalent: obscure and not obscure. That which is obscure is linked to form and the rest to two realms.

In the existence of form[27], that which is indeterminate is ambivalent: obscure and not obscure[28]: bodily and verbal (indeterminate) action, being material because the action is material, are twofold, obscure and not obscure: i.e. obscure means [813a] covered by affliction and produced by the afflictions. That which is otherwise is not obscure.

That which is obscure is linked to form: if obscure, it is only linked to the realm of form. Why? Afflictions to be abandoned through development[29] give rise to bodily and verbal action. The afflictions to be abandoned through development in this realm of desire are only unwholesome, and with unwholesome afflictions one cannot give rise to indeterminate actions.

The rest (is linked) to two realms: not obscure indeterminate action is both linked to the realm of desire and to the realm of form. Mental action is explained as the thoughts. They have

[26] *balavat.*
[27] *rūpabhava.*
[28] *nivṛta* and *anivṛta.*
[29] *bhāvanāheya.* The Chinese means: to be cut off through reflection.

been distinctly established somewhere else[30], and therefore they will not be explained here.

> (38) Let it be known that non-information of bodily and of verbal action is wholesome or unwholesome, and characterized by the three: (restraint) through trance, pure (restraint), and restraint of the code of discipline.

Let it be known that non-information of bodily and of verbal action is wholesome or unwholesome: when action is material, and furthermore when it has the nature of non-information, it is wholesome or unwholesome.

It is characterized[31] by the three: (restraint) through trance, pure (restraint), and restraint of the code of discipline[32]: restraint, which is non-information, has three characteristics: pure, produced through trance, and of the code of discipline. Pure: i.e. when restraint proceeds together with the path[33]: right speech, right action, and right livelihood[34]. Produced through trance: i.e. when it occurs within a trance, renouncing evil. The restraint of the code of discipline: i.e. the restraint of the realm of desire.

> (39) Let it be known that the non-information in the realm of desire and information dependent on two existences, are no companions of thought. That is to say, the others are called companions of thought.

That is to say, the non-information of the realm of desire is no companion of thought[35]. Why? Wholesome thoughts, unwholesome thoughts and indeterminate thoughts do[36] occur in the restraint after being ordained[37], but it is not the companion of

---

[30] See stanzas 20-22; cf. AH2 840b.

[31] *lakṣaṇa*.

[32] The three kinds of *saṃvara*: *dhyāna* (ja) °, *anāsrava*°, *prātimokṣa* (调御: discipline, *dama*), *saṃvara* (威仪戒: restraint relating to proper deportment).

[33] i.e. *āryamārga*. MAH 889b explains: *śaikṣa*°, *aśaikṣamārga*.

[34] *samyagvāc*, *samyakkarmānta*, *samyagājīva*.

[35] *cittānuparivartin*.

[36] We follow the reading of the 3 editions: 唯: *eva*.

[37] *upasaṃpanna*. The *prātimokṣasaṃvara* is meant.

wholesome, unwholesome, or indeterminate ones. Information both in the realm of desire and in the realm of form is not a companion of thought. Why? Because it is dependent on the body. The non-information of the realm of form and the pure one[38] are companions of thought. Why? Because they depend on (such) thoughts. It is not the case that they occur with different thoughts.

We have distinctly established all actions. How one accomplishes actions will now be explained.

> (40) Pure restraint is accomplished by the vision of the truths, and the (restraint) produced through trance (is accomplished) when obtaining a trance. The one of keeping the precepts is produced in the realm of desire.

Pure restraint is accomplished by the vision of the truths[39]: vision of the truths: i.e. when pure vision views the noble truths. When producing a pure vision for the first time, one views the truth of suffering[40] in the realm of desire. Therefore all the noble accomplish pure restraint.

The (restraint) produced through trance (is accomplished) when obtaining a trance: i.e. he who obtains a trance accomplishes the restraint through trance.

The one of keeping the precepts[41] is produced in the realm of desire: when someone is ordained[42], he[43] accomplishes the restraint of the realm of desire.

We have briefly explained their accomplishment[44]. How they can be obtained as past, present, and future [813b], will know be explained.

---

[38] i.e. the *saṃvara* which is *dhyānaja,* and the *anāsrava* one.
[39] *satyadarśana*; 戒律仪 means *saṃvara*.
[40] *duḥkhadarśana*. See also stanza 104.
[41] i.e. *prātimokṣasaṃvara*.
[42] *upasaṃpanna*.
[43] We follow the reading of the 3 editions: 彼: he.
[44] 成就, a translation for *samanvāgama*.

(41) Let it be known that the non-information of the one who abides in the restraint (of the code), as it is in the present, is permanently accomplished. Or again, having ended, it is past.

Let it be known that the non-information of the one who abides in the restraint (of the code)[45], as it is in the present, is permanently accomplished: when abiding in the restraint (of the code), one accomplishes at every moment the restraint which is non-information. It is never abandoned. One is attached to it until life's end.

Or again, having ended, it is past: or the accomplished past restraint which is non-information, when it has ended, is not lost. I.e. when the beginning has ended, it is the case that one accomplishes what has passed. Another term for what has passed is what has ended.

(42) When someone brings about information, he immediately establishes the middle period. Let it be known that one establishes what has passed when (the information) has ended without being abandoned.

When someone brings about information[46], he immediately establishes the middle period: when one brings about bodily or verbal information, at that moment one immediately accomplishes present information. Another term for the present is the middle period.

Let it be known that one establishes what has passed when (the information) has ended without being abandoned: when the information has ended but is not lost, at that moment then one accomplishes what has passed.

(43) It is said that he who has obtained the non-information through trance, accomplishes what is

---

45 *(Prātimokṣa)saṃvara.* We follow the reading of the 3 editions: 威仪戒.

46 Abiding in *prātimokṣasaṃvara*.

> extinguished and what is not yet reached, and when he is engaged in right sensation, (he accomplishes) what is intermediate. The information is as explained before.

It is said that he who has obtained the non-information through trance[47], accomplishes what is extinguished and what is not yet reached[48]: when one obtains the one through trance, he accomplishes what has passed and what has not yet come[49]. Why? (The accomplishing of) the restraint is just like the accomplishing of the trance[50].

When he is engaged in right sensation[51], (he accomplishes) what is intermediate: another term for the present is what is intermediate. When he is engaged in concentration, at that moment[52] he accomplishes present non-information. Why? Because it is a companion of concentration.

The information is as explained before[53]: as when abiding in the restraint (of the code)[54] –when bringing about information, at that moment one accomplishes present information; but when not bringing about information, at that moment one does not accomplish present information. When it has ended without being lost, at that moment one accomplishes what has passed, but when it has not ended or if, having ended, it is lost, at that moment one does not accomplish it- it is the same when one abides in the restraint through trance.

> (44) Let it be known that it is accomplished by all who have obtained the path, if it has not yet been produced. What is intermediate, is in the thoughts of the path. When

---

47 i.e. *dhyānajasaṃvara*, which is *cittānuparivartin*.
48 i.e. *atīta* and *anāgata,* past and future.
49 See note 48.
50 e.g. when one can obtain a future *dhyāna,* one will also obtain the *dhyānasaṃvara.*
51 *samādhi*.
52 We follow the reading of the 3 editions, i.e. without 空.
53 Stanza 42.
54 *(prātimokṣa)saṃvara.*

it has ended without being abandoned, (then) it is of the previous period.

Let it be known that it[55] is accomplished by all who have obtained the path, if it has not yet been produced[56]: all who have obtained the path accomplish future pure non-information. Why? (The accomplishing of) the restraint is just like the accomplishing of the pure thoughts.

What is intermediate is in the thoughts of the path: when, in harmony with the path, one has engaged in concentration[57], [813c] at that moment one accomplishes the present.

When it has ended without being abandoned, (then) it is of the previous period: the previous period is the past. When, regarding this non-information, it has ended without being lost, one accomplishes past non-information, just like someone who has obtained a noble fruition and falls away[58].

> (45) When he who has established restraint performs what is evil and unwholesome, he accomplishes the two, as long as he is bound by his ties. Let it be known that they have ended after their destruction

When he who has established restraint performs what is evil and unwholesome, he accomplishes the two: he who thus abides in the restraint (of the code), or he who abides in the restraint through trance, or he who abides in pure restraint[59] may bring about unwholesome and unclean heavy ties[60]. When at that moment he produces non-information relating to the unwholesome, he accomplishes information and non-information.

---

55 i.e. *anāsravasaṃvara*, which is *cittānuparivartin*.
56 i.e. future.
57 *Samāhita*.
58 "Falling away" may translate *parihāṇi*.
e.g. when an *anāgāmin* has attained the *arhattvaphala* and falls away to be a *sakṛdāgāmin*. cf. infra stanzas 110 et seq., and 185.
59 (prātimokṣa)*saṃvara*°, *dhyānasaṃvara*°, *anāsravasaṃvarastha*.
60 Seems to mean *saṃyojana* (scil. *kleśa*).

If they are not unclean heavy ties, he does not produce non-information[61].

Question: For how long does he accomplish them?

Answer: As long as he is bound by his ties. When he is bound by his ties, he accomplishes what can be obtained accordingly.

Let it be known that they have ended after their destruction: when these ties are destroyed, then the information and the non-information have ended.

> (46) Abiding in non-restraint, non-information is accomplished in the middle -being evil it has an unlovely fruition- and also as past, when it has ended.

Abiding in non-restraint[62], non-information is accomplished in the middle[63] -being evil it has an unlovely fruition[64]: when dwelling in non-restraint, at that moment one accomplishes unwholesome non-information. Unwholesome means having an unlovely fruition.

Also as past, when it has ended: when extinguished and not when not extinguished.

> (47) When, with information, it is visible in the moment, it is said to be accomplished in the middle, and also as past, when it has ended. When wholesome, it is the opposite of the above.

When, with information, it[65] is visible in the moment, it is said to be accomplished in the middle, and also as past, when it has ended: the information is as explained before[66].

---

[61] *avijñapti* is "heavy", cf. stanza 35 note 12, and stanza 36 note 26.
[62] *asaṃvara.* The Chinese means: restraint not relating to proper deportment.
[63] i.e. as present.
[64] cf. stanza 20.
[65] i.e. *asaṃvara*.
[66] Stanza 42.

When wholesome, it is the opposite of the above[67]: just as dwelling in restraint is said to be unwholesome, so dwelling in non-restraint is said to be wholesome as long as the wholesome thought (lasts).

> (48) Now, what is performed by one who abides in-between, is accomplished in the middle period, and also (accomplished) as past, when it has ended. It is either the two or one[68].

One who dwells in between[69]: he who abides in neither-restraint-nor-non-restraint[70] abides in what is contained in between. When he abides in that which is wholesome, they say that which is wholesome is either twofold, both with information and without information, or it is only information. It is either both wholesome and unwholesome, or one[71].

Question: How does one obtain the restraint of the realm of form, and how does one abandon it? Is it obtained through the fundamental trances[72] or through other applications[73]?

Answer: Not only through the fundamental trances.

> (49) The wholesome thoughts in the realm of form obtain the restraint through concentration. When the former are lost, the latter is also lost. For the pure one there are six thoughts.

[814a] The wholesome thoughts in the realm of form obtain the restraint[74] through concentration: when one obtains the wholesome thoughts of the realm of form, whether having

---

[67] Stanza 45. In this case, the *asaṃvarastha* who performs that which is *kuśala,* wholesome, is meant.
[68] 2: present and past *vijñapti* and *avijñapti* } AH2 841b; cf. MAH 890ab.
1: present *avijñapti* } AH2 841b; cf. MAH 890ab.
[69] *madhyastha.* i.e. one who dwells in the middle, i.e. in *naivasaṃvaraṇāsaṃvara.*
[70] *naivasaṃvaraṇāsaṃvara.*
[71] *kuśala* or *akuśala.* cf. MAH 890ab.
[72] *mauladhyāna.*
[73] Besides the four fundamental trances, there are the *anāgamyadhyāna* and the *dhyānāntara.*
[74] 威仪戒: *saṃvara.*

renounced desire or not having renounced desire, they all obtain the restraint of the realm of form. Why? In all wholesome thoughts of the realm of form, the restraint is always a companion.

Question: How is it lost?

Answer: When the former are lost, the latter is also lost.

Question: What about the pure one[75]?

Answer: For the pure one there are six thoughts. Pure restraint is obtained together with the pure thoughts of six stages[76].

Question: How is it lost?

Answer: When the former are lost, the latter is also lost.

Six stages: the pre-trance, the intermediate trance, and the four fundamental trances[77].

Question: At how many moments are these restraints abandoned?

Answer: (50) The Awakened One has expounded that the restraint of the code of discipline is abandoned at five moments, and that the one produced by trance and the pure one (are abandoned) at two moments.

The Awakened One has expounded that the restraint of the code of discipline[78] is abandoned at five moments: the restraint (of the code) is abandoned at five moments: refusing the moral rules[79], breaking the precepts[80], at the moment of death[81], when

---

[75] *anāsrava* (*saṃvara*).

[76] *bhūmi*. See infra for the 6.

[77] i.e. the *anāgamya*, the *dhyānāntara* and the 4 *mauladhyānas*.

[78] 調御: *prātimokṣa;* 威仪戒: *saṃvara*. cf. note 32.

[79] *śikṣāpratyākhyāna*. 道: path, *scil. śikṣāpada*, the moral rules. AH2 841c: when abandoning the precepts, *śikṣānikṣepaṇa*.

[80] This seems to mean: in the case of a *patanīya*, a fundamental offence (*āpatti*). According to the *Kośa* IV 95, this view is held by the Sautrāntikas, not by the *Vaibhāṣikas* in *Kāśmīra*. See also MAH 892b.

[81] *Cyuti*.
AH2 841c: when abandoning the *nikāyasabhāga*, the appropriate kind.

that which is wrong is increased[82], and when the law vanishes[83].
The one produced by trance and the pure one (are abandoned) at two moments: restraint through trance is abandoned at two moments: when falling away[84] and when born in a higher stage. Pure restraint is also abandoned at two moments: when falling away and when obtaining a fruition[85].

Question: How are the other actions abandoned?

Answer: (51) For the restraint which is unwholesome , there are two (moments). The same applies to the wholesome formless one. For the defiled one they mention one moment, when the action is in the mind.

For the restraint which is unwholesome [86], there are two (moments): when failing to achieve application[87], and also the moment of death.

The same applies to the wholesome formless one[88]: wholesome formless action is also abandoned at two moments: when the wholesome roots are cut and when one is born in a higher stage[89].

---

[82] This seems to agree with *ubhayavyañjanotpatti*; i.e. in the case of a hermaphrodite.
AH2 841c: when both organs are produced
MAH 892b: when both figures are produced.
Another possibility: in the case of *mūlaccheda*, cutting down the wholesome roots.

[83] *saddharmāntardhāna*. AH2 841c also lists this moment, adding that the masters of the *Vibhāṣā* in Kāśmīra do not list it. MAH 892b does not list this moment, but informs us that it is listed by the 持律者: *(Vinayadhara)*, not by the *Ābhidhārmikas*. *Kośa* IV 95 says that *Dharmaguptakas* list this moment. The 5 moments listed in AH2 841c: 1. *nikāyasabhāgatyāga;* 2. *śikṣānikṣepaṇa*; 3. *mūlaccheda*; 4. *ubhayavyañjanotpati*; 5. *saddharmāntardhāna*. MAH892 lists: 1.*śikṣānikṣepaṇa*; 2. *nikāyasabhāgatyāga*; 3. *mūlaccheda*; 4. *ubhayavyañjanotpatti*. *Kośa* IV 94-95 also lists these 4 moments.

[84] *parihāṇi*.
AH2 841c says that some people add a third moment, i.e. *indriyasaṃcāra,* perfecting the faculties.
MAH 892b mentions these 3 moments. Idem *Kośa* IV 100.

[85] i.e. from *srotaāpattiphala* up to *arhattvaphala*. See MAH 892b.

[86] i.e. *asaṃvara*.

[87] This may mean: when failing to do that which one was going to do.
方便 may translate *kriyākāra*.

For the defiled one[90] they mention one moment, when the action is in the mind: defiled mental action is abandoned at one moment: the moment of renouncing desire[91].

We have explained the nature of all actions, and also how they are accomplished. We will now explain that the World-Honored One has distinctly established different types of such actions.

> (52) Let it be known that, when actions bear an unpleasant fruition, they are evil conduct. That which is predominant in evil mental conduct, is covetousness, hatred, and wrong view.

Let it be known that, when actions bear an unpleasant fruition, they are evil conduct[92]: i.e. when actions are unwholesome, all are said to be evil conduct. That which is unwholesome has an unpleasant fruition.

That which is predominant in evil mental conduct, is covetousness, hatred and wrong view[93]: unwholesome volition[94] is evil mental conduct. Now, evil mental conduct is said to be threefold: covetousness, hatred, and wrong view.

> (53) The Most Victorious One has expounded that the opposite of this is good conduct. Now, that which is supreme in it, is called the ten paths.

The Most Victorious One has expounded that the opposite of this is good conduct[95]: all wholesome actions are the opposite of this,

---

88 *kuśalārūpa,* action.
89 *mūlaccheda* and *ūrdhvajanman*.
90 *kliṣṭa* action.
91 MAH 893a says that a defiled immaterial (*arūpa*) action is abandoned when renouncing desire (*vairāgya*), and by the coming into existence of the antidote (*pratipakṣotpāda*).
92 *duścarita*.
93 *abhidhyā*, *vyāpāda*, *mithyādṛṣṭi*.
94 *cetanā*.
95 *sucarita*.

[814b] and also absence of covetousness, absence of hatred, and right view[96].

Now, that which is supreme in it, is called the ten paths: now, the supreme actions among unwholesome actions are called paths of action[97], such as: taking life, taking what is not given, wrong conduct, false speech, slander, harsh words, frivolous talk, covetousness, hatred, and wrong view. Among them, taking life[98]: when, conscious of the fact that it is a being and with the intention of doing away with[99] a being, one puts an end to someone else's life, accomplishing the action with premeditation[100]. Taking what is not given[101]: when things owned by someone else are not given but abruptly taken, while one is conscious of the fact that they belong to someone else. Wrong conduct[102]: when a woman who belongs to someone else is offended in relation to intercourse, or when one's own (woman) is offended from time to time in relation to a wrong way of intercourse[103]. False speech[104]: when speaking, one is conscious of the fact that it is false, and one has the intention of imposing on someone else. Slander[105]: when, out of hatred for another, one speaks taking pains to bring about a separation from oneself. Harsh words[106]: unkind words out of hatred for another. Frivolous talk[107]: the senseless words of one with unwholesome thoughts. Covetousness[108]: the desire of the realm of desire. Hatred[109]: anger[110]. Wrong view[111]: when denying cause and

---

[96] *anabhidhyā, avyāpāda, samyagdṛṣṭi.*
[97] *karmapatha.*
[98] *prāṇātipāta.*
[99] *parityaj°.*
[100] *prayoga.*
[101] *adattādāna.*
[102] *mithyācāra.*
[103] Only the *yonimārga* is not *amārga.* Other ways are wrong. See *Kośa* IV157.
[104] *mṛṣāvāda.*
[105] *paiśūnya.* Chinese: being double-tongued.
[106] *paruṣavacana.*
[107] *saṃbhinnapralāpa.*
[108] *abhidhyā.*
[109] *vyāpāda.*
[110] *dveṣa.*
[111] *mithyādṛṣṭi.*

effect[112]. They are the paths of action. The rest are not paths of action, i.e. when the preparation[113] for these deeds is undertaken, or when drinking spirits, and so forth.

The volition[114] for an action that is not right is the fundamental action. It takes those ten as its paths.

> (54) Such actions involve retribution in the present, or they are subsequently experienced as retribution after being reborn. The same applies to later retribution. It is said that the rest are not fixed.

I.e. an action can accomplish its fruition in the present, but sometimes it is not fixed[115].

Question: The three actions as expounded by the World-Honored One: with pleasant retribution, with unpleasant retribution, and with neither unpleasant nor pleasant[116] retribution, what about these?

Answer: (55) Now, those which are wholesome in the realm of desire, and three stages of the realm of form must involve pleasant retribution. That which is experienced is either fixed or it is not fixed.

Now, those which are wholesome in the realm of desire, and three stages of the realm of form must involve pleasant retribution: the wholesome actions of the realm of desire produce a retribution accompanied by happiness, and also the first trance, the second and the third one of the realm of form produce

---

[112] See stanza 71.
Denying, *apavāda*.
[113] *prayoga*.
[114] *cetanā*.
[115] *karman* is *niyata*, fixed, (*dṛṣṭadharmavedanīya*, to be experienced in the present; *upapadyavedanīya*, to be experienced after being reborn; *apạraparyāyavedanīya*, to be experienced a later time), or *aniyata*, not fixed. See AH2 842b.
[116] Pleasant, *sukha*; unpleasant, *duḥkha*; neither unpleasant nor pleasant, aduḥkhāsukha.

retribution accompanied by happiness. These are all said to possess pleasant retribution[117].

Question: Are they also fixed[118]?

Answer: That which is experienced is either fixed or it is not fixed. Whether fixed or not fixed, the wholesome (actions) in these four stages all possess a pleasant retribution.

> (56) That which produces neither suffering nor happiness is precisely in that which is wholesome at a higher stage. When they experience unpleasant retribution, they are said to be unwholesome actions.

That which produces neither suffering nor happiness [119] is precisely in that which is wholesome at a higher stage: the wholesome actions in the stage of the fourth trance and also in formlessness have a neither unpleasant nor pleasant retribution. They produce retribution accompanied by neither suffering nor happiness. In it there is no pleasant feeling[120].

When they experience unpleasant retribution, they are said to be unwholesome actions: unwholesome actions involve unpleasant retribution. They are certain to be accompanied by unpleasant feelings[121]. The retribution experienced is also either fixed [814c] or it is not fixed, as explained earlier[122].

Question: The World-Honored One has expounded four actions: black with black retribution, white with white retribution, black and white with black and white retribution, and neither black nor white without retribution[123]. What about these actions[124]?

---

[117] *sukhavipāka.*
[118] *niyata.* cf. note 115.
[119] *aduḥkhāsukha.*
[120] *sukhavedanā.*
[121] *duḥkhavedanā.*
[122] Stanza 55d.
[123] *kṛṣṇakṛṣṇavipāka, śuklaśuklavipāka, kṛṣṇaśuklakṛṣṇaśuklavipāka, akṛṣṇāśuklāvipāka.*
[124] We follow the reading of the 3 editions, adding 业.

Answer: (57) When there is wholesome action in form, it is white and involves white retribution. Black and white is in the realm of desire. That which is not clean is said to involve black retribution.

When there is wholesome action in form, it is white and involves white retribution: the wholesome actions of the realm of form involve white retribution, because they are absolutely without strife[125], and because they are free from that which is unwholesome. When they only involve extremely good retribution, they are said to be white, with white retribution.

Black and white is in the realm of desire: the wholesome actions of the realm of desire are black and white, with black and white retribution. Why? They are spoilt by what is unwholesome, because they are weak. For that reason they are called black and white. Because they experience mixed retribution, both lovely and unlovely, they are said to involve black and white retribution.

That which is not clean[126] is said to involve black retribution: that which is unwholesome, in other words, that which is not clean, is black, because it makes evil grow. It is said to involve black retribution because of its vileness.

(58) When volitions reject[127] them, they[128] leave absolutely

---

[125] We follow the 3 editions: 不诤. *āniñjya*, immovable. See *Kośa* IV129. 诤 is the usual translation for *raṇa.* AH2 842c 无恼: without vexation; MAH 896b 无瞋恚: without hatred (or anger). Does AH understand *anindya*?

[126] *aśubha.*

[127] 舍离, a possible translation for *pratikṣip*°. AH2 842c: 破坏: and MAH 896b: 坏: to destroy.

Volition, *cetanā*, associated with the *ānantaryamārgas* of the *āryamārga* (*darśana*° and *bhāvanāmārga*), is called the fourth action (*karman*). In the *darśanamārga* there are 8 *ānantaryamārgas* (i.e. the 8 *kṣāntis*. Cf. stanzas 104 et seq.) and in the *bhāvanāmārga* 81 (i.e.*kāmadhātu*, 4 *dhyānas,* 4 *ārūpyas*: 9 in each *bhūmi.* 9: see prose to stanzas 107 et seq.). The *cetanā* meant here is associated with 4 *kṣāntis* of the *darśanamārga*, and with 13 *ānantaryamārgas* of the *bhāvanāmārga*, i.e. the 9 of the *kāmadhātu* and the ninth *ānantaryamārgas* of the 4 *dhyānas.* The total adds up to 17.

AH2 842c explains: 4 *kṣāntis* (*darśanamārga*) + 8 of the *kāmadhātu* (*bhāvanāmārga*) cut short black actions (*akuśalakarman*).

The ninth *ānantaryamārgas* of the 4 *dhyānas* (*bhāvanāmārga*) cut short white actions (*kuśalakarman* of the *rūpadhātu*).

The ninth one of the *kāmadhātu* (*bhāvanāmārga*) cuts short black and white actions (*kuśalakarman* of the *kāmadhātu*).

[128] i.e. the 3 actions mentioned in the previous stanza: i.e. black with black retribution, white with white retribution, black and white with black and white retribution. See note 123.

> no remainder. Being in the immediate path they are called the fourth action[129]

This is to say, the path which can extinguish these three actions[130] is the immediate path[131]. All[132] its volitions, these volitions are the fourth action. In this respect, four volitions -in the path of development they extinguish the second action [133] -and thirteen[134]-with two paths: four in the path of the vision of the truths[135] and nine in the path of development[136]- are the pure[137] volitions. Because they do not make evil grow they are not black, and because they are not pleasant[138] they are not white. Because they are the opposite of that which is infinite[139], they are without retribution.

Question: The World-Honored One has expounded bodily, verbal and mental crookedness, uncleanliness, and impurity[140]. What about these?

Answer: (59) Crookedness is produced by deceit, and uncleanliness is produced by hatred. The World-Honored One has expounded that that which is produced by desire, is called impurity.

Crookedness is produced by deceit [141]: when an action is produced by deceit, it is crooked because it is an imposture.

---

[129] The *cetanās* associated with the 17 *ānantaryamārgas* mentioned in note 127, are the fourth action.

[130] i.e. black, white, black and white.

[131] *Ānantaryamarga*.

[132] 若有 or 所有.

[133] i.e. the ninth *ānantaryamārgas* of the 4 *dhyānas* extinguish in the *bhāvanāmārga* the white actions, the wholesome actions of the realm of form.

[134] See note 127, namely 1 (12 *cetanās*) and 3 (1 *cetanā*).

[135] i.e. 4 *kṣāntis* of the *darśanamārga*. cf. note 127.

[136] The 9 *ānantaryamārgas* (*bhāvanāmārga*) of the *kāmadhātu*.

[137] *Anāsrava*.

[138] *Amanojña*.
We follow the reading of the 3 editions: 可乐.

[139] AH2 842c 流转: *pravṛtti*, the process (of existence);
MAH 896b 堕界: *dhātupatita*, falling into the realms (of existence).

[140] *kauṭilya, doṣa, kaṣāya* (浊: turbidity).

[141] *śāñhya*.

Uncleanliness is produced by hatred[142]: when an action is produced by hatred it is unclean, because it only means strife.

The World-Honored One has expounded that that which is produced by desire[143], is called impurity: when an action is produced by desire it is impure, because it is totally filthy[144].

Question: The three purifications[145]: of body, of speech, and of mind, as expounded by the World-Honored One, what about these?

Answer: (60) The purifications are all good conducts. *mauneya* is of body and of speech. They say that the mental *mauneya* of one who has no more training to do is the thought of one who has no more training to do.

The purifications are all good conducts[146]: all[147] good conducts are all purifications, because they forsake the impurity[148] of the afflictions.

Question: What about *mauneya*[149]?

Answer: *mauneya* is of body and of speech. Bodily and verbal good conduct in the mind of one who has no more training to do[150] [815a] are called *mauneya*, because he has truly removed all obstructions.

---

142 *dveṣa*.
143 *rāga*.
144 尘垢 may translate *rajas*, durt.
145 *śauceya*.
146 *sucarita*, i.e. bodily, verbal, and mental.
147 See note 132.
148 *aśuci*: 不净.
149 满, a transcription for *mauneya*, sage (*muni*)-hood. *mauneya* means "quietness: 寂静", according to AH2 843a. In the stanza of AH2 we read 净: *jing*, but the 3 editions have the expected 靜: *jing*.
150 *aśaikṣa*.

They say that the mental *mauneya* of one who has no more training to do is the thought of one who has no more training to do: now, the mental *mauneya* of one who has no more training to do is the thought of one who has no more training to do. Why? Because the thought of one who has no more training to do has obtained that which is characteristic of a Muni.

We have explained the different terms for actions. Their fruition[151] will now be explained.

(61) Wholesome and evil, unwholesome actions, both have two (kinds of) fruition. Wholesome ones may bear three fruitions. The rest are said to have one fruition.

Wholesome and evil, unwholesome actions, both have two (kinds of) fruition: wholesome [152] actions bear two fruitions: the fruition which is the natural result [153] and the fruition of retribution[154]. Pure[155] actions also bear two fruitions: the fruition which represents the natural result and the fruition of disconnection[156] Unwholesome actions also bear two fruitions: the fruition which represents the natural result and the fruition of retribution[157]

Wholesome ones may bear three fruitions: i.e. when wholesome impure [158] actions can remove the afflictions, they bear three fruitions: the fruition which represents the natural result, the fruition of retribution, and the fruition of disconnection[159].

The rest are said to have one fruition: i.e. the rest, the indeterminate actions, have one fruition: the fruition which represents the natural result[160], and nothing else.

---

[151] *phala*.
[152] i.e. (*sāsrava*) *kuśala*. *Anāsrava* actions are as explained infra.
[153] *niṣyandaphala*. Chinese: fruition of that which is relied on. 所依 translates words such as *nissaya, niśraya*.
[154] *vipākaphala*.
[155] *anāsrava*.
[156] *niṣyandaphala* and *visaṃyogaphala*.
[157] *niṣyandaphala* and *vipākaphala*.
[158] *sāsrava*.
[159] *niṣyanda*°, *vipāka*°, *visaṃyogaphala*.
[160] See note 153.

Question: Bodily and verbal actions have the characteristic of being derivative form[161]. By which four great elements[162] are these actions produced?

Answer: (62) When one has the great elements of a particular stage, they are the basis for its bodily and verbal action. The pure ones are obtained according to one's power. They are namely its result.

When one has the great elements of a particular stage[163], they are the basis for its bodily and verbal action: now, in the realm of desire the actions depend on the great elements of the realm of desire, because they are produced by them. The same applies to the actions of the realm of form.

Question: What about the pure actions?

Answer: The pure ones are obtained according to one's power. They are namely its result: when the form of the pure ones is obtained on the basis of the four great elements, it depends on their stage. When one has attained the path dwelling in the realm of desire, his bodily and verbal actions are produced by the four great elements of the realm of desire. The same applies to all stages, i.e., when his life ends and he is born in the realm of formlessness, after his power has removed the desire of the realm of form and that of the realm of formlessness, and when he obtains the bodily and verbal actions not yet obtained, these bodily and verbal actions are produced by the four great elements of that stage[164].

---

161 造色: produced form (i.e. by the 4 great elements, *mahābhūtāni*), translates *bhautikarūpa* or *upādāyarūpa*, derivative form.

162 *mahābhūta*.

163 *svabhūmika*.

164 i.e. the stage of 力: the power. When the *ārya,* who has attained the path, is born in the realm of formlessness and attains the *anāsrava saṃvara*, which is future, not yet attained, bodily and verbal action (see stanzas 38, 40, and esp. 44), this bodily and verbal action is produced by the four great elements of the stage in which he has attained the path.

Question: What about the characteristics of the three obstructions, as explained by the World-Honored One: the obstruction of action, the obstruction of affliction, and the obstruction of retribution[165].

Answer: (63) Let it also be known that the immediate and irredeemable[166] actions, the afflictions one produces on a large scale, and the unwholesome retributions[167] experienced in the woeful courses[168], are obstructions.

With these three factors, the so-called obstructions, one surely will not experience the factors of the noble[169]. For that reason they are called obstructions.

Question: Which is the worst one among these actions?

Answer: (64ab) When one's action ruins the *saṃgha*, it is said to be the worst.

[815b] Namely the action which ruins the *saṃgha*[170] is the worst of the actions. One will dwell in the great avīci hell for a kalpa.

Question: Which is the finest one?

Answer: (64cd) Let it be known that volition in the summit of existence[171] is the finest.

The sphere of neither-perception-nor-non-perception[172] is the highest among existences. The volition comprised within that

---

165 *karmāvaraṇa, kleśāvaraṇa, vipākāvaraṇa.*
166 Immediate, *ānantarya*. One goes immediately to hell, according to AH2 843c. "Irredeemable" may translate *atrāṇa.*
167 We follow the reading of the 3 editions: 报.
168 *durgati.*
169 *āryadharma*. AH2 843b and MAH 898a have 圣道: the noble path, *āryamārga*.
170 Scil. *saṃghabheda*.
171 Volition, *cetanā.*
Summit of existence, *bhavāgra*
172 *naivasaṃjñānāsaṃjñāyatana.*

stage is the finest and brings the greatest fruition. Its retribution is a life of eighty thousand kalpas.

Treatise on the Essence of Scholasticism. Vol. I.

**业品第三**

已说诸行己性及由诸因缘生。今谓此有因能严饰果种生种生差别可得今当说。

| 33 | 业能庄饰世 | 趣趣在处处 |
|---|---|---|
| | 以是当思业 | 求离世解说 |

业能庄饰世趣趣在处处者三世于五趣中种种身差别严饰。是世严饰事唯业。是以当思业求离世解脱。

| 34 | 身业及口意 | 有有之所造 |
|---|---|---|
| | 是以生诸行 | 严饰种种身 |

身业及口意有有之所造者谓身口意业生生所造作。从是生诸行严饰种种身。
此业相今当略说。

| 35 | 身业教无教 | 当知二俱有 |
|---|---|---|
| | 口业亦如是 | 意业唯无教 |

身业教无教当知二俱有者身业性二种有教性无教性。于中有教者身动是善不善无记。善从善心生。不善从不善心生。无记从无记心生。无教者若作业牢固。转异心中此种子生如善受戒人不善无记心中彼犹相随。恶业人恶戒相随。口业亦如是者口业性亦二种。意业唯无教者意业性一向无教。所以者何。不现故思微相续故。
问。此五业几善几不善几无记。答。

| 36 | 教当知三种 | 善不善无记 |
|---|---|---|
| | 意无教亦然 | 余不说无记 |

教当知三种善不善无记者身口教说三种善不善无记。于中善身教者行施持戒等善心作身动。不善身教者杀身不与取非梵行等不善心作身动。无记身教者无记心作身动如威仪工巧伎术。如是口动善者如不虚言饶益相应应时言等从善心生口业不善者如妄言两舌恶口绮语等从不善心生口业。无记者从无记心生口业。意无教亦然者意业无教亦三种善不善无记。善心相应思是善。不善心相应思是不善。无记心相应思是无记。余不说无记者余有二身无教及口无教。彼二种善不善无无记。所以者何。无记心羸劣。彼不能生强力业谓转异心中彼相似相随。是故身无教口无教无无记。
问。无记业何等性。何处系。答。

| 37 | 色有无记二 | 隐没不隐没 |
|---|---|---|
| | 隐没系在色 | 余在于二界 |

色有无记二隐没不隐没者身口业是色性以业色性故二种隐没及不隐没。隐没者谓烦恼所覆亦从诸烦恼生。异者是不隐没。隐没系在色者若隐没一向系色界。所以者何。思惟断烦恼能起身口业。此欲界思惟断烦恼一向不善。不以不善烦恼能起无记业。余在于二界者不隐没无记业亦系在欲界亦系在色界。意业如心说。是余处分别。故今不说。

38 身口业无教 当知善不善
三相禅无漏 调御威仪戒

身口业无教当知善不善者业若色性于中若无教性是善不善。三相禅无漏调御威仪戒者无教戒有三相无漏禅生调御威仪。无漏者谓戒道共俱行正语正业正命。禅生者谓禅俱行离恶。调御威仪戒者谓欲界戒。

39 无教在欲界 教依于二有
当知非心俱 谓余心俱说

谓欲界无教是非心共俱。所以者何。谓受戒戒唯善心不善心无记心随行而不与善不善无记共俱。教者亦在欲界亦在色界但非心共俱。所以者何。由身故色界无教及无漏与心共俱。所以者何。由心故。此非余心中随行。

已分别诸业。若成就业今当说。

40 无漏戒律仪 见谛所成就
禅生若得禅 持戒生欲界

无漏戒律仪见谛所成就者见谛谓无漏见见圣谛。初生无漏见时见于欲界苦谛。是故一切圣人成就无漏戒。禅生若得禅者谓得禅是成就禅戒。持戒生欲界者若受戒者彼成就欲界戒。

已略说成就。如过去未来现在可得今当说。

41 谓住威仪戒 无教在于今
当知恒成就 或复尽过去

谓住威仪戒无教在于今当知恒成就者若住威仪戒一切时成就无教戒。彼终不离。至命尽所缚。或复尽过去者或成就过去无教戒若尽不失。谓初已尽是成就过去。过去者假名为尽。

42 若有作于教 即时立中世
当知成过去 已尽而不舍

若有作于教即时立中世。若作身口教尔时即成就现在教。现在者假名中世。当知成过去已尽而不舍者若彼教已尽不失尔时即成就过去。

43 谓得禅无教 成就灭未至
中若入正受 教亦如前说

谓得禅无教成就灭未至者若得禅彼成就过去未来。所以者何。如彼禅成就戒亦复尔。中若入正受者。现在假名中。彼若入定尔时成就现在无教。所以者何。与定俱故。教亦如前说者如住威仪戒。若作教尔时成就现在教若不作教尔时不成就教。若尽不失尔时成就过去。若不尽设尽便失尔时不成就。住禅戒亦复如是。

44　悉成就当知　得道若未生
　　中间在道心　尽不舍前世

悉成就当知得道若未生者一切得道成就未来无漏无教。所以者何。如彼无漏心成就戒亦复尔。中间在道心者已合道若入于定尔时即成就现在。尽不舍前世者前世是过去。彼于此无教若尽不失如得圣果及退者成就过去无教。

45　若作恶不善　立戒成就二
　　至彼缠所缠　尽已尽当知

若作恶不善立戒成就二者如此住威仪戒或住禅戒或住无漏戒或作不善浊重缠。尔时于不善中起无教即成就教及无教。若非浊重缠不起无教。
问。几时成就。答。至彼缠所缠。若缠所缠随可得成就。尽已尽当知者彼缠若尽教及无教亦随尽。

46　处不威仪戒　无教成就中
　　恶而不爱果　亦复过去尽

处不威仪戒无教成就中恶而不爱果者若住不威仪戒尔时成就不善无教。不善名不爱果。亦复过去尽者灭非不灭。

47　有教现于时　是说成就中
　　亦复尽过去　善于上相违

有教现于时是说成就中亦复尽过去者教谓如前说。善于上相违者如住威仪戒说不善如是住不威仪说善至彼善心。

48　若处中所作　即成就中世
　　亦复过去尽　或二亦复一

处中者不威仪亦非不威仪住是居中容。彼如善住说善或复二有教及无教或一向教。或善不善或一。
问。云何得色界戒云何舍。为根本禅得为余方便。答。非一向根本禅若得。

49　色界中善心　得定威仪戒
　　是失彼亦失　无漏有六心

色界中善心得定威仪戒者若得色界善心或离欲或不离欲彼一切得色界戒。所以者何。一切色界善心中戒常共俱。问。云何失。答。是失彼亦失。问。无漏云何。答。无漏有六心。无漏戒无漏六地心共得。问。云何失。答。是失彼亦失。六地者未来禅中间禅根本四禅。
问。此戒几时舍。答。

50 调御威仪戒 是舍于五时
禅生及无漏 二时觉所说

调御威仪戒是舍于五时者威仪戒五时舍罢道犯戒死时邪见增法没尽。禅生及无漏二时觉所说者禅戒二时舍退及上生。无漏戒亦二时舍退及得果。

问。余业云何舍。答。

51 不善戒有二 善无色亦然
秽污说一时 若业在于意

不善戒有二者不作方便及死时。善无色亦然者善无色业亦二时舍善根断时及上生。秽污说一时若业在于意者秽污意业一时舍离欲时。

已说诸业性及成就。如此业世尊种种分别今当说。

52 若业与苦果 当知是恶行
意恶行增上 贪瞋恚邪见

若业与苦果当知是恶行者谓业是不善尽说是恶行。不善者苦果。意恶行增上贪瞋恚邪见者不善思原是意恶行。复三种说意恶行贪瞋恚邪见。

53 此相违妙行 最胜之所说
若于中最上 是名为十道

此相违妙行最胜之所说者此相违一切善业及无贪无恚正见。若于中最上是名为十道者若于不善业中若业最上者是说业道。如杀生不与取邪行妄言两舌恶口绮语贪恚邪见。于中杀生者众生想舍众生意断他命求方便成业。不与取者物他所有他想不与辄取。邪行者妇女他所有犯于道若自所有时时犯非道。妄言者异想意欺诳他说。两舌者憎他故亲相离方便说。恶口者以瞋于他不爱言。绮语者不善心无义言。贪者欲界欲。恚者忿怒。邪见者谤因果。此是业道。余者非业道谓此行方便求及饮酒等。不正业思原者是根本业。此以彼十为道。

54 若业现法报 次受于生报
后报亦复然 余则说不定

谓业能成现法果时则不定。

问。如世尊说三业乐报苦报不苦不乐报此云何。答。

55 若欲界中善 及色界三地
是应有乐报 受者定不定

若欲界中善及色界三地是应有乐报者。欲界善业生报与乐俱。及色界初禅第二第三。亦生报与乐俱。此总说乐报。问此亦是定耶。答受者定不定。若定若不定是四地中。善一切有乐报

56 生不苦不乐 谓在于上善

若受于苦报　　是说不善业

生不苦不乐谓在于上善者第四禅地善业及无色中是不苦不乐报。是生报与不苦不乐俱。于中无乐痛。若受于苦报是说不善业者不善业是苦报。必与苦痛俱。受报此亦定不定如上。
问。世尊说四业黑黑报白白报黑白黑白报不黑不白无报。此业云何。答。

57　色中有善业　　是白有白报
黑白在欲界　　黑报说不净

色中有善业是白有白报者色界善业是白报一向不净故及离不善故。彼一向极妙报是谓白有白报。黑白在欲中者欲界善业黑白黑白报。所以者何。是不善所坏羸劣故故说黑白。彼杂受报爱不爱故说黑白报。黑报说不净者不善谓不净是黑增恶故。鄙贱故是说黑报。

58　若思能舍离　　是尽无有余
彼在无碍道　　谓是第四业

谓道能灭此三业是无碍道。若有思此思是第四业。于中四思思惟道灭第二业十三有二道见谛道四思惟道九是无漏思。不增恶故不黑。不可乐故不白。与无穷相违故无报。
问。世尊说身口意曲秽浊。此云何。答。

59　曲生于谄伪　　秽从瞋恚生
欲生谓为浊　　世尊之所说

曲生于谄伪者若业从伪生是曲欺诳故。秽从瞋恚生者若业从恚生是秽一向诤故。欲生谓为浊世尊之所说者若业从欲生是浊一向尘垢故。
问。如世尊说三净身口意此云何。答。

60　净一切妙行　　满者是身口
谓无学意满　　即是无学心

净一切妙行者若有妙行是一切净离烦恼不净故。问。满云何。答。满者是身口。无学意中身口妙行是谓满善除一切挂碍故。谓无学意满即是无学心者若无学意满是无学心。所以者何。无学心者已逮得牟尼相故。
已说诸业假名。果今当说。

61　善恶不善业　　是俱有二果
善或成三果　　一果谓余说

善恶不善业是俱有二果者善业成二果所依果及报果。无漏业亦有二果所依果及解脱果。不善业亦有二果所依果及报果。善或成三果者谓善有漏业能除诸烦恼是三果所依果报果及解脱果。一果谓余说者谓余无记业是一果所依果无余。
问。造色相是身口业。是业何四大造。答。

62 自地若有大 依于身口业
无漏随力得 是彼谓之果

自地若有大依于身口业者若欲界诸业是依于欲界大此所造故。色界业亦如是。问。无漏诸业云何。答。无漏随力得是彼谓之果者无漏色若依四大得即依彼地。若住欲界得道彼
身口业欲界四大造。如是一切地。谓力除色界欲及无色界彼若命终生无色中若未得而得身口业是身口业即彼地四大造。
问。如世尊说三障业障烦恼障报障是相云何。答。

63 无间无救业 广能生烦恼
恶道受恶报 障碍亦应知

此三法障碍者必不受圣法。是故说障碍。
问。此业何等最大恶。答。

64 若业坏僧者 是说为极恶

谓业坏僧是业最恶。是阿鼻大地狱住劫。问。何者最大妙。答。

第一有中思 当知彼最大

非想非非想处于有第一。彼地摄思是大妙极大果彼八万劫寿报。
阿毗昙心论卷第一

Treatise on the Essence of Scholasticism. Vol. II, composed by Bhadanta Dharmaśreṣṭhin, translated on Mount Lu by Saṃghadeva of the Eastern Jin, with Huiyuan.

# CHAPTER IV. URGES[1]

We have explained the actions. The afflictions will now be explained.

> (65) The roots of all existence[2], the companions of the actions producing the hundred sufferings, the so-called ninety-eight urges are expounded by the Muni. Reflect on them[3]!

e.g. if one does not recognize hatred[4], harm is done, but if one recognizes it, one can leave it. The same applies to all afflictions. They must be known as enemies.

Question: How does one know them?

Answer: (66) Let it be known that in the class of all urges, two kinds[5] are established: the kind to be abandoned through the vision of the truths and the one to be abandoned through development.

All urges are either to be abandoned through vision or to be abandoned through development[6], i.e. when following the path of vision they are abandoned through vision, and when following the path of development[7] they are abandoned through development.

---

1 *Anuśayavarga*.
2 AH2 843c sums up: the existence of desire, of form, and of formlessness.
3 We follow the reading of the 3 editions: 当思.
4 *pratigha*.
5 *prakāra*.
6 *satyadarśanaheya* and *bhāvanāheya*.
7 *bhāvanāmārga*.

(67) In this respect they say that twenty-eight urges[8] are linked to the vision of suffering[9]. That is to say, they are abandoned at the moment of the vision of suffering, completely without any remainder.

(68) Let it be known that the ones to be abandoned through the vision of origination[10] (number) nineteen. The same applies to cessation[11]. Add three for the ones to be abandoned through the vision of the path[12]. Ten are said to be stopped through development[13].

They are namely the ninety-eight urges. We have explained their kinds. Their realms[14] will now be explained.

(69) Let it be known that there are ten afflictions of the first kind in desire. [815c] Of two kinds there are seven each. Another eight are to be abandoned through the vision of the path.

(70) Let it be known that in the realm of desire four are to be abandoned through development. That is to say, it must also be distinctly established that the rest are in two realms.

Let it be known that in the realm of desire four are to be abandoned through development: those thirty-six urges[15] are linked to the realm of desire.

---

[8] 结: fetters, according to the 3 editions.
[9] *duḥkhadarśana*.
[10] *samudaya*. The Chinese translates this as: practising.
[11] *nirodha*.
[12] *mārga*.
[13] *bhāvanā*.
[14] *dhātu*.
[15] 1. *darśanaheya* - vision of *duḥkha*: 10
- vision of *samudaya*: 7
- vision of *nirodha*: 7
- vision of *mārga*: 8
2. *bhāvanāheya*: 4

That is to say, it must also be distinctly established that the rest are in two realms: as for the remaining sixty-two urges, thirty-one of them are linked to the realm of form and thirty-one to the realm of formlessness. We have explained the realms. All urges will now be explained.

> (71) Let it be known that the view of extremes[16], the wrong view[17], the view of self[18], and two evil adherences[19] are the afflictions called view.

Unaware of the nature of all factors because of the continuity of causes, one either has the notion of their eternity or that of their annihilation[20]. Annihilation and eternity are the two extremes expounded by the World-Honored One. When a view here holds on to the extremes, it is called the view of extremes[21]. When it denies[22] the true meaning, this view is the wrong view[23].

When one is deluded in the species which has feelings and consciousness, and believes in a self[24], this is called the view of individuality[25]. When impure factors are experienced as being best[26], this view is evil adherence to wrong views[27]. When that which is not a cause is seen as a cause, this view is attachment

---

[16] *antagrāhadṛṣṭi*, Chinese: view of experiencing extremes.
[17] *mithyādṛṣṭi.*
[18] *ātmadṛṣṭi* (scil. *satkāyadṛṣṭi*). We follow the reading of the 3 editions: 吾我.
[19] *parāmarśa*, i.e. *dṛṣṭiparāmarśa* and *śīlavrataparāmarśa.*
[20] Eternity, *śāśvata*; annihilation, *uccheda.*
Notion, *saṃjñā*, 想, as read in the 3 editions.
[21] See note 16.
[22] *apavad°*.
[23] See note 17.
[24] *ātmagrāha.*
[25] *satkāyadṛṣṭi.*
[26] *parama.*
[27] *dṛṣṭiparāmarśa.*

to mere rules and ritual[28]. These five afflictions have the nature of wisdom[29], and so they are called views.

> (72) Desire, doubt, hatred, conceit, and foolishness are said to be no-view. Because they are differentiated by their ranges, one uses different terms for their process.

Desire, doubt, hatred, conceit, and foolishness are said to be no-view: desire [30] is called finding delight [31], longing and attachment to pleasure regarding the formations. The term doubt [32] is used when one reflects with uncertainty about something one has seen earlier. Hatred[33] is called anger when one's actions meet with opposition. Conceit[34] is called self-elevation. The term foolishness [35] is used for all ignorance. These five afflictions are said to be no-view. These[36] are all the afflictions.

Because they are differentiated by their ranges[37], one uses different terms for their process: of these ten afflictions some proceed within [38] suffering, some within origination, some within cessation, and some within the path[39]. Those among them which proceed within suffering, are abandoned through the vision of suffering, and so forth up to the path. The rest are abandoned through development[40].

> (73) All (proceed within) the suffering of the lower one. Apart from three views they proceed within two. For the

---

[28] *śīlavrataparāmarśa*.
[29] *prajñā*. cf. stanza 140.
[30] *rāga*.
[31] We follow the reading of the 3 editions: 爱念.
[32] *vicikitsā*.
[33] *pratigha*.
[34] *māna*.
[35] *moha* (or *avidyā*).
[36] i.e. 5 *dṛṣṭis* + the 5 afflictions mentioned in this stanza.
[37] *viṣaya*.
[38] AH2 844c 缘: to take as an object.
[39] i.e. *duḥkha*, *samudaya*, *nirodha*, *mārga*.
[40] *Bhāvanā*.

path one subtracts two views. Hatred does not proceed within the upper realms.

All proceed within the suffering of the lower one: the suffering of the lower one is the suffering of the realm of desire. In it proceed all ten afflictions. In respect to the suffering in the realm of desire, the common fool[41] does not understand causality and sees annihilation. He does not understand effects and sees eternity[42]. Denying[43] effects and denying suffering is the wrong view[44]. When suffering is experienced as being best, (that) is evil adherence to wrong views[45]. Speaking of one factor in relation to another factor [816a], considering as a cause what is not a cause, is attachment to mere rules and ritual[46]. One's own views mean desire, but someone else's views mean hatred. Uncertainty because of one's views means doubt[47]. Elevation of one's own view is conceit. Failure to understand is ignorance[48].

Apart from three views they proceed within two: seven[49] each proceed within origination and within cessation[50]. The view of individuality proceeds within the five aggregates which are visible. Origination is subtle, not visible. Therefore it does not proceed within it. The same applies to cessation. The view of extremes also proceeds within the visible. When attachment to mere rules and ritual proceeds within its range, this is also neither origination nor cessation.

---

[41] Scil. *pṛthagjana*, the common man.
[42] Annihilation, *uccheda*; eternity, *śāśvata*. *Satkāyadṛṣṭi* and *antagrāhadṛṣṭi* are meant.
[43] *apavad°*.
[44] *mithyādṛṣṭi*.
[45] *dṛṣṭiparāmarśa*. See stanza 71.
[46] *śīlavrataparāmarśa*. See stanza 71.
[47] We follow the reading of the 3 editions 疑: *vicikitsā*.
[48] *avidyā*.
[49] Ten minus *satkāyadṛṣṭi*, *antagrāhadṛṣṭi*, *śīlavrataparāmarśa*.
[50] *samudaya* and *nirodha*.

For the path one subtracts two views: the view of individuality and the view of extremes[51] do not proceed within the path, because of their impure ranges. Because of its similar path, attachment to mere rules and ritual[52] proceeds within the path, but it never understands the supreme nor does it see the right path.

Hatred does not proceed within the upper realms: the realms of form and formlessness are to be distinguished just as the realm of desire, (but) without hatred. In these there is no hatred, because the mind is appeased and softened.

The views and doubt[53] are not to be abandoned through development, but the other four in the realm of desire are to be abandoned through development, as well as three in the realm of form and three[54] in the realm of formlessness.

Question: How do they take their range as object?

Answer: (74) Being universal and relating to suffering and its cause, doubt, views and ignorance are developed by all kinds[55], finding delight in one stage.

The doubt, the views, and the ignorance of the kinds to be abandoned through the vision of suffering and to be abandoned through the vision of origination[56], these afflictions are universal[57]. In their particular stage all five kinds are proceeded

---

[51] *satkāyadṛṣṭi*, *antagrāhadṛṣṭi*.
[52] *śīlavrataparāmarśa*.
[53] 5 *dṛṣṭis* + *vicikitsā*.
[54] *bhāvanāheya*: in *kāmadhātu*: *rāga*, *pratigha*, *avidyā*, *māna*. In *rūpa*° and in *ārūpyadhātu*: idem, minus *pratigha*.
The Chinese text seems to be mistaken when it has 2 in the realm of formlessness, not 3. See MAH 900c.
[55] (缘: *ālambana* 所) 使: *ālaṃbanato'nuśerate*, developed (urged) by their object, the *ālambana* being of all 5 *prakāras* (*darśanaheya* 4; *bhāvanāheya* 1).
[56] *duḥkhadarśana*° and *samudayadarśanaheya*.
[57] *sarvatraga*.

in. Why? All impure factors mean suffering and origination by nature.

Question: Why do they proceed within their particular stage, not within another stage?

Answer: Because it is not their range they do not proceed within a higher one, and because they have renounced its desire they do not proceed within a lower one. They are namely the eleven[58] universal afflictions of the realm of desire, and the same applies to the realm of form and to the one of formlessness. The others are not universal, because their particular kind is their range.

> (75) That five kinds of the first afflictions[59] and the four said to be the second ones[60] have their range in a higher realm, (this) is expounded by the One who is not without Wisdom[61].

The wrong view to be abandoned through the vision of suffering in the realm of desire, denies[62] the suffering of the realm of form and of (the realm of) formlessness. The evil adherence to wrong views experiences it as being best, and the attachment to mere rules and ritual experiences it as a preparation[63] for deliverance. Doubt is uncertain about it, and ignorance does not understand it. The wrong view which must be abandoned through the vision of origination, denies[64] its cause in the realm of form and in the one of formlessness. The

---

[58] *duḥkhadarśanaheya*: 5 *dṛṣṭis*, *vicikitsā*, *avidyā*. *samudayadarśanaheya*: *vicikitsā*, *avidyā*. 2 *dṛṣṭis* (i.e. *mithyādṛṣṭi* and *dṛṣṭiparāmarśa*. cf. stanza 73).

[59] i.e. *duḥkhadarśanaheya* (cf. note 58): 1. *mithyādṛṣṭi*, 2. *dṛṣṭiparāmarśa* 3. *śīlavrataparāmarśa*, 4. *vicikitsā*, 5. *avidyā*.

[60] i.e. *samudayadarśanaheya* (cf. note 58): 1. *mithyādṛṣṭi*, 2. *dṛṣṭiparāmarśa*, 3. *vicikitsā*, 4. *avidyā*.

[61] Scil. the World-Honored One. AH2 845b has 普遍智: the One with Universal Knowledge, i.e. *sarvajña*.

[62] *apavad°*.

[63] *prayoga*.

[64] See note 62.

evil adherence to wrong views experiences its cause as being best. Doubt is uncertain about it, and ignorance does not understand it. It is thus for all stages of the realm of form and of the one of formlessness, up to the sphere of nothingness[65].

> (76) Let it be known that wrongness and doubt, (the ignorance) which is produced together with them, and also the ignorance which is special, to be abandoned through the two: appeasement[66] and the path, have a pure object.

The wrong view to be abandoned through the vision of cessation[67], denies[68] cessation. Because it takes cessation as its object it has a pure[69] object. Thus [816b] doubt is uncertain in relation to cessation. Also the ignorance associated with them[70] has a pure object. Likewise the special[71] ignorance to be abandoned through the vision of cessation[72], does not want *nirvāṇa*. It also has a pure object.

It is the same when they are abandoned through the vision of the path. These eighteen[73] urges have a pure object.

Question: How are the impure kinds[74] taken as objects[75] by the urges[76]?

---

[65] *ākiṃcanyāyatana.*
[66] *nirodha* is meant. 息止 translates *śam*°.
[67] *nirodhadarśanaheya.*
[68] See note 62.
[69] anāsrava.
[70] *saṃprayuktāvidyā.*
[71] *āveṇika.*
[72] See note 67.
[73] *mithyādṛṣṭi*², *vicikitsā*², their *saṃprayuktāvidyā* and *āveṇikāvidyā*. These 6 in: *kāma*°, *rūpa*°, and *ārūpyadhātu.*
[74] *prakāras* proceeding within the impure, *sāsrava. Anāsrava:* infra stanza 79.
[75] (缘): 缚: taken as object.
[76] i.e.: How do the *anuśayas* take *anuśayana*? How are they developed? There are 2 posibilities: *ālambanato'nuśerate,* 缘使: developed by their object, or *saṃprayogato'nuśerate,* 相应使: developed by association.

> (77) When the kinds[77] are in the realm of desire, all universal urges take them as objects in their particular stage. In a higher realm it is the same.

All universal[78] urges take as object all kinds in their particular stage, and they are developed by them[79].

> (78) Let it be known that all other urges are developed by an object of their own kind in their own realm, and that they are associated with that which is of their (own) class.

Let it be known that all other urges are developed by an object of their own kind in their own realm: all urges which are not universal, taking all factors within their own kind as objects, are developed by them.

And they are associated with that which is of their (own) class: the universal ones and the ones which are not universal are all developed by association[80] within their own class.

> (79) When the afflictions proceed within that which is pure and when they have their object in another stage, they are developed by association, because their range is disconnected.

When the afflictions proceed within that which is pure[81] and when they have their object in another stage, they are developed by association[82]: when urges have a pure object, and when they have their object in a higher stage, they are developed by association with that which is of their own class. They are not developed by their object[83]. Why?

---

[77] *prakāra*.
[78] *sarvatraga*. See stanza 74.
[79] i.e. *ālambanato'nuśerate*, developed by their object, *ālambana* (all *prakāras*).
[80] *saṃprayogato'nuśerate*.
[81] *anāsrava*. See stanza 76.
[82] See note 80.
[83] *ālambanato'nuserate*.

Because their range[84] is disconnected. These urges are not linked to[85] their range, but the pure factors are disconnected from the afflictions. The factors of a higher stage are disconnected from the afflictions of a lower stage.

Question: Must these urges be called unwholesome, or are they indeterminate[86]?

Answer: (80) The view of individuality, the view of extremes, and the ignorance associated with them, are indeterminate in desire. In form and in formlessness they all are (indeterminate).

The view of individuality, the view of extremes and the ignorance associated with them, are indeterminate in desire: in the realm of desire the view of individuality, the view of extremes, and their associated ignorance[87] are indeterminate. Why? The view of individuality is frequently assumed. If it were unwholesome, not one of the beings in the realm of desire would know happiness, because they would often perform the unwholesome. Furthermore, if it were unwholesome, it would be the opposite of merit[88]. Now, when someone believing in a self[89] performs that which is meritorious, he causes his self to obtain happiness[90]. Because the unwholesome is the opposite of the wholesome, the view of individuality is not unwholesome. The view of annihilation [91] is a view of impermanence. Disgust with birth and death, this is not unwholesome either. So (the view) is not unwholesome. Neither is the view of eternity[92] the opposite of the wholesome, [816c] in the same way as the view of individuality. Therefore

---

[84] *viṣaya*.
[85] We follow the reading of the 3 editions: 缚.
[86] *akuśala* or *avyākṛta*.
[87] *satkāyadṛṣṭi*, *antagrāhadṛṣṭi*, *saṃprayuktāvidyā*.
[88] *puṅya*.
[89] *ātmagrāha*.
[90] *sukha* means that the deed was *kuśala*.
[91] *ucchedadṛṣṭi*.
[92] *śāśvatadṛṣṭi*.

it is not unwholesome. The other afflictions of the realm of desire are only unwholesome.

In form and in formlessness they all are (indeterminate): the urges of the realm of form and of the realm of formlessness are all indeterminate. Why? Because they are destroyed[93] by right sensation[94]. That which is unwholesome experiences a painful retribution[95], and in them there is no suffering.
Question: Are all afflictions completely linked to all their particular ranges?

Answer: (81) Know that desire, hatred, and conceit may be linked to what has passed. As future they experience everything. The rest in both periods experience everything.

Know that desire, hatred, and conceit[96] may be linked to what has passed: i.e. past desire, hatred, and conceit do not necessarily arise in relation to all the particular former ranges. Desire cannot arise in relation to all former factors, because it is not produced by the unseen.

As future they experience everything: i.e. future desire, hatred, and conceit are linked to all impure factors. Why? Because they take everything which is impure as object.

The rest in both periods experience everything: the views, doubt, and ignorance[97] all take all factors as their objects. Therefore they are linked to past, to future, to all impure factors[98].

---

[93] AH2 846c: 制伏: checked.
[94] i.e. concentration, *samādhi.*
[95] A *vipāka* which is *duḥkhavedanā.*
[96] *rāga, pratigha, māna.* MAH 903a and *Kośa* V48 call them *svalakṣaṇakleśas.*
[97] *dṛṣṭi, vicikitsā, avidyā.* MAH 903a and *Kośa* V48 call them *sāmānyalakṣaṇa.*
[98] cf. MAH 903a.

As present urges are not specific[99], they are not mentioned, (but) when some experience something specific[100], they must be explained as the past ones[101].

We have explained the ranges of the urges. Their sequence will now be explained.

> (82) Gradually they are produced while in process: those of a particular stage in that particular stage. It must be distinctly established that those of a higher stage are also produced in a lower one.

Gradually they are produced while in process: those of a particular stage iṇ that particular stage: gradually following the afflictions of a particular stage, all afflictions may be attained. One gradually produces all (afflictions) one by one.

It must be distinctly established that those of a higher stage are also produced in a lower one: when their lives in the brahma-heaven end, all are subsequently produced in the realm of desire. While there the lives of defiled thoughts end, here only defiled thoughts continue[102]. The same applies to all stages.

We have explained the particular characteristics of the urges. Of such afflictions the World-Honored One has expounded many kinds for the purpose of conversion by instruction. They will now be distinctly established.

Question: The World-Honored One has expounded seven urges: desire for sensuous pleasure, hatred, desire for existence, conceit, wrong view, doubt, and ignorance[103]. What about them?

---

[99] 不（特）定: not specific, i.e. with a specific object. The *sāmānyakleśas*, general afflictions, seem to be meant.

[100] The *svalakṣaṇakleśas*, specific afflictions (*raga, pratigha, māna*) are meant. They arise in relation to a specific object.

[101] See this stanza ab.

[102] There: in the *rūpadhātu* (brahma-heaven). Here: in the *kāmadhātu*.

[103] *kāmarāga*, *pratigha*, *bhavarāga*, *māna*, *dṛṣṭi*, *vicikitsā*, *avidyā*.

Answer: (83)The fivefold desire in the realm of desire: this (urge) is called desire for sensuous pleasure. Desire for existence must be distinctly established in the same way in form and in formlessness.

The fivefold[104] desire in the realm of desire: this (urge) is called desire for sensuous pleasure[105]: abandoned through the visions of suffering, of origination, of cessation, and of the path, and (to be abandoned) through development[106].

Desire for existence[107] must be distinctly established in the same way in form and formlessness: the desire in the realm of form is fivefold. [817a] In the realm of formlessness it is the same.

> (84) Hatred, i.e. the urge hatred, is fivefold, as explained before. Conceit and ignorance are fifteenfold and in the three realms.

Hatred, i.e. the urge hatred[108], is fivefold, as explained before: hatred is also fivefold in the same way.

Conceit and ignorance[109] are fifteenfold and in the three realms: conceit is fivefold in the realm of desire, fivefold in the realm of form, and fivefold in the realm of formlessness. The same applies to ignorance.

> (85) The thirty-six (kinds) of the urge wrong view are said to be in all three realms. There are twelve (kinds) of the urge doubt. For the seven there are different terms.

---

104 i.e. of 5 kinds, *prakāra*.
105 *kāmarāga*.
106 *duḥkha*°, *samudaya*°, nirodha°, *mārgadarśanaheya*; *bhāvanāheya*.
107 *bhavarāga*.
108 *pratighānuśaya*.
109 *māna and avidyā*.

The thirty-six (kinds) of the urge wrong view[110] are said to be in all three realms: twelve wrong views in the realm of desire: five are to be abandoned through the vision of suffering, two through the vision of origination, two through the vision of cessation, and three through the vision of the path[111]. The same applies to the realms of form and of formlessness.

There are twelve (kinds) of the urge doubt[112]: in the realm of desire there are four: to be abandoned through the visions of suffering, origination, cessation, and the path. The same applies to the realms of form and of formlessness.

For the seven there are different terms: these afflictions are called attachments, graspings, floods, and impurities[113] .

Question: Why?

Answer: (86) The attachments, graspings, and floods unceasingly make all impure. The afflictions, which are attachments, graspings, and floods, are called impurities.

Because they bind all beings they are called attachments[114]. Because they are things with which one experience birth, they are called graspings[115]. Because they flow down in all beings they are called floods[116]. Because they unceasingly make all impure, they are called impurities[117].

We have explained their kinds[118] and the characteristics of their kinds. Their associated faculties[119] will now be explained.

---

[110] *dṛṣṭi.*
[111] cf. stanza 73.
[112] *vicikitsā.*
[113] *yoga; upādāna* (Chinese: experiencing); *ogha; āsrava.*
[114] *yoga.*
[115] *upādāna.*
[116] *ogha.*
[117] *āsrava.*
[118] *prakāra.*
[119] *indriya.*

(87) The urges in the three realms are all associated with the faculty evenmindedness. Faculties and urges are associated in the existence[120] of form according to its stage.

The urges in the three realms are all associated with the faculty evenmindedness[121]: all ninety-eight urges are associated with the faculty evenmindedness. In their final moment the afflictions are not based on seeking and are appeased.

Faculties and urges are associated in the existence of form according to its stage: the brahma-gods and the shining ones[122] have the faculty gladness[123]. The urges of those stages are associated with the faculty gladness as well as with the faculty evenmindedness. The entirely magnificent ones[124] have the faculty happiness[125]. The urges of that stage are associated with the faculty happiness. The urges of that stage are associated with the faculty happiness as well as with the faculty evenmindedness.

(88) The wrong view and ignorance mean happiness and suffering in the realm of desire. Hatred and doubt mean only suffering. That is to say, the rest mean only happiness.

The wrong view and ignorance[126] mean happiness and suffering[127] in the realm of desire: the wrong view and ignorance in the realm of desire, are associated with the faculty happiness as well as with suffering. The wrong view considers an evil action that has been committed to be joyful, and a clean

---

[120] We follow the reading of the 3 editions: 有: *bhava*, i.e. *rūpabhava*.

[121] *upekṣendriya*.

[122] *Brahmadeva* (in first *dhyāna*); *ābhāsvara* (in second *dhyāna*). Cf. stanza 177.

[123] *saumanasyendriya*.

[124] *śubhakṛtsna* (in third dhyāna).

[125] *sukhendriya*.

[126] *mithyādṛṣṭi* and *avidyā*.

[127] *sukha* and *duḥkha*.

action to be sorrowful. [817b] The same applies to the ignorance associated with it.

Hatred and doubt[128] mean only suffering[129]: for doubt, sorrow is basic. Because it is not certain, it is not joyful. The same applies to hatred.

That is to say, the rest mean only happiness[130]: the remaining urges of the realm of desire are only associated with happiness, not with suffering. For them joy is basic.

> (89) The twofold mixed ones are firmly attached to the body. The ones to be abandoned through vision are only associated with the mind. The afflictions of the realm of desire are associated with these faculties.

The twofold mixed ones [131] are firmly attached: viz. the afflictions to be abandoned through development[132]. They are associated with bodily feeling as well as [133] with mental feeling [134]. Among them, bodily feeling means the faculty happiness and also the faculty suffering[135], and mental feeling means the faculty gladness and also the faculty sadness[136].

Both[137] have the faculty evenmindedness[138]. All bodily feeling is to be abandoned through development[139], but for the mind one has the two[140].

---

[128] *pratigha* and *vicikitsā*.
[129] *duḥkha*.
[130] *sukha*.
[131] 熏 (AH2 847b) translates *kīrṇa* or *vyavakīrṇa* in *vyavakīrṇa* (mixed, scil. 杂) *bhāvanā* (development, scil. 修). See infra stanza 170.
The *kleśas* which are *bhāvanāheya* are meant, as the commentary explains. They are associated with both *kāyikī* and *caitasikī vedanā*. *Kāyikī* (身) *vedanā* is only *bhāvanāheya*.
[132] *bhāvanāheya*.
[133] We follow the reading of the 3 editions: 及心.
[134] *kāyikī vedanā* and *caitasikī vedanā*.
[135] *sukhendriya* and *duḥkhendriya*.
[136] *saumanasyendriya* and *daurmanasyendriya*.
[137] i.e. *kāyikī* and *caitasikī vedanā*.
[138] *Upekṣendriya*.
[139] See note 132.
[140] The 2 *prakāras*. *Caitasikī vedanā* is to be abandoned both through vision (*darśana*) and through development (*bhāvanā*). cf. AH2 847b.

The ones to be abandoned through vision are only associated with the mind: the fetters[141] to be abandoned through the vision of the truths[142], are only associated with the mind.

The afflictions of the realm of desire are associated with these faculties: they are the afflictions of the realm of desire.
We have distinguished the associated faculties. The secondary afflictions[143] will now be explained.

> (90) Shamelessness and absence of moral dread, sloth, remorse, and stinginess, envy, excitedness, and sleepiness[144] thrive[145] on the afflictions. Therefore they are called[146] secondary afflictions.

These eight things are called secondary afflictions. All urges are afflictions. Among them these secondary ones arise from them. They are the filth of the urges[147], depending on the urges.

Question: What is the filth of the urges?

Answer: (91) Sloth and excitedness are said to be companions of all afflictions. Shamelessness is a companion of the unwholesome ones. The same applies to absence of moral dread.

Sloth and excitedness[148] are said to be companions of all afflictions: excitedness[149] is called non-appeasement[150] in

---

[141] *Saṃyojana*, scil. *kleśa*.
[142] *Satyadarśanaheya*.
[143] *Upakleśa*. Chinese: higher affliction.
[144] *Āhrīkya*, *anapatrāpya*, *styāna*, *kaukṛtya*, *mātsarya*, *īrṣyā*, *auddhatya*, *middha*.
[145] 盛 *sheng*: to be abundant, to thrive. AH2 847b has the expected 上 *shang*: the highest (among the afflictions).
[146] We follow the reading of the 3 editions: 说.
[147] *Anuśayamala*.
[148] *styāna* and auddhatya.
[149] auddhatya.
[150] avyupaśama.

thoughts. It is associated with all afflictions, an affliction being non-appeasement. Although sloth [151] is called heavy-mindedness[152], still it is associated with all afflictions, because heavy-mindedness produces[153] the afflictions.

Shamelessness [154] is a companion of the unwholesome ones. The same applies to absence of moral dread [155]: the term shamelessness is used when one is not ashamed for someone else when he does evil. The term absence of moral dread is used when one is not disgusted with and not ashamed of[156] one's own evil. These two secondary afflictions are only associated with the unwholesome ones, not with the indeterminate ones.

> (92) Remorse, i.e. suffering in the mind, is to be abandoned through development. Sleepiness exists only in a desirous mind. The rest are all established by themselves.

Remorse [157], i.e. suffering in the mind, is to be abandoned through development[158]: the term remorse is used when, doing good or doing evil, the thing is not accomplished but regretted. Because one cannot say it is joyful, it is only associated with suffering. It is associated with the faculty sadness[159] in the mind. Because it is produced by evil deeds it is said to be abandoned through development[160]. Because it is associated with suffering one should know it is of the realm of desire.

---

[151] *styāna*. We follow the reading of the 3 editions: 睡.
[152] 沈: *guru*. AH2 847c seems to have *akarmaṇyatā* here. MAH 904b has *cittākarmaṇyatā*. cf. Kośa II 161.
[153] We follow the reading of the 3 editions: 便生…
[154] *āhrīkya*.
[155] *ȧnapatrāpya*.
[156] We follow the reading of the 3 editions: 羞: *lajjā*.
[157] *kaukṛtya*.
[158] bhāvanāheya.
[159] *daurmanasyendriya*.
[160] See note 158.

Sleepiness[161] exists only in a desirous mind: because a sleepy mind is closed[162], [817c] sleepiness exists only in the realm of desire in the mental stage. It is associated with all afflictions of the realm of desire. All afflictions proceed at the moment of sleepiness.

The rest are all established by themselves: i.e. the two remaining secondary afflictions, envy and stinginess[163]. Envy is called the burning inside when one sees someone else being happy. The term stinginess is used for hoarding and parsimonious attachment[164]. They are both established by themselves. They are not associated with other afflictions.

Question: How many consciousnesses[165] are the afflictions associated with?

Answer: (93) Let it be known that desire, hatred, and ignorance are based on the six consciousnesses, i.e. when in desire they are to be abandoned through development. In form they agree with that which can be obtained.

Let it be known that desire, hatred, and ignorance[166] are based on the six consciousnesses, i.e. when in desire they are to be abandoned through development[167]: the desire, hatred, and ignorance in the realm of desire, to be abandoned through development, are associated with the six consciousnesses.

In form they agree with that which can be obtained[168]: in the realm of form, desire and ignorance are in accord with that

---

[161] *middha*.
[162] *abhisaṃkṣipta*? This would be a view held by the masters in Gandhāra. *Kośa* VII 18.
[163] *āgraha*.
[164] *īrṣyā* and *mātsarya*.
[165] *vijñāna*.
[166] *rāga*, *pratigha*, *avidyā*.
[167] See note 158.
[168] Scil. of the consciousnesses.

which can be obtained: in the brahma-heaven[169] with four consciousnesses[170]. There[171], these two afflictions are associated with four consciousnesses. The other afflictions stand in relation to mind-consciousness[172].

We have explained the afflictions. How they are abandoned[173] will now be explained.

> (94) In one moment one abandons the afflictions, and then one is disconnected. The One with right Knowledge has expounded that (this) is attained at countless moments.

In one moment one abandons[174] the afflictions, and then one is disconnected [175]: these afflictions are abandoned by the immediate path[176] in one moment. It is not the case that, when already abandoned, they are to be abandoned again.

The One with right Knowledge[177] has expounded that (this) is attained[178] at countless moments: they[179] are destroyed[180] at several moments. e.g. the ones of the realm of desire to be abandoned through vision: one obtains the realization of their destruction[181] at five moments: their own[182] and those of the

---

[169] Brahma-heaven: first *dhyāna*.
[170] According to MAH 879ab: *cakṣur*°, *śrotra*°, *kāya*°, *manovijñāna*.
[171] AH2 847c adds that in the higher stages (i.e. second *dhyāna*, etc) they are only associated with *manovijñāna*.
[172] *manovijñāna*.
[173] *prahā*°.
[174] See note 173.
[175] *visaṃyukta*.
[176] *Ānantaryamārga*.
[177] Same in MAH 905c. AH2 847c: The One with Expedient Knowledge.
[178] Scil. *visaṃyoga*, disconnection (from the afflictions).
[179] i.e. *kleśas*.
[180] 尽: *kṣaya*, *destruction*, i.e. 灭: *nirodha* (scil. *visaṃyoga*).
[181] See note 180.
[182] i.e. when producing their *pratipakṣas* (对治: antidotes), the different *dharmajñānas* (*vimuktimārga)*. See infra stanza 105. See AH2 848a. cf. *Kośa* V 109 note 1.

four fruitions of *śramaṇaship*[183]. It is thus for all (of them), as explained in the chapter: the Noble[184].

> (95) The noble say that the disconnections in the realm of desire represent four full overcoming comprehensions. Let it be known that renunciation in the realm of form and in the one of formlessness, means five full overcoming comprehensions.

Destruction[185] everlasting and complete, they call it full overcoming comprehension[186]. In this respect, when the destruction of the (afflictions) of the realm of desire, which are to be abandoned through the visions of suffering and of origination[187], is completely obtained, the disconnections[188] represent one full overcoming comprehension. A second (full overcoming comprehension) is for the ones which are to be abandoned through the vision of cessation, a third one for the ones which are to be abandoned through the vision of the path, and a fourth one for the ones which are to be abandoned through development[189]. For the ones which are to be abandoned through the visions of suffering and of origination in the realms of form and of formlessness, there is one full overcoming comprehension. A second one is for the ones which are to be abandoned through the vision of cessation, a third one for the ones which are to be abandoned through the vision of the path, a fourth one for the ones which are to be abandoned through development in the realm of form, and a fifth one for the ones which are to be abandoned through development in the realm of formlessness.

---

[183] i.e. when obtaining the 4 fruitions of *śramaṇaship, śrāmaṇyaphala*. See infra stanzas 107 et seq.

[184] Chapter 5: *Āryavarga*.

[185] See note 180.

[186] *Prahāṇaparijñā*. Chinese: knowledge which means a cutting off (*prahāṇa*).

[187] i.e. the kleśas of the *kāmadhātu* which are *duḥkha*° and *samudayadarśanaheya*.

[188] *visaṃyoga*.

[189] *bhāvanāheya*.

Question: Why do they use the term [190] full overcoming comprehension[191] for the abandonment?

Answer: Because comprehension is its result, it is called full overcoming comprehension, in the same way that when someone is born to the Gautama-clan [192], he too is called Gautama[193].

Question: Are these urges associated with thought or are they not associated[194]?

Answer: They are associated.
Why?

> (96) Urges afflict the thoughts. They are obstructions and opposed to that which is clean[195], [818a] although that which is wholesome can be obtained. They must be known as associated urges.

Urges afflict[196] the thoughts: if urges were not associated with thought, then they would not afflict the thoughts. When they afflict the thoughts, they are therefore associated.

As for the term obstruction[197]: if urges were not associated with thought, they would not obstruct the wholesome factors [198]. When they obstruct them, wholesome factors are not produced. Without such obstruction, they would let them be produced. Therefore they are associated.

---

[190] We follow the reading of the 3 editions: 名.
[191] See note 186.
[192] We follow the reading of the 3 editions: 姓: *gotra*.
[193] i.e.: the *parijñā* causes *prahāṇa,* which is then also called *parijñā*. The Gautama-clan gives birth to someone, who is then also called Gautama. cf. *Kośa* V 110.
[194] i.e. *cittasaṃprayukta* or *cittaviprayukta*.
[195] We follow the reading of the 3 editions: 净相违. See further the explanation of this verse. cf. AH2 848b.
[196] *Kliś°*.
[197] *Āvaraṇa*. cf. supra stanza 63.
[198] *Kuśaladharmāḥ*.

They are opposed to that which is clean, although that which is wholesome can be obtained: if urges were not associated, they would not be opposed to that which is wholesome. If they were not opposed to that which is wholesome, wholesome thoughts should (as yet) be produced. If they were not opposed[199] and did not have the nature of bringing affliction, they would also not cause ailment. When their opposition continues uninterruptedly, one does not produce that which is wholesome; but when it does not continue, one produces that which is wholesome[200]. Because of these facts they are associated[201] urges.

[199] We follow the reading of the 3 editions: 若不相违非是.

[200] cf. *Kośa* V 5.

[201] i.e. with thought.

**阿毗昙心论卷第二**

尊者法胜造
东晋僧伽提婆
共慧远于庐山译

**使品第四**

已说诸业。诸烦恼今当说。

65 一切有根本 业侣生百苦
九十八使者 文尼说当思

譬怨不识则害成。若识则得离。诸烦恼亦然。当知如怨家。
问。云何知。答。

66 一切诸使品 当知立二种
见谛所断种 亦思惟所断

若有使者尽见断及思惟断。谓从见道是见断从思惟道是思惟断。于中

67 说二十八结 是系在见苦
谓当见苦时 断灭尽无余

68 见习断当知 十九灭亦然
增三见道断 十说思惟止

是谓九十八使。已说种。界今当说。

69 第一烦恼种 在欲当知十
二种种有七 余八见道断

70 在欲界当知 四是思惟断
谓余在二界 是亦当分别

在欲界当知四是思惟断者此三十六使是欲界系。谓余在二界是亦当分别者余六十二使于中三十一色界系三十一无色界系。
已说界。诸使今当说。

71 受边见邪见 及与吾我见
二盗应当知 是烦恼说见

从因相续不识诸法性于中或有常想或有断想。断常是二边世尊之所说。于中若见受边是谓受边见。诽谤真实义此见是邪见。若有情识类愚于中计我是谓身见。有漏法受第一此见是见盗。非因见因此见是戒盗。此五烦恼是慧性故说见。

72 欲犹豫瞋恚 慢痴说非见

是界差别故　　转行种种名

欲犹豫瞋恚慢痴说非见者欲名爱念想思于诸行中乐著。犹豫名如前所见于中或思惟。瞋恚名所作相违忿怒。慢名自举。痴名所有不识。此五烦恼说非见。是谓一切诸烦恼。是界差别故转行种种名者是十烦恼或从苦行或从习或从灭或从道。于中若从苦行者是见苦断如是至道。余思惟断。

73　下苦于一切　　离三见行二
道除于二见　　上界不行恚

下苦于一切者下苦是欲界苦。于中行一切十烦恼。凡愚于欲界苦不了因见断。不了果见常。谤果谤苦邪见。苦受第一见盗。谓法于法非因计因戒盗。自见欲他见恚。从见中或疑。自见举慢。不了无明。离三见行二者习及灭各七行。身见行于现五阴。习者细微不现。是故于中不行。灭亦如是。受边见者亦行于现。戒盗行于界彼亦非习灭。道除于二见者身见边见不行于道有漏境界故。戒盗者行于道似道故。终竟不解至不见正道。上界不行恚者如欲界分别色无色界亦尔除其恚彼中无恚意止柔软故。诸见及疑非思惟所断。余欲界四思惟所断。色界三无色界二。
问。云何彼缘境界。答。

74　普遍在苦因　　疑见及无明
是一切种使　　乐在一地中

见苦断种及见习断疑见及无明此烦恼是普遍。一切五种行于自地。所以者何。一切有漏法是苦习性。问。何故行于自地非他地。答。非境界故不行于上。离欲故不行于下。是谓欲界十一一切遍烦恼。色无色界亦尔。余不一切遍自种境界故。

75　初烦恼五种　　四说为第二
境界于上界　　未离慧所说

欲界见苦。断邪见谤色无色界苦见盗受第一。戒盗受解脱方便。疑惑无明不了。见习断邪见谤色无色界因。见盗于因受第一。疑惑无明不了。如是色无色界一切地乃至无所有处。

76　邪疑是俱生　　及不共无明
息止道二断　　当知无漏缘

见灭断邪见谤于灭。是缘灭故无漏缘。如是疑惑于灭。及彼相应无明无漏缘。如是见灭断不共无明谓不欲于涅槃。彼亦无漏缘。见道断亦复如是。是十八使无漏缘。
问。云何有漏种诸使所缚。
答

77　若种在欲界　　一切诸遍使

缘缚于已地　　在上界亦然
诸一切遍使是于自地中缘使一切种。

78　其余诸结使　　当知自种缘
所使于自界　　及是相应品
其余诸结使当知自种缘所使于自界者一切不遍使自于种中缘诸法即彼所使。及是相应品者一切遍及不一切遍是一切自品中相应所使。

79　若无漏所行　　及他地缘恼
是相应所使　　境界解脱故
若无漏所行及他地缘恼是相应所使者若使无漏缘及上地缘是自品相应所使非缘使。所以者何。境界解脱故。此使不缚于境界。无漏诸法解脱一切烦恼。上地诸法解脱下地烦恼。
问。此使当言不善为无记。答。

80　己身见边见　　此相应无明
是欲中无记　　色无色一切
己身见边见此相应无明是欲中无记者欲界身见边见及相应无明是无记。所以者何。己身见数数行。若当不善者欲界众生应无有乐多作不善故。复次若不善者相违于福此中计我人行福令我得乐。不善者相违于善是以身见非不善。断见是无常见。厌于生死是亦非不善。是故非不善。有常见亦不于善如身见。是故非不善。余欲界烦恼一向不善。色无色一切者色界无色界诸使尽无记。所以者何。正受所坏故。不善者受苦痛报。彼中无苦痛。
问。一切诸烦恼尽缚自所有境界为不。答。

81　贪欲瞋恚慢　　知或过去缚
未来受一切　　余二世尽受
贪欲瞋恚慢知或过去缚者谓过去爱恚慢是不必于前一切自境界起。爱者不能于前一切法中起非以不见生故。未来受一切者谓未来受恚慢缚一切有漏法。所以者何。缘一切有漏故。余二世尽受者见疑及无明总缘一切法。是故缚过去未来诸有漏法。现在使不定故不说。若有者受自相彼应说如过去。
已说诸使境界。次第今当说。

82　次第是转生　　自地于自地
上地亦生下　　此事当分别
次第是转生自地于自地者一切诸烦恼于自地烦恼次第缘可得。一一次第生一切。上地亦生下此事当分别者梵天上命终次第生欲界一切。若彼中秽污心命终此中一向秽污心相续。如是一切地。
已说诸使自相。如此烦恼世尊教化故多种说。今当分别。

问。世尊说七使欲爱恚有爱慢见疑及无明。此云何。答。

83 欲界五种欲 此说欲爱使
色无色如上 有爱当分别

欲界五种欲此说欲爱使者见苦习灭道思惟断。色无色如上有爱当分别者色界爱五种。无色界亦尔。

84 恚即是恚使 五种如前说
骄慢及无明 十五在三界

恚即是恚使五种如前说者瞋恚亦如是五种。骄慢及无明十五在三界者慢欲界五种色界五种无色界五种。无明亦尔。

85 见使三十六 说普在三界
疑使有十二 此七有异名

见使三十六说普在三界者欲界十二见五见苦断二见习断二见灭断三见道断。色无色界亦尔。疑使有十二者欲界有四见苦习灭道断。色无色界亦尔。此七有异名者此烦恼说扼受流漏。
问。以何等故。答。

86 扰缚及受流 漏一切无穷
诸扼及受流 烦恼是说漏

系一切众生故说扼。受生具故说受。流下一切众生故说流。漏一切无穷故说漏。
已说种种相。相应根今当说。

87 诸使在三界 尽护根相应
随地诸根使 相应于色有

诸使在三界尽护根相应者一切九十八使尽护根相应。诸烦恼后时依于无求而止。随地诸根使相应于色有者梵天及光曜有喜根。彼地诸使喜根相应及护根。遍净有乐根。彼地诸使乐根相应及护根。

88 邪见及无明 欲界中乐苦
瞋恚疑唯苦 谓余一向乐

邪见及无明欲界中乐苦者欲界邪见无明乐根相应及苦。邪见者作恶业为喜净业为忧。
彼相应无明亦尔。瞋恚疑唯苦者疑忧戚为本。不决定故不喜。瞋恚亦尔。谓余一向乐者欲界余使一向乐相应非苦。彼欢喜为本。

89 二熏坚著身 见断唯应意
欲界诸烦恼 此根是相应

二熏坚著名诸烦恼思惟断。彼身痛相应及心痛。于中身痛者乐根及苦根。心痛者喜根及忧根。俱有护根。一切身痛思惟断。意俱有。见断唯应意者见谛断结唯意相应。欲界诸烦恼此根是相应者是谓欲界诸烦恼。
已分别相应根。上烦恼今当说。

90 无惭亦无愧 睡悔及与悭
嫉掉眠烦盛 故说上烦恼

此八事说上烦恼。诸使是烦恼。于中此上从中起。此是使垢依于使。
问。何者使垢。答。

91 一切烦恼俱 说睡及与掉。
无惭不善俱 无愧亦复然

一切烦恼俱说睡及与掉者掉名于心不止息。是一切烦恼相应烦恼是不止息。睡虽名沈意彼亦一切烦恼相应以沈心便生烦恼。无惭不善俱无愧亦复然者无惭名行恶时不惭他无愧名自恶不厌不羞。此二上烦恼一向不善相应非无记。

92 谓苦在于意 悔思惟所断
眠唯在欲意 余各自建立

谓苦在于意悔思惟所断者悔名作善作恶事不成而悔。不可说是喜故一向苦相应。是意忧根相应。从恶行生故说思惟断。苦相应故当知是欲界。眠唯在欲意者眠意闭故眠是一向欲界在意地。彼于欲界一切烦恼相应。一切诸烦恼行于眠时。余各自建立者谓余二上烦恼嫉及悭。嫉名见他乐生热。悭名守护惜著。彼俱自建立非余烦恼相应。
问。诸烦恼几识相应。答。

93 欲瞋恚无明 当知依六识
谓欲思惟断 色中随所得

欲瞋恚无明当知依六识谓欲思惟断者欲界思惟所断爱恚无明六识相应。色中随所得者爱无明色界随所可得梵天上四识。彼中此二烦恼四识相应。余烦恼在意识中。
已说诸烦恼。如所断今当说。

94 一时断烦恼 而于中解脱
无量时所得 正智之所说

一时断烦恼而于中解脱者此烦恼无碍道一时断。非已断复断。无量时所得正智之所说者此得尽数数如欲界见断五时得尽证自分及四沙门果。如是一切如坚圣品说。

95 欲界中解脱 圣说四断智
离色无色界 当知五断智

永尽无余谓之断智。于中若欲界见苦习所断若尽得无余解脱是一断智。见灭断二。见道断三。思惟断四。色无色界见苦习断一断智。见灭断二。见道断三。色界思惟断四。无色界思惟断五。问。以何等故于断名断智。答。智果故说断智如瞿昙姓中生亦名瞿昙此亦复尔。
问。此诸使为心相应为不相应。答。相应。所以者何。

96 心为使烦恼 障碍净相违
诸妙善可得 当知相应使

心为使烦恼者若使心不相应不以烦心。若烦心者是故相应。障碍名若使心不相应不障碍诸善法。若障碍者善法不生。不障碍使生。是故相应。净相违诸妙善可得者若使不相应不与善相违。若不与善相违者善心亦应生。若不相违非是烦恼性亦不应作患。若相违常相随不生善。不相随则生善。因此事故是相应使。

# CHAPTER V. THE NOBLE[1]

We have set out the chapter on the urges. The chapter: The noble will now be explained.

> (97) Thus[2] the noble eliminate hardship[3], the root of all fear. The right knowledge of the preparatory applications[4] will now be explained. Listen well!

Among those who have not settled[5] their thoughts, no one can produce right vision[6]. Therefore:

> [7](98) First see to it that your thoughts, tied to[8] the places[9] of your body, are concentrated, and when you want to bind them to the base of consciousness[10], you will attain destruction of the enemies[11] which are the afflictions.

---

1 *āryavarga*.

2 As explained in the text which follows.

3 i.e. *kleśa*, affliction.

4 等: *saṃ*°, 方便: *prayoga*.
The stanza 98-100 (4 *smṛtyupasthānas*) and 101-103 (4 *kuśalamūlas*) explain the preparatory path leading to the *darśanamārga*, the path of viewing (the 4 noble truths).

5 停: *upasṭhita*?

6 Meaning the *darśanamārga*.

7 Our text takes 98 and 99 together. Their subject: 4 *smṛtyupasthānas*. AH2 848c, explaining the term *ādikārmika* (始业: beginner, not mentioned in AH, even though stanza 98 starts with 始), does not do so. Its first stanza deals with the 3 practices: *aśubhabhāvanā, ānāpānasmṛti*, and *dhātuvyavasthāna* (界入: engaging in the elements, i.e. of one's own person). Its second stanza deals with *smṛtyupasthāna*.
MAH 907c-908 starts the chapter by explaining the 3 kinds of ascetics: *ādikārmika, kṛtaparijaya,* and *atikrāntamanaskāra* (the last two not mentioned in AH2). Then it has a concordance for AH 97. After that, MAH has a stanza which agrees with AH 98, and explains *aśubhabhāyanā, ānāpānasmṛti* and *dhātuvyavasthāna* (界方便观: the contemplation which is application to one's elements). The following stanza deals with *smṛtyupasthāna.*
*dhātuvyavasthāna*: see MAH 908b.

8 *baddha*.

9 *pradeśa*.

10 识: *vijñāna,* 足: *pada*. AH2 848c and MAH 908a explain this as 一缘: *ekālambana*, one object.

11 *doṣa*.

> (99) In this application[12] one is constantly concentrated on the true characteristics[13] of the body. The feelings, the thoughts, and the factors[14] are to be contemplated in the same way.

The body has the characteristics of being unclean, impermanent, painful, and selfless[15]. These characteristics are decidedly true. Those who bind their thoughts to one place of their body and who do away with disturbed thoughts[16], truly contemplate the characteristics of their body for the first time. Consequently they contemplate feeling, and after that they contemplate the thoughts and their companions, what depends on them and what is associated with them, the other factors which constitute thought's concomitants [17]. They also contemplate the formations not associated with thought[18]. In accordance with their nature and their characteristics all are such. The applications of mindfulness[19] to the body, to feeling, to thought, and to the factors, are produced one after another.

> (100) Engaging in the contemplation in relation to the factors in general, one contemplates the common characteristics of the factors. The four (characteristics) are: impermanent, void, selfless, and unpleasant.

Engaging in the contemplation in relation to the factors in general, one contemplates the common characteristics[20] of the factors: engaging in the application of mindfulness to the factors, the noble one contemplates the characteristics of the formations[21] in general. Having contemplated the characteristics of the

[12] *prayoga*, i.e. *smṛtyupasthāna*, especially *kāyasmṛtyupasthāna*.
[13] *lakṣaṇa*.
[14] Meant are: *vedanā*°, *citta*°, *dharmasmṛtyupasthāna*.
[15] *Aśubha, anitya, duḥkha, anātmaka*. cf. 4 *viparyāsas*, infra. stanza 199.
[16] 心: citta; 乱: *vikṣepa*.
[17] *caitasika dharma*.
[18] *cittaviprayuktasaṃskāra*.
[19] *smṛtyupasthāna*. We follow the reading of the 3 editions: 意止: fixation of the mind.
[20] *sāmānyalakṣaṇa*.
[21] *saṃskāra*.

formations and raising his thoughts [22] more and more, he produces the flawless eye of knowledge, and all bodies, feelings, thoughts, and factors are contemplated in general.

Question: How?

Answer: The four [23] are: impermanent, void, selfless, and unpleasant[24]. [818b] Because, as these bodies, feelings, thoughts, and factors continue in existence, they are produced one after another, they are impermanent. Because they are not self-existing, they are void. Because of their evil calamities, they are painful.

> (101) After that, a factor called warmth is then produced in the mind. Its aspects are the sixteen aspects, and it intuitively realizes the four truths.

After that, a factor called warmth[25] is then produced in the mind: while thus contemplating, he produces wholesome warmth. The fire of pure knowledge that will be produced here, burns the firewood of all formations.

Question: Which are its aspects[26] and what is its range[27]?

Answer: Its aspects are the sixteen aspects, and it intuitively realizes[28] the four truths.

Its aspects are the sixteen aspects[29] and its range is the four truths. Four aspects when realizing suffering: because this suffering is by nature defective[30] and produced by causes and conditions[31], it

---

[22] We follow the reading of the 3 editions: 心.
[23] *kāya*, *vedanā*, *citta*, *dharma*.
[24] *anitya*, *śūnya*, *anātmaka*, *duḥkha*.
[25] *uṣmagata*, the first of the 4 wholesome roots, *kuśalamūlas*.
[26] *ākāra*, aspect. 行: mode.
[27] *viṣaya*.
[28] 正观: correctly contemplating, a translation for *abhisameti*.
[29] The *ākāras* which will be explained are:
*duḥkha*: *anitya*, *duḥkha*, *śūnya*, *anātmaka*.
*samudaya*: *hetu*, *samudaya*, *prabhava*, *pratyaya*.
*nirodha*: *nirodha*, *śānta*, *praṇīta*, *niḥsaraṇa*.
*mārga*: *mārga*, *nyāya*, *pratipatti*, *nairyāṇika*.
[30] 劣 often translates *hīna*.
[31] *hetupratyaya*.

is impermanent; because ruined by the power of impermanence, it is painful; because in relation to the inner[32] it is free from a personality[33], it is void; because not self-existing it is selfless. Four aspects when realizing origination: because this origination bears a similar fruition, it is a cause; because[34] it forms a series[35] while proceeding, it means origination; because all births and deaths may be obtained without end it means existence; because things which are not similar form a series[36], it is a condition. Four aspects when realizing cessation: because this cessation covers the end of all calamities, it means cessation; because it removes the fire of all affliction, it means appeasement; because it excels all factors, it is excellent; because it abandons birth and death it means leaving. Four aspects when realizing the path: because this path reaches *nirvāṇa*[37] it is the path; because it is not wrong[38] it is right[39]; because all the noble traverse it, it is a track; because the process of the calamities of birth and death is abandoned, it leads to escape[40]. These are namely the sixteen aspects within which it[41] proceeds. The wholesome root which has as its range the four truths, is called the factor warmth.

> (102) When it has arisen and it is established, one brings forth the summit, and subsequently patient acceptance. Obtaining the highest worldly factor, one relies on its uniqueness.

When it has arisen and it is established, one brings forth the summit[42], and subsequently patient acceptance[43]: when one has accomplished the factor warmth, one then brings forth further in the realm of desire a wholesome root as a summit, realizing also the four truths in their sixteen aspects[44]. Because it surpasses the

---

[32] *adhyātma*.
[33] i.e. there is nothing one may call a personality in the 5 *skandhas*.
[34] The reading of the 3 editions: 故.
[35] 相续 may translate such words as *saṃtati*, *saṃtāna*, etc.
[36] See note 35.
[37] 非品: rankless, meaning *nirvāṇa*.
[38] 顛倒: reversed, i.e. wrong. This is the usual translation for *viparyāsa*, *viparīta*.
[39] AH2 849a has 正: right. 如 or 如理 means 'right'.
[40] *nairyāṇika*. Chinese: it is a conveyance.
[41] Scil. *uṣmagata*.
[42] *mūrdhan*.
[43] *kṣānti*.
[44] *ākāra*. cf. note 29.

factor warmth it is called a summit. Having increased, the summit produces a wholesome root called patient acceptance, also realizing the four truths in their sixteen aspects [45]. Because one is forbearing, it is called patient acceptance. Patient acceptance having been established and attaining the highest worldly factor[46], one relies on its uniqueness[47]. As the most excellent one among all the worldly qualities[48], one produces the wholesome root called the highest worldly factor. Because, as it opens the gate to *nirvāṇa*, it is that which excels most in the mind of the common man[49], it is called the highest factor.

Question: Why do they say that one relies on its uniqueness?

Answer: In the mind of the common man there is no other comparable second quality[50]. If there were, it should also open the gate to *nirvāṇa*, but it does not. Therefore they say one relies on its uniqueness.

Question: How many aspects[51] and which object[52] does it have? Within which stage is it comprised[53]?

Answer: [818c] (103ab) It proceeds within the four aspects of suffering, and they say it is comprised within six stages and relies upon them.

It proceeds within suffering: it takes the truth of suffering as its object, nothing else.

The four aspects[54]: it proceeds within the range of the truth of suffering, which is impermanent, etc. Why? Its object is like that of the first pure thought[55].

---

[45] See note 44.
[46] *laukikāgradharma*.
[47] 一: *eka*, 相: *lakṣaṇa*.
AH2 849b and MAH 909c *kṣaṇa* (*ekakṣaṇa*), not *lakṣaṇa*.
[48] *guṇa*.
[49] *pṛthagjana*.
[50] See note 48.
[51] See note 44.
[52] *ālambana*.
[53] *saṃgṛhīta*.
[54] See note 44.

They say it is comprised within six stages and relies upon them: this factor is comprised within six stages: pre-trance, intermediate trance, and the fundamental four trances[56], not within the realm of desire, because it is a realm that is not certain[57], and not within the realm of formlessness, because it is without the path of vision[58].
Question: Within which stages are the other wholesome roots comprised?

Answer: (103cd) Patient acceptance is also comprised within six stages. The others rely on seven.

Patient acceptance is also comprised within six stages: patient acceptance that goes with[59] the truths, is comprised within six stages, just as the highest worldly factor.

The others rely on seven: warmth and the summit[60] are comprised within seven stages: within these six and within the realm of desire, when desire had not yet been removed; but when one had removed desire in the realm of desire, within the realm of form.

(104)[61] After the highest worldly factor one is certain to produce patient acceptance of the law. After the patient

---

[55] The first *anāsrava citta*, i.e. *duḥkhe dharmakṣānti*, the object of which is the suffering in the realm of desire. cf. stanza 104.
[56] i.e. *anāgamyadhyāna*; *dhyānāntara*; 4 mauladhyānas.
[57] *niścita*, certain, i.e. without doubt.
AH does not have the term *nirvedhabhāgīya*, sharing (the quality of) penetration, for the *kuśalamūlas*.
AH2 849c has 达: *nirvedha* (penetration), 分: *bhāgīya* (sharing in), 善根: *kuśalamūla*. MAH 910a has 決定: *nirvedha* (certainty) 分善根.
[58] *darśanamārga*.
[59] *anuga*.
[60] *uṣmagata* and *mūrdhan*.
[61] With this stanza the actual noble path begins. It is subdivided into a 有学道: *śaikṣamārga* (stanzas 104-112) and a 无学道: *aśaikṣamārga* (stanzas 113-end).
The first one is further subdivided into a *darśanamārga* and a *bhāvanāmārga*. The *darśanamārga* consists of 8 *kṣāntis* (ānantaryamārga) and 7 *jñānas* (vimuktimārga).
The eighth *jñāna* is already *bhāvanāmārga*.

*darśanamārga*:

acceptance one produces the knowledge. Both realize the lower suffering.

After the highest worldly factor[62] one is certain to produce a patient acceptance of the law[63]: after the highest worldly factor one produces a pure[64] patient acceptance of the law, called patient acceptance of the law in relation to suffering[65].. Because that which has not yet been realized is patiently accepted when now realized, they call it patient acceptance. It is namely the first pure[66] immediate path[67].

After the patient acceptance one produces the knowledge: after that, one produces the knowledge of the law in relation to suffering[68], the path of deliverance[69], in the same range[70] experiencing the true nature.

Question: What is the object[71] of that patient acceptance and of the knowledge?

---

| | *duḥkhadarśanaheya* (*kleśa*) | *samudaya*° |
|---|---|---|
| *kāmadhātu* | 1. *duḥkhė dharmakṣānti* | 5. *samudaye...* |
| | 2. *duḥkhe dharmajñāna* | 6. *samudaye...* |
| *rūpa*° & *ārūpyadhātu* | 3. *duḥkhe'nvayakṣānti* | 7. *samudaye...* |
| | 4. *duḥkhe'nvayajñāna* | 8. *samudaye...* |

| | *nirodha*° | *mārga*° |
|---|---|---|
| *kamadhātu* | 9. *nirodhe dharmakṣānti* | 13. *mārge…* |
| | 10. *nirodhe dharmakṣānti* | 14. *mārge…* |
| *rūpa*° & *ārūpyadhātu* | 11. *nirodhe'nvayakṣānti* | 15. *mārge…* |
| | 12. *nirodhe'nvayajñāna* | 16. (*marge* 'nvayajñāna in bhāvanāmārga) |

[62] *laukikāgradharma.*
[63] *dharmakṣānti.*
[64] *anāsrava.*
[65] *duḥkhe dharmakṣānti.*
[66] See note 64.
[67] *ānantaryamārga.*
[68] *duḥkhe dharmajñāna.* For the meaning of *dharma* in *dharmajñāna*: cfr. stanza 157d and stanza 124.
[69] *vimuktimārga.*
[70] *viṣaya.*
[71] *ālambana.*

Answer: Both realize the lower suffering.

The lower suffering: the suffering of the realm of desire is taken as object by both.

> (105) The same applies to the upper suffering. It is the same with its cause, cessation, and path. All these ways of intuitive realization are called the sixteen clean thoughts.

The same applies to the upper suffering: the upper suffering is the suffering of the realms of form and of formlessness. In the same way one produces there an immediate path[72] which is a patient acceptance, and a path of deliverance[73] which is a knowledge: subsequent patient acceptance in relation to suffering and subsequent knowledge in relation to suffering[74].

(It is the same with) its cause[75]: this is the truth of origination[76]. In relation to it, one also produces four paths, just as with suffering: patient acceptance of the law in relation to origination, knowledge of the law in relation to origination, subsequent patient acceptance in relation to origination, and subsequent knowledge in relation to origination[77].

Cessation: in relation to cessation one in the same way also produces four paths: patient acceptance of the law in relation to cessation, knowledge of the law in relation to cessation, subsequent patient acceptance in relation to cessation, and subsequent knowledge in relation to cessation[78].

---

[72] See note 67.
[73] See note 69.
[74] *duḥkhe'nvayakṣānti* and *duḥkhe'nvayajñāna*.
未知智: knowledge of what was not yet known.
[75] *hetu*.
[76] *samudayasatya*.
[77] *samudaye dharmakṣānti, samudaye dharmajñāna.*
*samudaye'nvayakṣānti, samudaye'nvayajñāna.*
[78] *nirodhe dharmakṣānti, nirodhe dharmajñāna.*
*nirodhe'nvayakṣānti, nirodhe'nvayajñāna.*

It is the same with the path: in relation to the path one in the same way also produces four paths: patient acceptance of the law in relation to the path, knowledge of the law in relation to the path, subsequent patient acceptance in relation to the path, and subsequent knowledge in relation to the path[79].

All these ways of intuitive realization[80] are called the sixteen clean thoughts: they are ways of viewing[81]. They call the ways of viewing intuitive realization[82]. This is [819a] another term for viewing.

> (106) The keen faculties of the law-follower are in relation to fifteen thoughts. As for the faith-follower, let it be known that his weak vision is also within them.

The keen faculties[83] of the law-follower[84] are in relation to fifteen thoughts: when at the moments[85] of those fifteen thoughts he possesses keen faculties, (the noble) is called a law-follower.

As for the faith-follower[86], let it be known that his weak[87] vision is also within them: i.e. when at the moments of those fifteen thoughts he has weak faculties, he is called a faith-follower.

> (107) Not yet having renounced the desire of the realm of desire, they progress towards the first fruition. Having abandoned six, they progress to the second one. Progress is made towards the third when the nine are pure.

---

79 *mārge dharmakṣānti, mārge dharmajñāna.*
*mārge'nvayakṣānti, mārge'nvayajñāna.*
80 *abhisamaya.*
81 *darśana.*
82 See note 80.
83 *tīkṣṇendriya.*
84 *dharmānusārin.* Chinese: one who walks following the law.
85 The 3 editions: 顷.
86 *śraddhānusārin.* Chinese: one who walks following his faith.
87 *mṛdu.* Chinese: dull.

Not yet having renounced the desire of the realm of desire, they progress towards the first fruition[88]: when the faith-follower[89] and the law-follower [90] progress towards the fruition of *śramaṇaship*[91], not yet having renounced desire, they both progress towards the *srotaāpatti*-fruition[92].

Having abandoned six, they progress to the second one: the afflictions of the realm of desire are ninefold: weak-weak, weak-medium, weak-strong[93], medium-weak, medium-medium, medium-strong, strong-weak, strong-medium, and strong-strong[94]. When at the moment of being common men[95] they have renounced six kinds, and when afterwards they progress towards realization[96], they both progress towards the second fruition[97].

Progress is made towards the third when the nine[98] are pure: when they have renounced the nine kinds, they both progress to the *anāgāmi*-fruition[99].

> (108) When they have reached the sixteenth thought, they are called people who dwell in the fruition. One given to faith is one with weak vision. One with sharp vision is called one who has attained correct views.

When they have reached the sixteenth thought, they are called people who dwell in the fruition[100]: the sixteenth thought is

---

88 *prathamaphalapratipanna*.
89 See note 86.
90 See note 84.
91 *śrāmaṇyaphala*.
92 The first fruition: *srotaāpattiphala*, the fruition of streamwinning. *Kośa* VI p. 194-195.
93 We follow the 3 editions: 微上中.
94 Weak: *aṇu*; medium: *madhya*; strong: *adhimātra*. 微 translates *aṇu* rather than *mṛdu* (软).
95 *pṛthagjana*.
96 证: realization, *niyāma*.
AH2 850a 入 (to enter); 决定 (certainty): *niyāmapratipanna*, meaning: entering the *darśanamārga*. See *Kośa* VI 180.
97 i.e. *sakṛdāgāmiphala*, the fruition of returning once.
98 i.e. the 9: weak-weak, etc., of the realm of desire.
99 *anāgāmiphala*, the fruition of not returning.
100 *phalastha* (not *phalapratipannaka*. cf. stanza 107).

called subsequent knowledge in relation to the path[101], associated with thought. When they have produced it, they are called people who dwell in the fruition[102]. Not having renounced the desire of the realm of desire, they are both *srotaāpannas* [103]. Having renounced six kinds they are both *sakṛdāgāmins* [104]. Having renounced the nine kinds completely, they are both *anāgāmins*[105].

One given to faith [106] is one with weak [107] vision. One with sharp[108] vision is called one who has attained correct views[109]: when at the moment of his progression[110] he followed his faith[111] with weak faculties[112], he is one who is given to faith[113]. When following the law[114] with keen faculties[115], he is one who has attained correct views[116].

> (109) He who is reborn seven times at the most, has not yet destroyed what is to be abandoned through development. One (destined to be reborn) in several families, has destroyed three. Both are in a fruition of the path.

He who is reborn seven times at the most [117], has not yet destroyed what is to be abandoned through development: when the one who is given to faith[118] and the one who has attained correct views[119] have not yet renounced an affliction which is to

---

[101] *mārge'nvayajñāna*.
[102] See note 100.
[103] Streamwinners. Cf. note 92.
[104] People who return once. Cf. note 97.
[105] People who do not return. Cf. note 99.
[106] *śraddhādhimukta*. Chinese: delivered by faith.
[107] *mṛdu*. We follow the 3 editions: 软.
[108] *tīkṣṇa*.
[109] *dṛṣṭiprāpta*.
[110] 趣: *pratipad°*.
[111] See note 86.
[112] *mṛdvindriya*.
[113] See note 106.
[114] See note 84.
[115] See note 83.
[116] See note 109.
[117] *saptajanmabhavaparama*. Chinese: one who is at the most reborn in seven births and deaths.
[118] See note 106.
[119] See note 109.

be abandoned through development in the realm of desire, they are reborn in seven births and deaths. Because they have seven rebirths in heaven and among men, they are said to be reborn seven times at the most[120].

One (destined to be reborn) in several families[121], has destroyed three: when the three kinds: strong-weak, strong-medium and strong-strong[122], are destroyed, they are called (destined to be reborn) in several families. [819b] Because they obtain *parinirvāṇa* after they are reborn in either two families or in three families in heaven and among men, they are called (destined to be reborn) in several families.

Both are in a fruition of the path: both the one who has seven existences at the most[123] and the one (destined to be reborn) in several families, are said to dwell in *srotaāpatti*[124].

> (110) When six are destroyed they come and go once. He who has renounced eight is said to germinate one more time. When the nine are extinguished they do not return, having emerged from the mud of desire.

When six are destroyed they come and go[125] once: when they have destroyed six kinds: the strong three and the medium three[126], they are *sakṛdāgāmins*[127]. To them remains one birth. They are called *sakṛdāgāmins* because after one birth in heaven, they obtain *parinirvāṇa*, having come and gone once among men.

He who has renounced eight is said to germinate one more time[128]: when eight kinds are destroyed they germinate one more

---

[120] See note 117.
[121] *kulaṃkula*.
[122] cf. supra stanza 107.
[123] *saptakṛtvobhavaparama*.
[124] i.e. they dwell in the fruition of streamwinning, *srotaāpattiphala*. They are *srotaāpannas* (note 103).
[125] 往来 is the usual translation for *āgatigati*.
[126] cf. supra stanza 107.
[127] See note 104.
[128] *ekabījin*. This is the term used in Prākrit. The Saṇskrit term is *ekavīcika*, having one single interval. Cf. *Kośa* VI 208 note 4.

time. Because to them only one birth remains, no more, they are said to germinate one more time[129].

When the nine are extinguished they do not return[130]: when all nine kinds are destroyed, they are *anāgāmins*[131]. Because they do not come to the realm of desire again, they are called *anāgāmins*. Why? They have emerged from the mud of desire[132].

> (111) The World-Honored One has expounded that when such nine afflictions are in the upper eight stages, they are extinguished by two paths.

When such nine afflictions are in the upper eight stages: the nine afflictions, from weak-weak to strong-strong[133], are in the upper realms just as in the realm of desire.

The eight stages (are): the brahma-world, the shining ones, the entirely magnificent ones, the ones having great fruition, the sphere of unlimited space, the sphere of unlimited consciousness, the sphere of nothingness, and the sphere of neither-perception-nor-non-perception[134].

The World-Honored One has expounded that they are extinguished by two paths: all these afflictions are extinguished by two paths in the realm of desire and in the realms of form and of formlessness. After their extinction through the immediate path[135], the path of deliverance[136] is realized.

---

AH2 850b and also MAH 911c have *ekabījin.*
[129] See note 128.
[130] *anāgam°*.
[131] See note 105.
[132] *kāmapaṅka*.
[133] cf. supra stanza 107. Weak: 软, as in the 3 editions.
[134] In *rūpadhātu* (cf. stanza 177) : 1. *brahmaloka* (*dhyāna* 1); 2. *ābhāsvara* (dhyāna 2); 3. *śubhakṛtsna* (*dhyāna* 3); 4. *bṛhatphala* (*dhyāna 4*).
In *ārūpyadhātu*: 1. *ākāśānantyāyatana*; 2.*vijñānānantyāyatana*; 3. *ākiṃcanyāyatana*; 4. *naivasaṃjñānāsaṃjñāyatana*.
[135] *ānantaryamārga*.
[136] *vimuktimārga*.

Question: Are these paths worldly or are they pure[137]?

Answer: (112) With both the stained and the stainless path one can renounce eight stages. He who dwells in them is called a bodily witness, i.e. when he has obtained the attainment of cessation.

(Eight stages): the stage of the realm of desire: 1. The stages of the realm of form: 4. Stages of the realm of formlessness: 3. They are extinguished by both the worldly path and by the pure one[138]. When even the common man[139] can renounce them by following his worldly path, how much more readily can the noble[140] do so.

He who dwells in them is called a bodily witness[141], i.e. when he has obtained the attainment of cessation[142]: when the so-called one in training[143] who abides in the renouncement[144] of the eight stages, has obtained the attainment of cessation, he is a bodily witness[145]. Why? Because the factor[146] resembles *nirvāṇa* and because his body is in contact with it, he is called a bodily witness.

> (113) [147] After the diamond-like concentration one is sure to obtain the knowledge of extinction. In a mind in which it has been produced, the births of a self are destroyed, having left all impurities.

[819c] After the diamond-like concentration[148] one is sure to obtain the knowledge of extinction[149]: diamond-like

---

[137] *laukika* (i.e. sāsrava) or *anāsrava*.
[138] See note 137.
[139] See note 95.
[140] ārya.
[141] kāyasākṣin.
[142] nirodhasamāpatti.
[143] śaikṣa.
[144] vairāgya.
[145] See note 141.
[146] Scil. nirodhasamāpatti.
[147] From this point on the *aśaikṣamārga*, the path without training, is explained.
[148] *vajropamasamādhi*.

concentration is called the last thought of one in training[150], the ninth immediate path[151] at the moment of renouncing desire in the sphere of neither-perception-nor-non-perception[152]. There all afflictions are completely destroyed for evermore. Because all noble deeds[153] have ended, it is called diamond-like *samādhi*[154]. After this, one produces the first knowledge of one who has no more training to do[155]: the knowledge of extinction[156].

In a mind in which it has been produced, the births of a self are destroyed, having left all impurities[157]: all births of a self are destroyed by the concentrated mind in which it has been produced. At that moment it is without attachment[158], delivered from all impurities[159].

Question: How many kinds of the ones without attachment[160] are there?

Answer: (114) There are six kinds of the ones without attachment. The five who are born having followed their faith, obtain two knowledges. Let it be known that they are temporarily released.

There are six kinds of the ones without attachment[161]: the World-Honored One has mentioned six ones without attachment: one who falls away, one who wants (to end his existence), one who guards, one who abides unshakable, one who will penetrate, and

---

[149] *kṣayajñāna*.
[150] *śaikṣacitta*.
[151] See note 135.
[152] *naivasaṃjñānāsaṃjñāyatana*.
[153] 行: car°.
[154] AH2 850c says: "The last *śaikṣacitta* is called *vajropamasamādhi*, just as a diamond has nothing which it cannot destroy". MAH 913c says: "Because it does not have one thing which it does not destroy, the term *vajra* is used".
[155] *aśaikṣajñāna*.
[156] See note 149.
[157] *āsrava*.
[158] 无著: without attachment (*asakta, arakta*), meaning delivered (loose from): an old rendering of an equivalent of Sanskit *arhat*.
[159] See note 157.
[160] See note 158.
[161] See note 158.

the immovable one[162]. Among them: when he falls away when with weak[163] knowledge and with weak vigorous pursuit[164] he is endowed with falling away, he is therefore called one who falls away[165]. Because with weak knowledge and with weak vigorous pursuit[166] he again and again dislikes his body, and because disliking his body he cherishes[167] its destruction, he is called one who wants (to end his existence)[168]. Because with weak knowledge and with extensive[169] vigorous pursuit he constantly guards his thoughts with the power of his vigorous pursuit, he is called one who guards[170]. Because with medium knowledge and with equal vigorous pursuit he does neither increase nor decrease, but abides in the middle path remaining equal, he is called one who abides unshakable[171]. Because with little sharpness[172] but with extensive[173] vigorous pursuit he will certainly attain immovability[174], he is called one who will penetrate[175]. Because with sharp[176] knowledge and with extensive[177] vigorous pursuit he for the first time attains immovability, he is called an immovable one[178].

The five who are born having followed their faith, obtain two knowledges: five from among them have walked following their faith[179]. They have two knowledges: the knowledge of

---

[162] a. *parihāṇadharman* (退: to recede), b. *cetanādharman* (念: to cherish), c. *anurakṣaṇādharman*, d. *sthitākampya* (Chinese: one who dwells remaining equal), e. *prativedhanādharman* (Chinese: one who will certainly ascend), f. *akopyadharman*.
[163] *mrdu*.
[164] 进: seems to mean *vīrya*.
[165] See note 162a.
[166] See note 163.
[167] 念 opposite 恶. AH2 851a: 欲念.
[168] See note 162b.
[169] ati°.
[170] See note 162c.
[171] See note 162d.
[172] 利: *tīkṣṇa* (scil. knowledge). Cf. AH2 851a.
[173] See note 169.
[174] I.e. he will become an *akopyadharman,* the sixth kind of *arhat.*
[175] See note 162e.
[176] See note 172.
[177] See note 169.
[178] See note 162f.
[179] They were *śraddhānusārins*.

extinction[180] and the view which is common to those who have no more training to do[181].

Let it be known that they are temporarily released[182]: the one who must be known as temporarily released searches for an occasion[183] and cannot on every occasion apply himself as he desires to that which is good.

> (115) Having keen faculties the immovable one is finally released. He has obtained three knowledges and accomplishes an equal deliverance.

Having keen faculties[184] the immovable one[185] is finally released[186]: i.e. the one who has keen faculties only is the immovable one. He is not temporarily released, but he can on all occasions apply himself as he desires to that which is good. He does not search for an occasion[187].

He has obtained three knowledges: he has the three knowledges: knowledge of extinction, knowledge of non-production[188], and the view which is common to those who have no more training to do[189].

He accomplishes an equal deliverance[190]: i.e. being temporarily released, the five who are without attachment accomplish an equal emancipation of mind[191]. The so-called immovable one accomplishes an immovable deliverance.

---

[180] See note 149.
[181] *aśaikṣī samyagdṛṣṭi*. AH2 851a has 正见. cf. *Kośa* VI 240 note 2.
[182] *samayavimukta*. Chinese: occasionally delivered.
[183] i.e. his *vimukti* or deliverance depends on certain circumstances, as e.g. a certain place, a certain moment, a companion, the exposition of the doctrine, clothing and food etc.
See AH2 851a.
[184] *tīkṣṇendriya*.
[185] See note 162f.
[186] *asamayavimukta*. Chinese: not occasionally delivered.
[187] The opposite of note 183.
[188] *kṣayajñāna* and *anutpādajñāna*.
[189] See note 181.
[190] i.e. being *akopya* his deliverance is equally *akopya*, immovable.
[191] i.e. being *samayavimukta*, temporarily released, their *cetovimukti*,

(116) Let it be known that he who is emancipated through wisdom has not obtained the attainment of cessation. [820a] Only the twice-delivered one has accomplished the attainment of cessation.

Let it be known that he who is emancipated through wisdom[192] has not obtained the attainment of cessation[193]: when those six without attachment have not accomplished the attainment of cessation[194], they are called emancipated through wisdom[195]. They are emancipated through the power[196] of wisdom, not through the power of concentration.

Only the twice-delivered one[197] has accomplished the attainment of cessation[198]: when those six without attachment have obtained the attainment of cessation, they are called twice-delivered[199]. They are delivered by both powers[200]: the power of wisdom and the power of concentration.

We have explained the noble persons. Their factors will now be explained.

(117) The factors of the faith-follower, the factors of the law-follower, and the path of the vision of the truths in the noble path[201], have the characteristics of all being one and the same.

The factors of the faith-follower[202] and the factors of the law-follower[203] are called the path of vision.

---

emancipation of mind, is also *sāmayıkī*, occasional.

[192] *prajñāvimukta*.
[193] *nirodhasamāpatti*.
[194] See note 193.
[195] See note 192.
[196] bala.
[197] *ubhayatovimukta*.
[198] See note 193.
[199] See note 197.
[200] See note 196.
[201] With the *darśanamārga* begins the noble (*ārya*) path (*mārga*).
[202] *śraddhānusārin*. cf. stanza 106.
[203] *dharmānusārin*. cf. stanza 106.

> (118) The organic factors which are there, are called the faculty "I shall come to understand the not yet understood". They say Buddha calls the other factors of one in training the faculty of understanding.

The organic factors which are there[204], are called the faculty "I shall come to understand the not yet understood"[205]: the faculties[206] and that which is organic among the factors of the path of vision, such as thought, feelings, and the five faculties, faith etc.[207], are the faculty "I shall come to understand the not yet understood"[208].

They say Buddha calls the other factors of one in training[209] the faculty of understanding[210]: in relation to the factors of one in training other than the factors of one in training in the path of vision, this faculty[211] is called the faculty of understanding[212].

> (119) Let it be known that the faculty of one who has fully understood, is among those of the one who has no more training to do. One must say that, having obtained a fruition, one abandons the previous paths.

Let it be known that the faculty of one who has fully understood[213], is among those[214] of the one who has no more training to do[215]: among the factors of one who has no more

---

204 In the *darśanamārga*.

205 *anājñātam* (未知) *ājñāsyāmīndriya*.

206 *indriya*.

207 *citta* or *manas*; vedanā (i.e. sukha, *saumanasya*, *upekṣā*); the 5: *śraddhā*, *vīrya*, *smṛti*, *samādhi*, *prajñā*. Cf. infra stanza 204. See also *Kośa* II 116.

208 See note 205.

209 *śaikṣa*.

210 *ājñendriya*.

211 See note 207. In the *darśanamārga* it is called *anājñātam ājñāsyāmīndriya*, and in the *bhāvanāmārga* it is called *ājñendriya*. In the *aśaikṣamārga*: *ājñātāvīndriya*.

212 See note 210.

213 *ājñātāvīndriya*. The Chinese translates *a*°, i.e. one who has nothing which he should know. One can understand this when one knows that the *indriya* 无知 is of the saint 无学(*aśaikṣa*).

214 i.e. *dharmas*.

215 *aśaikṣa*.

training to do, this faculty[216] is called the faculty of one who has fully understood.

One must say that, having obtained a fruition[217], one abandons the previous paths: when one makes progress in the pure[218] factors and obtains a fruition, one abandons that which was comprised[219] within the immediate path and within the path of deliverance[220].

> (120) That which is destroyed is disconnected. Its attainment is comprised within one fruition. One must say that that which is not defiled is extinguished by the ninth one.

That which is destroyed[221] is disconnected[222]. Its attainment is comprised within one fruition: in the immediate path and in the path of deliverance[223], there one obtains the destruction of the afflictions, but at the moment of attaining a fruition all afflictions are destroyed, and one attains one fruition which is a disconnection[224].

One must say that that which is not defiled[225] is extinguished by the ninth one: we have said that the afflictions are extinguished by a ninefold path[226], but that which is not defiled is abandoned by the ninth immediate path in one moment, not gradually.

> (121) When he has a similar name, he can obtain immovability. [820b] When the one without attachment

---

[216] See note 211.
[217] From srotaāpattiphala to *arhattvaphala*.
[218] *anāsrava*.
[219] *saṃgṛhīta*.
[220] *ānantaryamārga* and *vimuktimārga*.
[221] *kṣīṇa*.
[222] *visaṃyukta*.
[223] See note 220.
[224] *visaṃyogaphala*.
[225] That which is not defiled (*kliṣṭa*), i.e. factors which are not *kleśas*, such as impure wholesome factors.
[226] cf. stanza 107.

and the one who is given to faith have the same nature, they grow in the path.

When he has a similar name, he can obtain immovability[227]: i.e. not all the ones without attachment[228] can obtain immovability. Only[229] the one who will penetrate[230] obtains it, as he has a name which is similar.

When the one without attachment and the one who is given to faith[231] have the same nature, they grow in the path: i.e. of the ones given to faith only the one who has the nature of one who will penetrate[232] increases[233] his faculties and obtains (the state of) one who has attained correct views[234], no one else[235].

Question: How does one know the gradual viewing of the truths?

Answer: (122ab) Establishing the meritorious ones and the faulty ones[236], one gradually views the truths.

It is not the case that, at the moment of viewing the meritorious ones, one views the faulty ones. At the moment of viewing the faulty ones, one does not view the meritorious ones. Neither is it the case that one first intuitively realizes[237] those faulty ones in a

---

[227] *akopya.*
[228] i.e. *arhat.* See stanza 114.
[229] 3 editions: 惟.
[230] *prativedhanādharman.*
[231] *śraddhādhimukta.*
[232] See note 230.
[233] *saṃcāra, vivṛddhi.*
[234] i.e. becomes a *dṛṣṭiprāpta.*
[235] A *śraddhādhimukta*, who is *mṛdvindriya* in the *bhāvanāmārga*, may become a *dṛṣṭiprāpta*, who is *tīkṣṇendriya* in the *bhāvanāmārga*, when his nature is the same as the nature of a *prativedhanādharman*, who, being *samayavimukta* and *mṛdvindriya*, becomes an *akopyadharman*, who is *asamayavimukta* and *tīkṣṇendriya.*
[236] 功德: *guṇa*; 悪: *doṣa.*
The faulty ones are the *duḥkha*° and the *samudayasatya*. The meritorious ones are the *nirodha*° and the *mārgasatya*. See AH2 852a and MAH 916b.
[237] *abhisameti.*

general way[238], nor is it the case that they are all disliked in one moment.

It is also not the case that a complete meritorious one[239] equals all meritorious ones, nor is it the case that they are combined in one moment. Therefore, establishing the meritorious ones and the faulty ones, one gradually views the truths.

Question: How does one know a formed and an unformed fruition[240]?

Answer: (122cd) Through the power of the immediate path one obtains a formed and an unformed fruition.

The power of the immediate path[241] attains both a formed fruition and an unformed fruition[242]. Therefore, one attains a formed and an unformed fruition through the power of the immediate path.

Treatise on the Essence of Scholasticism: Vol. II.

---

[238] E.g. when intuitively realizing the *duḥkhasatya*, one gradually contemplates its *ākāras:anitya, duḥkha, śūnya, anātmaka.* cf. stanza 101.

[239] i.e. with its 4 *ākāras*. cf. stanza 101.

[240] The fruition of *śramaṇaship* (śrāmaṇya) is *saṃskṛta* and *asaṃskṛta*. See also *Kośa* VI 241-242.

[241] *ānantaryamārga*.

[242] kośa VI 242: the *ānantaryamārgas* for the *kleśas* constitute *śramaṇaship*, *śrāmaṇya*. The *vimuktimārgas* are the formed (*saṃskṛta*) fruitions, and the *pratisaṃkhyānirodha* or destruction of the *kleśas*, is the unformed (*asaṃskṛta*) fruition.
MAH 916b says: "The *pratisaṃkhyānirodha* of the *kleśas* and the *vimuktimārga* are both obtained through the power of the *ānantaryamārga*. Therefore both are called *śrāmaṇyaphala*."
See also AH2 852a.

**贤圣品第五**

已说使品。贤圣品今当说。

97 如此圣断劳 众恐怖之本
等方便正智 今当说善听
不亭心者无能起正见。是以

98 始自身处所 系缚心令定
亦欲缚识足 及尽烦恼怨

99 是方便于身 真实相常定
诸痛及此心 法亦如是观
此身不净相无常相苦相无我相。是相定真实。彼自身一处系心离心乱始真实观身相。次观痛后观心彼伴彼依及彼相应余心数法。观亦诸心不相应行。如其性如其相所有如是彼身痛心法意止次第生。

100 入法中总观 同观诸法相
此四是无常 空无我非乐
入法中总观同观诸法相者入法意止中彼圣总观诸行相。观诸行相已增长养心生无垢智眼。一切身痛心法总观。问。云何。答。此四是无常空无我非乐。此身痛心法展转相生故无常不自在故空。非主故无我。恶灾患故苦。

101 从是名暖法 即是意中生
行是十六行 正观四真谛
从是名暖法即是意中生者彼如是观生善暖。于中当生无漏智火能烧一切行薪。问。彼何行何境界。答。行是十六行正观四真谛。彼行是十六行境界四真谛。四行观苦谛。此苦性劣从因缘生故无常。无常力所坏故苦。内离人故空。不自在故无我。四行观习。此习成相似果故因。行相续故习。一切生死无穷可得故有。不相似事相续故缘。四行观灭。此灭覆一切患尽故灭。除一切烦恼火故止。胜一切法故妙。舍生死故离。四行观道。此道至非品故道。非颠倒故如。一切圣所履故迹。生死患转出故乘。是谓彼行十六行。境界四真谛善根谓之暖法。

102 彼起已成立 生顶及于忍
得世第一法 依倚于一相
彼起已成立生顶及于忍者若已成暖法于中复于欲界生善根如顶亦十六行观四真谛。胜暖法故说顶。已增上顶生善根名为忍亦十六行观四真谛。堪任故说忍。若忍已成立得世第一法依倚于一相。一切世俗功德中最胜生善根名世间第一法。开涅槃门故于凡夫意中最胜故说第一法。问。以何等故说依倚于一相。答。于凡夫意中更无有比二功德。若有者彼亦应开涅槃门而不开。是故说依倚于一相。
问。彼几行何缘何地所摄。

103 彼行苦四行 说摄依六地
彼行苦者彼即缘苦谛非余。四行者谓行苦谛境界无常为首。所以者何。如初无漏心缘彼亦复尔。说摄依六地者彼法摄于六地未来禅中间禅根本四禅。非欲界不定界故。非无色界无见道故。
问。余善根何地所摄。答。

忍亦摄六地 余则依于七
忍亦摄六地者谛顺忍六地所摄如世间第一法。余则依于七者暖及顶七地所摄此六及欲界未除欲。欲界已除欲色界。

104 世第一法次 必兴起法忍
忍次生于智 俱观于下苦
世第一法次必兴起法忍者世间第一法次第生无漏法忍名苦法忍。彼未曾观今观时堪任故曰忍。是谓初无漏无碍道。忍次生于智者彼次第生苦法智同境界受真实性解脱道。问。彼忍及智何缘。答。俱观于下苦。下苦者欲界苦彼同缘。

105 上苦亦如是 因灭道亦然
是正观诸法 说十六净心
上苦亦如是者上苦是色无色界苦。彼亦如是生忍无碍道智解脱道苦未知忍及苦未知智。因者是习谛。彼亦如是生四道如苦习法忍习法智习未知忍习未知智。灭者灭亦如是生四道灭法忍灭法智灭未知忍灭未知智道亦然者道亦如是生四道道法忍道法智道未知忍道未知智。是正观诸法说十六净心者是见法。见法者谓之正观。是见异名。

106 从法行利根 此在十五意
从信行当知 钝见亦在中
从法行利根此在十五意者彼十五心顷若利根是说从法行。从信行当知钝见亦在中者即彼十五心顷若钝根是说从信行。

107 未离欲界欲 趣向于始果
舍六趣至二 三向九无漏
未离欲界欲趣向于始果者彼从信行及从法行趣沙门果时若未离欲俱趣须陀洹果。舍六趣至二者欲界烦恼九种微微微中微上中微中。中中上。上微上中上上。彼若凡夫时已离六种彼于后若趣证是俱趣第二果。三向九无漏者若已离九种是俱趣阿那含果。

108 若至十六心 是名住于果

信解脱软见　　　　见到说利见

若至十六心是名住于果者十六心名道未知智心相应。彼生已说住于果。未曾离欲界欲俱须陀洹。已曾离六品俱斯陀含。尽离九品俱阿那含。信解脱软见见到说利见者若彼趣时从信行钝根是信解脱。若彼从法行利根是见到。

109　未尽思惟断　　　　极生生死七
家家有三尽　　　　俱在道迹果

未尽思惟断极生生死七者彼信解脱及见到未离欲界思惟所断烦恼是生生死七。彼有天上七生及人中故说极生生死七。家家有三尽者若三种尽上微上中上上是说家家。彼天上及人中或生二家或生三家后般涅槃故说家家。俱在道迹果者极七有及家家当言俱住须陀洹。

110　六尽一往来　　　　离八谓一种
九灭尽不还　　　　已出欲污泥

六尽一往来者若有六种尽上三中三是斯陀含。彼余一生。天上一生人中一往来已般涅槃故说斯陀含。离八谓一种者若八品尽是一种。彼余唯一生无余故说一种。九灭尽不还者若一切九品尽是阿那含。彼不复来欲界故说阿那含。所以者何。已出欲污泥。

111　如是九烦恼　　　　若在上八地
彼双道所灭　　　　世尊之所说

如是九烦恼若在上八地者如欲界九种烦恼软软至上上上界亦如是。八地中梵世光曜遍净果实无量空处无量识处无所有处非想非非想处。彼双道所灭世尊之所说者此一切烦恼欲界及色无色界双道所灭。以无碍道灭解脱道得证。

问。此道为世俗为无漏。答。

112　有垢无垢道　　　　俱能离八地
住中说身证　　　　谓获灭尽定

欲界地一色界地四无色界地三。亦世俗道灭亦无漏。凡夫从世俗道尚得远离况复圣贤住中说身证谓获灭尽定者住于八地无欲中谓学得灭尽定是身证。所以者何。法似涅槃身所触故说身证。

113　金刚喻定次　　　　必逮得尽智
生意我生尽　　　　离于一切漏

金刚喻定次必逮得尽智者金刚喻定名非想非非想处离欲时第九无碍道最后学心。于中一切诸烦恼永尽无余。一切圣行毕竟故说金刚喻三摩提。此次第生尽智最初无学智。生意我生尽离于一切漏者彼生定意我一切生尽。彼于尔时无著解脱一切漏。

问。无著有几种。答。

114　　无著有六种　　　　是从信生五
　　　逮得于二智　　　　当知时解脱

无著有六种者世尊说六无著退法念法护法等住必升进不动法。于中若软智及软进是得退具便退故说退法。软智及软进数数恶身恶身已念坏故说念法。软智面广进进力常自护心故说护法。中智及等进是不增不损等住于中道故说等住。少利而广进彼必得不动故说必升进。利智及广进是始得不动故说不动。是从信生五逮得于二智者于中五曾从信行。彼有二智尽智及无学等见。当知时解脱者彼当知时解脱是求时不能一切时随所欲学善。

115　　不动法利根　　　　是不时解脱
　　　获得于三智　　　　成就等解脱

不动法利根是不时解脱者谓一向利根是不动法。彼不时解脱能一切时随所欲学善。不求时。获得于三智者彼有三智尽智无生智无学等见。成就等解脱者谓此五无著时解脱是成就等意解脱。谓不动法是成就不动解脱。

116　　慧解脱当知　　　　不得灭尽定
　　　唯有俱解脱　　　　成就灭尽定

慧解脱当知不得灭尽定者此六无著若不成就灭尽定是说慧解脱。是慧力解脱非定力。唯有俱解脱成就灭尽定者此六无著若得灭尽定是说俱解脱。彼具力解脱慧力及定力。
已说贤圣人。法今当说。

117　　从信行诸法　　　　及从法行法
　　　圣道见谛道　　　　是尽同一相

从信行法从法行法是说见道。

118　　于中诸根法　　　　是名未知根
　　　谓余有学法　　　　佛说已知根

于中诸根法是名未知根者于见道法中谓根根数如心及痛信等五根是未知根。谓余有学法佛说已知根者离见道学法诸余学法中即彼根说已知根。

119　　当知无知根　　　　在于无学中
　　　已得果便舍　　　　前道应当说

当知无知根在于无学中者无学法中即彼根说无知根。已得果便舍前道应当说者此无漏法升进得果时舍无碍道所摄及解脱道。

120　　已尽为解脱　　　　得摄于一果
　　　不秽污第九　　　　灭尽应当说

已尽为解脱得摄于一果者无碍道至解脱道于其中间得烦恼尽。但得果时一切烦恼尽得一解脱果。不秽污第九灭尽应当说者说诸烦恼九种道所灭。但不秽污第九无碍道一时断不渐渐。

121　　若有相似名　　彼能获不动
　　　　无著及信脱　　彼同性增道

若有相似名彼能获不动者谓无著不能一切得不动惟必升进得。彼是相似名。无著及信脱彼同性增道者谓信解脱一向性必升进是增益诸根逮得见到非余。

问。云何知渐渐见谛。答。

122　　建立功德恶　　次第见真谛

非以见功德时见恶。亦不以见恶时见功德。亦非初总观彼恶。亦非一时一切厌。亦非总功德诸功德。亦非一时合。是以建立功德恶次第见真谛。问。云何知有为无为果。答。

　　　　无碍道力得　　有为无为果

无碍道力得有为果及无为果。是故以无碍道力得有为无为果。

阿毗昙心论卷第二

Treatise on the Essence of Scholasticism. Vol. III, composed by Bhadanta Dharmaśreṣṭhin, translated on Mount Lu by Saṃghadeva of the Eastern Jin, with Huiyuan .

# CHAPTER VI. KNOWLEDGE[1]

(123) When one can understand the nature of knowledge, one clearly contemplates all that exists. The existing and that which is non-existent[2], *nirvāṇa*, their characteristics will now be explained.

Knowledge has namely been explained briefly in the chapter: The Noble[3]. Its ranges[4], the existing and that which is non-existent, will now be explained.

(124) Three knowledges are expounded by Buddha, the supreme and the best mind: knowledge of the law, subsequent knowledge, and conventional knowledge.

These three knowledges comprise all knowledges. Among them, knowledge of the law[5] is called the pure[6] knowledge which takes the suffering, origination, cessation, and the path[7] in the realm of desire as its range. Because in its range one experiences for the first time the characteristics of the law, [820c] it is called knowledge of the law. After the knowledge of the law, when that which is visible for the faculties[8] is seen, comes subsequent knowledge[9], in which that which is not visible for the faculties is still seen. Subsequent knowledge is called the pure[10] knowledge

---

1 *jñānavarga*.
2 cf. AH2 852ab; MAH 916c.
3 See stanzas 104, 105, 114, and 115.
4 *viṣaya*.
5 *dharmajñāna*.
6 *anāsrava*.
7 *duḥkha, samudaya, nirodha, mārga*.
8 *indriya*.
9 *anvayajñāna*.
10 See note 6.

which takes suffering, origination, cessation, and the path[11] in the realms of form and of formlessness as its range. Because in its range one experiences the characteristics of the law at a later point, it is called subsequent knowledge. Impure[12] knowledge is called conventional knowledge[13]. It mostly[14] grasps what is conventionally true[15] by distinguishing[16] male or female, long or short, etc.

> (125) The Delivered Master[17] has explained that, as suffering, origination, appeasement, and the path can be obtained by two knowledges, these names are given to four knowledges.

As the two knowledges, the knowledge of the law and subsequent knowledge[18], proceed within the truths, they are thus designated by such names[19]. When the truth of suffering is their range, they are called knowledge of suffering. When the truth of origination is their range, they are called knowledge of origination. When the truth of cessation is their range, they are called knowledge of cessation. When the truth of the path is their range, they are called knowledge of the path[20]. They are explained by the Delivered Master.

> (126) It is said that, when knowledges contemplate the thoughts of others, they are based on three. The knowledges of extinction and of non-production are a pair. Their ranges rest in the four categories.

It is said that, when knowledges contemplate the thoughts of others, they are based on three: of the knowledges of the thoughts of others[21], the one with an impure range is (called)

---

[11] See note 7.
[12] *sāsrava*.
[13] *saṃvṛtijñāna*.
[14] *prāyeṇa*. The *saṃvṛtisatya* has all factors as its objects.
[15] *saṃvṛtisatya*.
[16] The 3 editions: 知.
[17] AH2 852b: The Muni, i.e. *Śākyamuni*.
[18] *dharmajñāna* and *anvayajñāna*.
[19] *duḥkhe dharmajñāna* and *duḥkhe'nvayajñāna*: *duḥkhajñāna*. Etc…
[20] The 4 knowledges: *duḥkhajñāna*, *samudayajñāna*, *nirodhajñāna*, *mārgajñāna*.
[21] *paracittajñāna*.

conventional knowledge[22]. The one which takes the path in the realm of desire as its range, is knowledge of the law[23]. The one which takes the path in the realm of form as its range, is subsequent knowledge.

The knowledges of extinction and of non-production[24] are a pair: the two knowledges of one who has no more training to do[25], are the knowledge of extinction and the knowledge of non-production[26]. Among them, the knowledge of one who has no more training to do, experienced when that which should be done is done[27], is the knowledge of extinction[28]. The knowledge of one who has no more training to do, which is experienced when one does not do it again, is the knowledge of non-production[29]. They represent also the knowledge of the law and subsequent knowledge[30].

Question: Which truths are the ranges of the knowledge of extinction and of the knowledge of non-production?

Answer: Their ranges rest in four categories[31]. The four truths are the ranges of these two knowledges: suffering, origination, cessation, and the path[32].

We have explained the ten knowledges. Their aspects[33] will now be explained.

> (127) Two knowledges: the knowledge of the law and subsequent knowledge have the sixteen aspects. The one

---

[22] See note 13.
[23] See note 5.
[24] *kṣayajñāna* and *anutpādajñāna*.
[25] aśaikṣa.
[26] See note 24.
[27] *kṛtaṃ karaṇīyam*.
[28] *kṣayajñāna*.
[29] *anutpādajñāna*.
[30] See note 18.
[31] 门 may translate *paryāya*.
[32] See note 7.
[33] *ākāra*. cf. stanza 101.

either having such aspects or not, is said to be conventional knowledge.

Two knowledges: the knowledge of the law and subsequent knowledge [34], have the sixteen aspects [35]: by nature the knowledge of the law[36] has the sixteen aspects: four aspects when experiencing suffering, four aspects for origination, four aspects for cessation, and four aspects for the path[37]. The same applies to subsequent knowledge[38] in the realms of form and of formlessness.

The one either having such aspects or not, is said to be the conventional knowledge [39]: the aspects of the conventional knowledge which is comprised within warmth, the summit, patient acceptance, and the highest factor[40], and its pure[41] aspects, when comprised within two truths [42], are the sixteen aspects. When it is comprised within the highest factor [43], it has four aspects. The conventional knowledge through learning, reflection, and development[44] has the sixteen aspects. The other conventional knowledge besides this one does not have the sixteen aspects: i.e. giving, morality, friendliness[45], and so forth.

(128) It is explained with certainty by those who proceed within them, that four knowledges have four aspects.

---

[34] See note 18.
[35] See note 33.
[36] See note 5.
[37] cf. stanza 101.
[38] See note 9.
[39] See note 13.
[40] *uṣmagata*, *mūrdhan*, *kṣānti*, (laukika) *agradharma*: the 4 *kuśalamūlas*. cf. *stanzas* 101-102.
The *laukikāgradharma* proceeds within 4 *ākāras*, infra and in stanza 103ab.
[41] *anāsrava*.
[42] *saṃvṛtisatya* and *paramārthasatya*.
[43] (*laukika*) *agradharma*. cf. note 40.
[44] *śrutamaya°*, *cintāmaya°*, *bhāvanāmaya°*. The Chinese translates both *cintā* and *bhāvanā* as 思: reflection. For this reason, it gives 余思惟: the other reflection, when rendering *bhāvanā*.
[45] *dāna*, *śīla*, *maitrī*.
戒 may also translate *saṃvara*.

> [821a] The knowledge which intuitively realizes the thoughts of others is either like this or not.

It is explained with certainty by those who proceed within them, that four knowledges have four aspects: the knowledge of suffering[46] has four aspects, as we have explained earlier[47]. The same applies to origination, cessation, and the path[48].

The knowledge which intuitively realizes[49] the thoughts of others[50] is either like this or not: pure[51] knowledge of the thoughts of others has four aspects, as does the knowledge of the path[52]. But when it is impure[53], it does not.

> (129) The knowledge of extinction and the knowledge of non-production are said to have fourteen aspects, leaving out the aspects voidness and selflessness. The characteristics experienced prevail.

The knowledge of extinction and the knowledge of non-production[54] are said to have fourteen aspects, leaving out the aspects voidness and selflessness[55]: the knowledge of extinction and the knowledge of non-production have fourteen aspects, subtracting the aspects voidness and selflessness. Why? They proceed within the conventional truth[56]: "I have already done it, and I will not do it again"[57]. They do not proceed within voidness and selflessness.

---

[46] *duḥkhajñāna.*
[47] Because *duḥkhajñāna* proceeds within *duḥkha*, it has the 4 *ākāras* of *duḥkha*. cf. stanza 101.
[48] i.e. *samudaya°*, *nirodha°*, *mārgajñāna.*
[49] *abhisameti.*
[50] *paracittajñāna.*
[51] See note 41.
[52] *mārgajñāna.*
[53] *sāsrava.*
[54] See note 24.
[55] *śūnya*, *anātmaka.*
[56] *saṃvṛtisatya.*
[57] See supra stanza 126.

The characteristics[58] experienced prevail: it is not the case that all pure[59] knowledges exist in relation to the sixteen aspects. The sixteen aspects are general [60] aspects. There are also pure knowledges which experience sixteen characteristics, such as the application of mindfulness to the body[61]. They are knowledges of the particular characteristics[62]. In relation to the sixteen aspects they do not first experience the sixteen aspects. Because the particular characteristics, when pure knowledges proceed within them, are experienced first[63], they prevail.

We have explained their sixteen aspects. The manner of obtaining these knowledges will now be explained.

> (130) The first pure thought may accomplish one. The second one may accomplish three. At higher stages they are increased by one.

The first pure thought[64] may accomplish one: the first pure thought is associated with patient acceptance of the law in relation to suffering[65]. Having not yet renounced desire[66], one accomplishes conventional knowledge [67] only. Having renounced desire, one accomplishes the knowledge of the thoughts of others[68].

The second one may accomplish three: the second pure thought is associated with the knowledge of the law in relation to

---

[58] *lakṣaṇa.*
[59] See note 41.
[60] 总: *sāmānya.*
[61] *kāyasmṛtyupasthāna.* See stanza 98.
[62] *svalakṣaṇa* (scil. of the object).
[63] an *anāsrava jñāna* first experiences the 'particular characteristics' and only after that does it come to the 16 *ākāras*, which are general.
[64] *anāsravacitta.* See stanza 104.
[65] *duḥkhe dharmakṣānti.*
[66] i.e. as a *pṛthagjana*, a common man, not having renounced desire (*virakta*) by following the *laukika* (=*sāsrava*) *mārga.* See *Kośa* VII 47.
[67] *saṃvṛtijñāna.*
[68] i.e. as a *pṛthagjana* having renounced desire by following the *laukika mārga.* Such a one also accomplishes *paracittajñāna* (comprised within the fundamental *dhyānas.* cf. stanza 131).

suffering[69]. Having not yet renounced desire, one accomplishes the three: knowledge of the law, knowledge of suffering, and conventional knowledge [70]. Having renounced desire one accomplishes knowledge of the thoughts of others[71].

At higher stages they are increased by one: at higher stages one is mentioned in addition at four moments. The four moments[72]: obtaining subsequent knowledge in relation to suffering one obtains subsequent knowledge. With the knowledge of the law in relation to origination one obtains the knowledge of origination. With the knowledge of the law in relation to cessation one obtains the knowledge of cessation. With the knowledge of the law in relation to the path one obtains the knowledge of the path. In patient acceptance one does not obtain knowledge.

Question: Within which stages[73] are these knowledges comprised?

Answer: (131) The noble say that nine knowledges rely on upper stages. Ten knowledges are in the trances, and eight in the stage of formlessness.

The noble say that nine knowledges rely on upper[74] stages: in the pre-trance and in the intermediate trance [75] there is no

---

[69] *duḥkhe dharmajñāna.*
[70] *dharmajñāna, duḥkhajñāna, saṃvṛtijñāna.*
[71] *paracittajñāna.*
They are: *duḥkhe'nvayajñāna, samudaye dharmajñāna, nirodhe dharmajñāna, mārge dharmajñāna.*
The knowledges which are added at these moments are: *anvayajñāna, samudayajñāna, nirodhajñāna, mārgajñāna.*
Bringing all this information together:
Not yet having renounced desire (cf. note 66):
First citta (*duḥkhe dharmakṣānti*): *saṃvṛtijñāna.*
Second citta (*duḥkhe dharmajñāna*): *dharma*°, *duḥkha*°, and *saṃvṛtijñāna.*
Fourth citta (*duḥkhe'nvayajñāna*): the 3 + *anvayajñāna.*
Sixth citta (*samudaye dharmajñāna*): the 4 + *samudayajñāna.*
Tenth citta (*nirodhe dharmajñāna*): the 5 + *nirodhajñāna.*
Fourteenth citta (*mārge dharmajñāna*): the 6 + *mārgajñāna.*
Having renounced desire (cf. note 68).
In each instance one must add *paracittajñāna.*
[73] *bhūmi.*
[74] AH2 853a: 二: two.

knowledge of the thoughts of others[76], because it is comprised within the fundamental trances[77].

Ten knowledges are in the trances: the ten knowledges are in the fundamental trances[78].

Eight in the stage of formlessness[79]: in the stage[80] of formlessness there are eight knowledges, [821b] subtracting the knowledge of the law and the knowledge of the thoughts of others[81]. Knowledge of the law takes the realm of desire as its range, not the one of formlessness. Having taken the realm of desire as its range, knowledge of the thoughts of others proceeds to form[82], and in the stage of formlessness there is no form.

We have explained their stages. Their development[83] will now be explained. There are two kinds of development[84]: development which means acquisition[85] and development which involves practice[86]. Development which means acquisition[87]: i.e. when a quality[88] which was not yet obtained, is obtained, and when, after its acquisition, the other qualities which rely on it are also obtained. After its acquisition, they are later produced although not striven for. Development which involves practice[89]:

---

[75] *anāgamyadhyāna* and *dhyānāntara*.
[76] See note 71.
[77] *mauladhyāna*.
[78] See note 77.
[79] *ārūpya*.
[80] See the 3 editions: 地.
[81] *dharmajñāna* and *paracittajñāna*.
[82] *rūpa*.
[83] bhāvanā.
[84] AH2 853a mentions 6 kinds (as the western masters do. See *kośa* VII 65): *pratilambha°*, *niṣevaṇa°*, *pratipakṣa°*, *vinirdhāvana°*, *saṃvara°*, *vibhāvanābhāvanā*. Then it continues (AH2 853b): "We only take 2 of them: *pratilambha°* and *niṣevaṇabhāvanā*".
[85] *pratilambhabhāvanā*.
[86] *niṣevaṇabhāvanā*.
[87] See note 85.
[88] *guṇa*.
[89] See note 86.

i.e. when a quality which has been obtained is now present[90] and practiced.

Question: How are these knowledges developed?

Answer: (132) When the knowledges which are in noble vision are developed after their acquisition, they are developed as future. The same applies to the patient acceptances.

When the knowledges which are in noble vision[91] are developed after their acquisition[92], they are developed as future: when a knowledge in the path of the vision of the truths, from the knowledge of the law to the knowledge of the path[93], is developed as present, then it is developed as future.

The same applies to the patient acceptances[94]: When patient acceptance of the law in relation to suffering[95] is developed as present, then a patient acceptance of the law in relation to suffering is developed as future. It is not the case that the knowledge[96] or another patient acceptance (are developed). The same applies to all (patient acceptances[97]).

> (133) It is in three thoughts that one performs development which means acquisition in relation to conventional knowledge. It is explained by the last thought that one develops seven or six.

It is in three thoughts that one performs development which means acquisition[98] in relation to conventional knowledge: at

---

90 *saṃmukhībhūta*.
91 i.e. in the *darśanamārga*.
92 We follow the 3 editions: 已得. The *bhāvanā* meant here is *pratilambhabhāvanā*.
93 i.e. this is the case for the knowledges from *dharmajñāna* to *mārgajñāna*.
94 *kṣānti*.
95 *duḥkhe dharmakṣānti*.
96 i.e. *duḥkhe dharmajñāna*.
97 *kṣānti*.
98 See note 85.

the moments[99] of three thoughts in the path of vision of the truths [100], one develops conventional knowledge as future: subsequent knowledge in relation to suffering, subsequent knowledge in relation to origination, and subsequent knowledge in relation to cessation[101]. When proceeding within these three truths one performs the development which means acquisition of conventional knowledge. Why? When these three truths, not the truth of the path[102], have been practiced and intuitively realized, (one develops) in the said stages in the path of vision[103] the conventional knowledge of those stages and also of the realm of desire[104].

It is explained by the last thought that one develops seven or six: in subsequent knowledge in relation to the path[105], the one who has renounced desire develops seven knowledges[106], i.e. the ones comprised within the *ānāgami*-fruition[107]. The one who has not yet renounced desire[108] develops six knowledges, subtracting the knowledge of the thoughts of others[109]. Because there in the path of neither-perception-nor-non-perception[110] one obtains a fruition

---

[99] 3 editions: 顷.
[100] See note 91.
[101] *duḥkhe', samudaye', nirodhe'nvayajñāna.*
[102] i.e. *duḥkha*°, *samudaya*°, and *nirodhasatya*, not the *mārgasatya*.
[103] *darśanamārga.*
[104] e.g. realizing the *darśanamārga* on the basis of the fourth *dhyāna*, one develops as future or one acquires the *saṃvṛtijñāna* of 7 stages, i.e. *anāgamya, dhyānāntara*, 4 *dhyānas,* and *kāmadhātu.* See *Kośa* VII 52-53, MAH 919a, and AH2 853b. In AH2 853b and MAH 919a the *saṃvṛtijñāna* in this case is called *abhisamayāntika* (at the end of *abhisamaya*)*jñāna.* See *Kośa* VII 50.
[105] *mārge'nvayajñāna*, the 16th. *anāsrava citta* and the beginning of the bhāvanāmārga.
[106] One who has renounced the desire of the *kāmadhātu* (cf. note 67) develops (i.e. *pratilambhabhāvanā*) seven, i.e. the 10 minus *saṃvṛti*°, *kṣaya*° and *anutpādajñāna.* See AH2 853b. cf. *Kośa* VII 54.
[107] *anāgāmiphala.* cf. stanza 107.
[108] cf. note 66.
[109] *paracittajñāna.*
[110] i.e. when developing the path of that which is opposed to the *naivasaṃjñānāsaṃjñāyatana.* See MAH 919b. There: the 16th. *citta.*

of *śramaṇaship*[111], one does not develop conventional knowledge[112].

> (134) Let it be known that in seventeen pure thoughts in the higher path of development, one develops seven. Six are developed while increasing one's faculties.

Let it be known that in seventeen pure thoughts[113] in the higher path of development, one develops seven: at the moments[114] of seventeen thoughts[115] of the path of development[116] above the *srotaāpatti*-fruition[117], one develops seven knowledges. Because this path is comprised within the pre-trance[118], there is no knowledge of the thoughts of others[119]. One who has no more training to do[120] has the knowledge of extinction and the knowledge of non-production[121]. Therefore one does not have them. The remaining seven knowledges are sure to be developed. Why? In that mind [821c] these qualities[122] are permanent, not discontinued. If they were not developed, if they were abandoned after being obtained and had not yet been obtained anew, in-between they would be discontinued, but they are not discontinued. Therefore they are sure to be developed.

Six are developed[123] while increasing[124] one's faculties: they call it increasing one's faculties when one who is given to faith[125] increases his faculties and becomes one who has attained correct

---

[111] *śrāmaṇyaphala*. See stanza 107.
[112] *saṃvṛtijñāna*, being impure, is not opposed to the *kleśas* of the *bhavāgra*. *Kośa* VII 56; AH2 853b; MAH 919b.
[113] i.e. 9 *ānantaryamārgas* and 8 *vimuktimārgas*. The ninth *vimuktimārga* means the *anāgāmiphala*. See infra stanza 135a.
[114] See note 99.
[115] See note 113.
[116] *bhāvanāmārga*.
[117] *srotaāpattiphala*. See stanza 107; cf. note 113.
[118] *anāgamyadhyāna*.
[119] See note 109.
[120] *aśaikṣa*.
[121] *kṣaya*° and *anutpādajñāna*.
[122] *guṇa*.
[123] 3 editions: 修.
[124] *saṃcāra*, *vivṛddhi*.
[125] *śraddhādhimukta*.

views[126]. He has nine immediate paths and nine paths of deliverance[127]. In all these immediate paths and in all these paths of deliverance he develops six knowledges. Because this is said when he has not yet renounced desire[128], he has no knowledge of the thoughts of others[129]. At that moment[130] he applies himself to the path, but he does not apply himself in order to abandon affliction. Because he has not yet performed development which means acquisition[131] of the quality[132], nor obtained it already, he does not develop conventional knowledge.

> (135) At the moment of obtaining the fruition of one who does not return, when leaving seven stages, and in the paths considering super-knowledge, the deliverances develop eight (knowledges).

At the moment of obtaining the fruition of one who does not return[133]: when obtaining the fruition of one who does not return, one develops eight knowledges. Because there one surely obtains fundamental trance[134], one develops the knowledge of the thoughts of others[135]. The other knowledges are as explained previously[136].

When leaving seven stages: all nine paths of deliverance[137] at the moments of renouncing desire in the four trances and in three formlessnesses[138], develop eight knowledges. There they all develop those of the trance of a lower stage[139].

---

[126] *dṛṣṭiprāpta*.
[127] *ānantaryamārga* and *vimuktimārga*. cf. Kośa VI 270.
[128] i.e. when he is not yet an *anāgāmin*. cf. *Kośa* VII 56.
[129] See note 109.
[130] i.e. of *indriyasaṃcāra* in the *bhāvanāmārga*.
[131] See note 85.
[132] *guṇa*, seems to mean application, making efforts to abandon the *kleśas*. cf. AH2 853c.
[133] *anāgāmiphala*.
[134] *mauladhyāna*.
[135] See note 109.
[136] In the previous stanza 134abc.
The 3 editions: 如前说.
[137] *vimuktimārga*.
[138] 4 *dhyānas* and the first 3 *ārūpyas*.
[139] See infra stanza 137cd.

In the paths considering superknowledge[140], the deliverances[141] develop eight (knowledges): all nine paths of deliverance[142] of the three superknowledges: the base of psychic power, heavenly eye, and heavenly ear[143], develop eight knowledges. Why? Because they are comprised within the fundamental trances[144].

> (136) In these[145] immediate paths and in the eight paths of deliverance which extinguish the summit of existence, one develops seven of the said ones.

In all immediate paths[146] at the moments of renouncing desire in seven stages[147], one develops seven knowledges, subtracting the knowledge of the thoughts of others[148]. Why? When these immediate paths are developed, they cast off the fetters[149], but the practicing[150] of the knowledge of the thoughts of others does not mean that one casts off the fetters. Therefore it is not developed. The sphere of neither-perception-nor-non-perception[151] is the summit of existence[152]. In eight paths of deliverance[153] when renouncing desire, one develops seven knowledges, subtracting conventional knowledge[154]. Why? Conventional knowledge is set aside from the sphere of neither-

---

140 *abhijñā*.
141 *vimukti*.
142 See note 137.
143 *ṛddhipāda* (如意: as one wishes; 足: foot, step), *divyacakṣus, divyaśrotra*. AH2 853c and MAH 919bc differ from AH.
For the translation of *ṛddhipāda*: see stanza 191c, but especially AH2 862a and MAH 937c.
144 See note 134.
145 The previous stanza has explained *vimuktimārgas*. Here their ānantaryamārgas are meant.
146 *ānantaryamārga*.
147 See stanza 135b.
148 See note 109.
149 结 may mean *saṃyojana*.
150 3 editions: 习.
151 *naivasaṃjñānāsaṃjñāyatana*.
152 *bhavāgra*.
153 i.e. 8 *vimuktimārgas*, not the ninth one.
154 *saṃvṛtijñāna*.
Subtracting, i.e. from the 8 knowledges in stanza 135. The stanza 136d itself has 说者.

perception-nor-non-perception[155], because it is not opposed[156] to it.

> (137) When renouncing the summit of existence, six are developed in the immediate paths. Let it be known that, while ascending, one develops those of a lower stage.

When renouncing the summit of existence[157], six are developed in the immediate paths[158]: in the nine immediate paths at the moments of renouncing desire in the summit[159], one develops six knowledges, subtracting knowledge of the thoughts of others and conventional knowledge[160].

Let it be known that, while ascending, one develops those of a lower stage: when these are developed, in all stages –as one should know-one develops the knowledges pertaining to the stage (itself) and the ones comprised within a lower stage. I.e. he who renounces desire on the basis of the first trance develops the qualities of two stages: the ones comprised within his own stage and the ones within the pre-trance[161]. It is like this up to the sphere of nothingness[162].

> (138) [822a] In the first thought of one who has no more training to do one develops the qualities, impure or pure, of all stages. This is a mind with subsequent knowledge.

In the first thought of one who has no more training to do[163] one develops the qualities, impure or pure[164], of all stages: the

---

[155] See note 151.
[156] 3 editions: 敌. AH2 854a, 对治: *pratipakṣa.*
[157] See note 152.
[158] See note 146.
[159] agra, i.e., *bhavāgra*.
[160] i.e. subtracting *paracittajñāna* and *saṃvṛtijñāna* from the 8 *jñānas* of stanza 135.
[161] *anāgamyadhyāna*.
[162] *ākiṃcanyāyatana*.
[163] *aśaikṣa*. The first thought of such a one is the ninth and last *vimuktimārga* in the *bhavāgra*, when the fruition of *arhatship* or *arhattvaphala* is obtained.
[164] *sāsrava* and *anāsrava*.

moment one obtains the fruition of being without attachment[165], one develops (the qualities) in the nine stages[166], i.e. in the stage itself and in all stages. Why? In the stage of the sphere of neither-perception-nor-non-perception [167] one is opposed to affliction[168]. In all stages a mind with afflictions is not clear, but a mind without afflictions is clear. Therefore, having renounced them, one develops everything.

Question: With which knowledge is this first thought of one who has no more training to do associated?

Answer: This is a mind with subsequent knowledge[169]. It is the case that the first thought of one who has no more training to do, is associated with subsequent knowledge. It brings about this thought: "My birth is extinguished"[170], i.e. the conditions for birth in the sphere of neither-perception-nor-non-perception. Why? Because it is the final destruction. So, it is associated with subsequent knowledge in relation to suffering[171].

Question: The World-Honored One has further spoken about vision, knowledge, and wisdom[172]. Are these three of one kind or are they of different kinds?

Answer: These are three distinctions of wisdom[173] and have the nature of wisdom. However, because of certain elements[174] the World-Honored One sometimes calls it vision or he sometimes calls it knowledge.

Question: What does this mean?

---

[165] *arhattvaphala.*
[166] From *kāmadhātu* to *bhavāgra.*
[167] See note 151.
[168] *kleśa.*
[169] *anvayajñana.*
[170] *kṣīṇā me jātiḥ.* 3 editions: 尽.
[171] *duḥkhe'nvayajñāna.*
cf. *Kośa* VII 6.
[172] a. *darśana*, b. *jñāna*, c. *prajñā.*
[173] *prajñā.*
[174] *vastu.*

Answer: (139) That is to say, one knows with certainty that the patient acceptances do not have the nature of knowledge. The knowledge of extinction does not represent vision, and the same applies to the knowledge of non-production.

That is to say, one knows with certainty that the patient acceptances[175] do not have the nature of knowledge[176]: because, when developing the eight patient acceptances[177], one is seeking[178], they represent vision, and because one is considering[179], they represent wisdom. However, they do not represent knowledge, because they are not certain[180]. Why? Because of the first reason[181].

The knowledge of extinction does not represent vision, and the same applies to the knowledge of non-production[182]: because the knowledge of extinction and the knowledge of non-production consider[183], they represent wisdom, and because they are certain[184] they represent knowledge, but they do not represent vision, because, as they form[185] nothing, they do not seek[186]. The other kinds of pure wisdom[187] have a threefold nature: vision, knowledge, and wisdom[188].

(140) Let it be known that wholesome worldly impure knowledge in relation to the mind, and the views also represent vision. They say all represent wisdom.

---

[175] *kṣānti*.
[176] *jñāna*.
[177] i.e. the 8 in the *darśanamārga*, i.e., *duḥkhe dharmakṣānti*, etc.
[178] 求 may translate *parimārg*°, *parimārgaṇa*.
[179] 视 often translates *īkṣ*° or compounds with *īkṣ*°.
[180] *aniścita*, because there is doubt, *vicikitsā*. See AH2 854b. "Certain" means *niścita*.
[181] i.e. because of the *parimārgaṇa*.
[182] *kṣayajñāna* and *anutpādajñāna*.
[183] See note 179.
[184] See note 180.
[185] *saṃskṛ*°.
[186] See note 178.
[187] *anāsrava prajñā*.
[188] See note 172.

Let it be known that wholesome worldly impure knowledge[189] in relation to the mind[190], and the views[191] also represent vision: wholesome impure wisdom[192] in the stage of mental consciousness[193] represents these three by nature: vision, knowledge, and wisdom[194]. The afflictions which are the five views[195] are by nature vision, because they contemplate[196]. They are also not separate from knowledge and from wisdom. The other kinds of impure wisdom[197] do not have the nature of vision. Why? The kind of wisdom which is associated with indeterminate mental consciousness[198] does not have the nature of vision, because it does not contemplate[199]. The kind of defiled wisdom[200] also does not have the nature of vision, because it is spoilt by affliction. The kind of wisdom which is associated with five consciousnesses[201] also does not have the nature of vision, because it does not contemplate[202], and it is not separate from the nature of knowledge.

They say all represent [822b] wisdom: i.e. in what we mentioned earlier something was not, as there was no knowledge in patient acceptance[203], no vision in the knowledge of extinction and in the knowledge of non-production[204], and no vision in the impure wisdom[205] apart from the stage of wholesome mental consciousness[206] and apart from the five views[207]. This is not the

---

[189] Wholesome *kuśala*, worldly *laukikī*, impure *sāsrava*, knowledge *jñāna*.
[190] *manas*.
[191] *drṣṭi*. i.e. the 5 *dṛṣṭis*. See stanza 71.
[192] *kuśala sāsrava prajñā*.
[193] *manovijñāna*.
[194] See note 172.
[195] See note 191.
[196] Meaning *upanidhyāna*.
[197] *sāsrava prajñā*.
[198] *avyākṛta manovijñāna*.
[199] See note 196.
[200] *kliṣṭa prajñā*.
[201] i.e. *cakṣur°*, *śrotra°*, *ghrāṇa°*, *jihvā*, *kāyavijñāna*.
[202] See note 196.
[203] See note 175.
[204] See note 182.
[205] See note 197.
[206] See stanza 140ab.
[207] See note 191.

case with wisdom. Why? Because all kinds of knowledge and all kinds of vision are kinds of wisdom.

Question: How many knowledges are taken as objects by the different knowledges?

Answer: (141) The knowledge of the law and subsequent knowledge understand nine knowledges. The knowledge of the cause and the knowledge of the effect have two knowledges as their range.

The knowledge of the law and subsequent knowledge [208] understand nine knowledges: contemplating nine knowledges the knowledge of the law takes nine knowledges as its object, subtracting subsequent knowledge. Why? Subsequent knowledge is neither of the result in the realm of desire, nor of the cause in the realm of desire, nor of the cessation in the realm of desire, nor of the path in the realm of desire[209].

The same applies to subsequent knowledge. It takes nine knowledges as its object, subtracting the knowledge of the law.

The knowledge of the cause and the knowledge of the effect[210] have two knowledges as their range: the knowledge of origination[211] is the knowledge of the cause. It takes impure knowledge of the thoughts of others [212] and conventional knowledge[213] as its object, because they share in origination[214]. The rest are not taken as object, because they are pure[215]. The same applies to the knowledge of suffering. This is namely the knowledge of the effect.

---

[208] a. *dharmajñāna*, b. *anvayajñāna*.
[209] In the *kāmadhātu*: *phala* (=duḥkha); *hetu* (=*samudaya*); *nirodha*; *mārga*.
[210] a. *hetujñāna* (*samudayajñāna*); b. *phalajñāṇa* (*duḥkhajñāna*).
[211] *samudayajñāna*.
[212] *sāsrava paracittajñāna*.
[213] *saṃvṛtijñāna*.
[214] *samudaya*.
[215] *anāsrava*.

(142) The knowledge of the path takes nine knowledges. The knowledge of deliverance takes none as its object. The One with certain knowledge has expounded that the rest have all as their range.

The knowledge of the path[216] takes nine knowledges: the knowledge of the path takes nine knowledges as its range. It does not take conventional knowledge[217] as its object, as it is impure[218], but all the others are taken as object, because they share in the truth of the path[219].

The knowledge of deliverance[220] takes none as its object: the knowledge of deliverance is the knowledge of cessation[221]. It does not take a knowledge as its object, because it takes the unformed[222] as its object.

The One with certain knowledge has expounded that the rest have all as their range: for the rest there are four knowledges which take all ten knowledges as their object. Conventional knowledge[223] takes the ten knowledges as its object, because it has all factors as its range. Knowledge of the thoughts of others[224] also takes the ten knowledges as its object, because it has all thoughts of others as its range. The knowledge of extinction and the knowledge of non-production[225] also take the ten knowledges as their objects, because all the formed[226] is their range.

Question: The World-Honored One has furthermore said that, when subsequent knowledge has renounced the sphere of

---

[216] *mārgajñāna.*
[217] See note 213.
[218] *sāsrava.*
[219] *mārgasatya.*
[220] *vimuktijñāna.*
[221] *nirodhajñāna.*
[222] *asaṃskṛta.*
[223] See note 213.
[224] *paracittajñāna.*
[225] See note 182.
[226] *saṃskṛta.*

neither-perception-nor-non-perception[227], one obtains the fruition of being without attachment[228]. The subsequent knowledge being that path, is it not the case that one can know from this that the subsequent knowledge alone is that path?

Answer: There are also knowledges of the law which are paths of the realms of form and of formlessness.

Question: Which?

Answer: (143) When knowledges of the law proceed within appeasement and the path, they extinguish the three realms, but it is not the case that desire (is extinguished by) subsequent knowledge.

When knowledges of the law proceed within appeasement and the path[229], they extinguish the three realms[230]: i.e. knowledge of the law in relation to cessation and knowledge of the law in relation to the path[231] cast off the fetters[232] of the three realms[233] in the path of development[234]. Some knowledges of the law renounce the desire of the realms of form and of formlessness. While they pay great attention to evil, [822c] in the realm of desire they reflect on cessation and on the path[235] and renounce the desire of the realms of form and of formlessness[236]. They are not knowledge in relation to suffering and they are not knowledge in relation to origination[237]. Why? Because they do not share in suffering and origination, but share in cessation and the path.

---

[227] *naivasaṃjñānāsaṃjñāyatana.*
[228] *arhattvaphala.*
[229] *nirodha* and *mārga.* 息止 : *śam.*
[230] *kāma°*, *rūpa°*, *ārūpyadhātu.*
[231] *nirodhe dharmajñāna* and *mārge dharmajñāna.*
[232] See note 149.
[233] See note 230.
[234] *bhāvanāmārga.*
[235] See note 229.
[236] cf. *Kośa* VII 14.
[237] i.e. *duḥkhe* and *samudaye.*

Question: Is there [238] a subsequent knowledge [239] which extinguishes the realm of desire?

Answer: It is not the case that desire (is extinguished by) subsequent knowledge. No subsequent knowledge can extinguish the realm of desire. Why? It may pay great attention to evil, but it does not oppose it[240].

Question: The divine superknowledges [241] have the nature of knowledge. For these it must also be explained how many knowledges each one represents.

Answer: (144) The base of psychic power represents conventional knowledge and the same applies to heavenly eye and ear. Six rest in the former lives. Five are called knowledge of the mental make-up of others.

The base of psychic power [242] represents conventional knowledge[243], and the same applies to heavenly eye and ear[244]: the base of psychic power is called conventional knowledge. The same applies to heavenly eye and ear. Pure knowledge[245] does not proceed within them.

Six rest in the former lives[246]: six knowledges rest in the superknowledge of the former lives[247]. Knowledge of the law

---

[238] 颇 : cf. *kim.* Japanese *moshi* (*ari*) *ya.*
[239] *anvayajñāna.*
[240] i.e. the evil in the realm of desire.
The 3 editions: 非 .
[241] *abhijñā.*
[242] *ṛddhipāda.*
[243] See note 213.
[244] *divyacakṣus* and *divyaśrotra.*
[245] *anāsrava jñāna.*
[246] *pūrvanivāsa* (*abhijñā*).
[247] AH2 855a says that the *abhidharma*-masters (论师) in Kaśmīra (i.e. the most important part of 罽宾) mention only *saṃvṛtijñāna* here. Cf. *Kośa* VII 101. MAH 920c: 6 *jñānas* according to *Ghoṣaka*, but only *saṃvṛtijñāna* according to the *abhidharma*-masters (scil. in Kaśmīra).
The 6: *dharma*°, *anvaya*°, *saṃvṛti*°, *duḥkha*°, *samudaya*°, *mārgajñāna.*

remembers[248] the part of the knowledge of the law. Subsequent knowledge remembers the part of subsequent knowledge. Conventional knowledge remembers the worldly. Knowledge of suffering remembers past suffering. Knowledge of origination remembers past origination. Knowledge of the path remembers the past path.

Five are called knowledge of the mental make-up of others[249]: five knowledges rest in the superknowledge which is knowledge of the mental make-up of others: [250]knowledge of the law knows the knowledge of the law in the thoughts of others, and also the factors which constitute thought and its concomitants[251], associated with it. The same applies to subsequent knowledge. Conventional knowledge knows the worldly factors which constitute other people's thoughts and their concomitants[252]. Knowledge of the path knows the pure[253] factors which constitute other people's thoughts and their concomitants[254]. Knowledge of the thoughts of others is (number) five.

> (145) The noble have expounded that nine knowledges represent superknowledge of the extinction of the outflows. Eight have their range in the body. The factors are ten, and nine knowledges are two.

The noble have expounded that nine knowledges represent superknowledge of the extinction of the outflows[255]: the superknowledge of the extinction of the outflows consists of nine pure[256] knowledges, because it is opposed to all impurity.

Question: The World-Honored One has furthermore said that the contemplation which is application of mindfulness

---

[248] *anusmṛ°*.
[249] *cetaḥparyāyajñāna*.
[250] *dharma°, anvaya°, saṃvṛti°, mārga°, paracittajñāna*.
[251] *cittacaitasikā dharmāḥ*.
[252] See note 251.
[253] *anāsrava*.
[254] See note 251.
[255] *āsravakṣayābhijñā*.
[256] See note 253.

contemplating the body in the body[257], represents wisdom[258]. The nature [259] of which knowledges does this application of mindfulness[260] have?

Answer: Eight have their range in the body. Eight knowledges contemplate the body. That another term for form[261] is body, is known by eight knowledges subtracting the knowledge of the thoughts of others and the knowledge of cessation[262]. When knowledge takes form [263] as its object, it is application of mindfulness to the body[264], but these two knowledges[265] do not take form as their object.

The factors are ten: in the application of mindfulness to the factors[266] are the ten knowledges. The factors are namely the factors other than form, feeling, and thought[267]. In this range are the ten knowledges. The knowledges [268] with the particular characteristics as their range [269] and also with that which is general in everything[270], represent application of mindfulness to the factors.

Nine knowledges are two: feeling and thought[271] mean nine knowledges, subtracting the knowledge of cessation[272]. i.e. when knowledge takes feeling as its object, it is application of

---

[257] 身: *kāye*; 身观: *kāyānupaśyī*; 意止: *smṛtyupasthāna*.
[258] *prajñā*.
[259] The 3 editions and the Ms. I, 8: 何智性.
[260] *smṛtyupasthāna*.
[261] *rūpa*.
[262] *paracittajñāna* and *nirodhjñāna*.
[263] See note 261.
[264] *kāyasmṛtyupasthāna*. Cf. *stanzas* 98-99.
[265] See note 262.
[266] *dharmasmṛtyupasthāna*.
[267] *rūpa*, *vedanā*, and *citta*. The mind is fixed on them in *kāya*°, *vedanā*°, and *cittasmṛtyupasthāna*.
[268] The 3 editions and the Ms. I, 11: 智.
[269] The Ms. has 界, and differs from the 3 editions: 境界.
[270] For the difference between contemplation of the particular characteristics (*svalakṣaṇa*) and contemplation of the general characteristics (*sāmānyalakṣaṇa*): see stanza 100.
[271] *vedanā* and *citta*.
[272] *nirodhajāna*.

mindfulness to feeling[273], and when knowledge takes thought as its object, it is application of mindfulness to thought[274].

Question: The Tathāgatas have the powers of knowledge[275]. How are the powers of the Tathāgatas established as knowledge, and how do [823a] the four fearlessnesses [276] of the Tathāgatas possess the nature of knowledge?

When I am, as they say, fully awakened[277] to these factors[278] -one does not see these attributes[279] when not yet fully awakened- all this [280] must also be distinctly established. Each one has the nature of how many knowledges?

Answer: (146) The power of what can be and what cannot be and the first of the fearlessnesses, these are the ten knowledges of the Buddha. The rest are distinctions within these.

The power of what can be and what cannot be[281] and the first of the fearlessnesses[282], these are the ten knowledges of the Buddha: the Buddha has the power of what can be and what cannot be which is the ten knowledges. As for the term knowledge of what can be[283]: when one experiences the true characteristics and the true aspects [284] of the factors, having experienced them, one knows that these factors possess such characteristics and such aspects. This is called knowledge of what can be. As for the

273 *vedanāsmṛtyupasthāna*.
274 *cittasmṛtypasthāna*.
275 *jñānabala*.
276 *vaiśāradya*.
277 *samyaksaṃbuddha*.
278 *jñānabala* and *vaiśāradya* are qualities of a Buddha only. Therefore they are called *āveṇika*, special or exclusive. cf. *Kośa* VII 66-67.
279 *nimitta*.
280 i.e. *jñānabala* and *vaiśāradya*.
281 *sthānāsthānabala*. Chinese: the power of right propositions and of wrong propositions.
282 The first *vaiśāradya*: *sarvadharmābhisaṃbodhivaiśāradya*. Kośa VII 75. cf. AH2 855b.
283 *sthānajñāna*.
284 *ākāra*.

term knowledge of what cannot be[285]: when other characteristics and other aspects of the factors cannot be obtained, one knows that it is not the case that these factors posses such characteristics and such aspects. This is called knowledge of what cannot be. They represent the ten knowledges of the Buddha. The first fearlessness [286] also represents ten knowledges, because it experiences fully and correctly.

The rest are distinctions within these: when the power of what can be and what cannot be is distinctly established, there are ten powers[287] within it. When the first fearlessness is distinctly established, there are four fearlessnesses[288] within it. Because knowledge of what can be and what cannot be has different ranges, ten kinds are distinguished, and because the first fearlessness has different ranges, four kinds are distinguished.

Question: The four analytical knowledges[289] also possess the nature of knowledge. They must also be distinctly established. How many knowledges does each one represent?

Answer: (147) Analytical knowledge of factors and analytical knowledge of expression represent one. Analytical knowledge of inspired speech and analytical knowledge of the meaning represent ten each. It is expounded by those whose knowledge is most excellent that the knowledge resulting from resolve represents seven knowledges.

Analytical knowledge of factors[290] and analytical knowledge of expression[291] represent one: the term analytical knowledge of factors is used when one is conscious of the names[292] of the

[285] *asthānajñāna.*
[286] See note 282.
[287] Mentioned in AH2 855b. *Kośa* VII 69ff.
[288] Mentioned in MAH 922c. See *Kośa* VII 75.
[289] *pratisaṃvid.* The Chinese actually means "eloquence" (*pratibhāna*).
[290] *dharmapratisaṃvid.* Chinese: eloquence concerning factors.
[291] *niruktipratisaṃvid.*
[292] *nāman.*

factors. It is conventional knowledge[293]. It is not the case that one experiences their names by means of pure knowledge[294]. The names in the world are mere designations. Pure knowledge does not proceed within them. The term analytical knowledge of expression is used when one is conscious of the right speech. Because this is conventional too, it is a mere designation for knowledge in the world.

Analytical knowledge of inspired speech[295] and analytical knowledge of the meaning[296] represent ten each: analytical knowledge of inspired speech is called the unhindered[297] and convenient[298] knowledge when contemplating and revealing. It represents the ten knowledges. The term analytical knowledge of the meaning is used when one is conscious of the reality of the factors. It is also the ten knowledges, because one experiences the true characteristics[299].
[[300]Some say that the two analytical knowledges, the one of expression and the one of inspired speech[301], correspond only to conventional knowledge[302], and that the two analytical knowledges, the one of factors and the one of the meaning[303], (correspond) to the ten knowledges.]

Question: How many knowledges are in the knowledge resulting from resolve[304]?

---

[293] *saṃvṛtijñāna*.
[294] See note 245.
[295] *pratibhānapratisaṃvid*. AH actually means: proper eloquence (*yuktapratibhāna*). AH2 855c has 乐 (说): joy, i.e. *paṭibhāna*, ready wit, or *pratibhāna* in *pratibhānapratisaṃvid*. AH 923b uses the term of our text, i.e. *yukta*°.
[296] *arthapratisaṃvid*.
[297] *asakta*.
[298] 方便: *yukta*.
[299] *bhūtalakṣaṇa*.
[300] This paragraph does not occur in the Ms. II, 7, but it occurs in the 3 editions. It is a commentary made by someone in later times. 其人: 经师: masters of the scriptural texts, according to the Ming edition.
[301] *nirukti*°, and *pratibhānapratisaṃvid*.
[302] See note 293.
[303] *dharma*°, and *arthapratisaṃvid*.
[304] *praṇidhijñāna*. cf. stanza 171.

Answer: It is expounded by those whose knowledge is most excellent that the knowledge resulting from resolve represents seven knowledges.

In the knowledge resulting from resolve there are seven knowledges, subtracting the knowledge of the thoughts of others, the knowledge of extinction, and the knowledge of non-production[305]. The knowledge resulting from resolve, being keen and prompt[306], has the three worlds as its range, and experiences all factors. It possesses the nature of seven knowledges[307].
[[308]Some say: only conventional knowledge. ]

---

[305] *paracitta*°, *kṣaya*° and *anutpādajñāna*.
[306] *tīkṣṇa*.
捷疾 translates such words as *java, śīghra, paṭu*.
[307] AH2 855c adds that this is expounded by the 论师: *abhidharma*-masters in Kāśmīra.
[308] Not in the MS II, 9. cf. note 300.

**阿毗昙心论卷第三**

尊者法胜造
东晋僧伽提婆
共慧远于庐山译

**智品第六**

123 智慧性能了 明观一切有
有无有涅槃 是相今当说

谓智坚圣品已略说。有无有境界今当说。

124 三智佛所说 最上第一意
法智未知智 及世俗等智

此三智摄一切智。于中法智名谓境界于欲界苦习灭道无漏智。境界是初受法相故曰法智。从法智根现见已非根现亦见未知智。未知智名谓境界色无色界苦习灭道无漏智。境界是后受法相故曰未知智。等智名谓有漏智。是多取等谛知男女长短为首。

125 苦习息止道 二智如可得
此名与四智 解脱师所说

此二智法智未知智若行于谛如是相似名所说。苦谛境界说苦智。习谛境界说习智。灭谛境界说灭智。道谛境界说道智。解脱师所说。

126 若智观他心 是从三中说
尽无生智二 境界在四门

若智观他心是从三中说者他心智谓有漏境界是等智。境界欲界道是法智。境界色界道是未知智。尽无生智二者无学二智尽智无生智。于中所作已竟受无学智是尽智。不复更作受无学智是无生智。是亦法智未知智。

问。尽智无生智何谛境界。答。境界在四门。此二智四谛境界苦习灭道。已说十智。行今当说。

127 二智十六行 法智未知智
如是行或非 是说为等智

二智十六行法智未知智者法智性是十六行四行受苦四行习四行灭四行道。未知智色无色界亦尔。如是行或非是说为等智者暖顶忍第一法中摄等智行无漏行二谛所摄十六行。第一法摄四行。闻思及余思惟等智十六行。离此余等智非十六行谓施戒慈如是比。

128 四智有四行 决定行所说
正观他心智 此或是或非

四智有四行决定行所说者苦智四行如上说。习灭道智亦如是。正观他心智此或是或非者无漏他心智四行如道智。有漏非。

129　尽智无生智　离空无我行
　说有十四行　受相为最胜

尽智无生智离空无我行说有十四行者尽智无生智十四行除空无我行。所以者何。彼行等谛我已作不复更作。空无我者不以此行。受相为最胜者非一切无漏智在十六行。十六行者是总行。更有无漏智受十六相如身意止。是自相智。不在十六行前受十六行。此自相行于诸无漏智前受故胜。

已说十六行。如此智所得今当说。

130　第一无漏心　或有成就一
　二或成就三　于上增益一

第一无漏心或有成就一者第一无漏心苦法忍相应。未离欲成就一等智。已离欲成就他心智。二或成就三者第二无漏心苦法智相应。未离欲成就三法智苦智等智。已离欲成就他心智。于上增益一者于上四时增说一。四时得苦未知智得未知智。习法智得习智。灭法智得灭智。道法智得道智。忍中不得智。

问。此智何地所摄。答。

131　九智圣所说　依倚于上地
　禅中有十智　无色地中八

九智圣所说依倚于上地者未来禅中间禅无他心智根本禅摄故。禅中有十智者根本四禅中有十智无色地中八者无色地中有八智除法智他心智。法智者境界于欲界不以无色。境界于欲界他心智行乘色。无色地中无色。

已说地。修今当说。修有二种得修行修。得修者谓功德未曾得而得。得已诸余功德彼所倚亦得。得已后时不求而生。行修者谓曾得功德今现在前行。

问。此诸智云何修。答。

132　若已得为修　智者诸圣见。
　彼即当来修　诸忍亦如是

若已得为修智者诸圣见彼即当来修者见谛道中谓智现在前修即彼当来修法智乃至道智。诸忍亦如是者忍亦如是苦法忍现在前修即苦法忍当来修。非智非余忍。如是一切。

133　是于三心中　得修于等智
　或修七或六　最后心所说

是于三心中得修于等智者即见谛道中三心顷当来修等智苦未知智习未知智灭未知智。行此三谛时得修等智。所以者何。此三谛习已观非道谛谓地见道即彼地等智及欲界。 或修七或六最后心所说者道未知智离欲修七智谓阿那含果所摄。未离欲修六智除他心智。彼中非想非非想道得沙门果。是以不修等智。

134 十七无漏心 于上思惟道
当知修于七 六修增益根

十七无漏心于上思惟道当知修于七者须陀洹果上思惟道十七心顷修七智。此道未来禅所摄。是以无他心智。尽智无生智是无学。以故无。余七智必修。所以者何。彼意此功德常不空。若不修者曾得已舍复未更得于其中间应空而不空。是以必修。六修增益根者增益根名谓信解脱增益诸根逮得见到。彼有九无碍道九解脱道。是一切无碍道一切解脱道修六智。此说未离欲。是以无他心智。尔时学道不学断烦恼。彼未曾得修功德非已曾得。是以不修等智。

135 得不还果时 远离于七地
思学诸通道 解脱修习八

得不还果时者若得不还果修八智。彼中要得根本禅。是以修他心智。余智如前说。远离于七地者四禅三无色离欲时一切九解脱道修八智。于中一切修下地禅。思学诸通道解脱修习八者三通如意足天眼天耳一切九解脱道修八智。所以者何。摄根本禅故。

136 此无碍道中 及灭第一有
彼八解脱道 说者修习七

七地离欲时一切无碍道中修七智除他心智。所以者何。此无碍道修灭结。习他心智非灭结。以故不修。非想非非想处第一有。彼离欲时八解脱道中修七智除等智。所以者何。等智于非想非非想处转。还以非敌故。

137 离于第一有 六修无碍道
乘上应当知 修习于下地

离于第一有六修无碍道者第一离欲时九无碍道中修六智除他心智及等智。乘上应当知修习于下地者此修一切地当知修自地诸智及下地所摄。谓依初禅离欲彼修二地功德自地所摄及未来禅。如是至无所有处。

138 漏无漏一切 诸地修功德
初无学心中 此未知智意

漏无漏一切诸地修功德初无学心中者得无著果时九地及自地亦一切诸地于中修。所以者何。非想非非想处地烦恼相违。一切地有烦恼意不明净。无烦恼意明净。是以离彼修一切。问。此无学初心何智相应。答。此未知智意。是初无学心未知智相应。彼作是念我生已尽。是非想非非想处生缘。所以者何。最后尽故。是以苦未知智相应。问。又世尊言见智慧。此三为一种为种种。答。此是慧之差别慧性所有。但以事故世尊或说见或说智。
问。此义云何。答。

139 谓决定能知 诸忍非智性
尽智则非见 无生智亦然

谓决定能知诸忍非智性者修行八忍能求故见能视故慧。但非智不决定故。所以者何。用始缘故。尽智则非见无生智亦然者尽智无生智视故慧决定故智。但非见不求故无所为故。余无漏慧种三性所有见智及慧。

140 善俗有漏智 在意及诸见
当知此则见 说一切是慧

善俗有漏智在意及诸见当知此则见者意识地中善有漏慧三性见智及慧。五见烦恼性此见所有观察故。亦不离智及慧。余有漏慧种非见性所有。所以者何。无记意识相应慧种非见性所有不观察故。秽污慧种亦非见性所有烦恼所坏故。五识相应慧种亦非见性所有不观察故亦不离智性。说一切是慧者谓前所说离如忍中离智尽智无生智离见除善意识地及五见已余有漏慧离见。慧不如是。所以者何。一切智种一切见种即是慧种故。
问。一一智几智缘。答。

141 法智未知智 晓了于九智
因智及果智 是二智境界

法智未知智晓了于九智者法智观九智缘九智除未知智。所以者何。未知智者非欲界果非欲界因非欲界灭非欲界道。未知智亦如是。九智缘除法智。因智及果智是二智境界者习智是因智。彼有漏他心智及等智缘同习故。余非缘无漏故。苦智亦如是。此即果智。

142 道智是九智 解脱智无缘
余一切境界 决定智所说

道智是九智者道智境界九智。不缘等智有漏故。余尽缘同道谛故。解脱智无缘者解脱智是灭智。非缘智缘无为故。余一切境界决定智所说者余有四智缘一切十智。等智缘十智境界一切法故。他心智亦缘十智具他心境界故。尽智无生智亦缘十智一切有为境界故。
问。又世尊言未知智如离非想非非想处得无著果。未知智是彼道非以此可知未知智是彼道非余耶。答。亦有法智是色无色界道。问。何者。答。

143 若息止及道 法智之所行
是灭于三界 非欲未知智

若息止及道法智之所行是灭于三界者谓灭法智及道法智在思惟道是灭于三界结。或有法智离色无色界欲。谓此重见恶是于欲界思惟灭及道离色无色界欲。非苦智非习智。所以者何。不同苦习同于灭道故。
问。颇有未知智灭欲界不。答。非欲未知智。无有未知智能灭于欲界。所以者何。 无彼重见恶而非此。
问。神通智性所有。彼亦应当说一一几智。答。

144 如意足等智 天眼耳亦然
六于宿命中 五说他心智

如意足等智天眼耳亦然者如意足说等智。天眼天耳亦如是。无漏智不以此行。六于宿命中者宿命通有六智。法智忆法智分未知智忆未知智分。等智忆俗。苦智忆过去苦。习智忆过去习。道智忆过去道。五说他心智者他心智通有五智。法智知他心中法智及彼相应心心数法。未知智亦如是。等智知他俗心心数法。道智知他无漏心心数法。他心智五。

145 九智漏尽通 圣人之所说
八境界于身 法十九智二

九智漏尽通圣人之所说者漏尽通无漏九智一切漏相违故。问。又世尊言身身观意止观者是慧。此意止何智性所有。答。八境界于身。八智观身。色假名为身。是八智所知除他心智及灭智。若智缘色者是身意止。此二智不缘色。法十者法意止有十智。离色痛心余法谓法。是境界有十智。自相境界及一切总智是法意止。九智二者痛及心九智除灭智。谓智缘痛是痛意止。谓智缘心是心意止。
问。诸如来有智力。云何如来力施设智及如来四无所畏智性所有。如所说我等正觉此诸法未等正觉不见此相如是一切此亦应当分别。一一几智性所有。答。

146 是处非处力 及无畏第一
此是佛十智 余此中差别

是处非处力及无畏第一此是佛十智者佛有十智是处非处力。是处智名受诸法真实相真实行受知此法如是相如是行。是谓是处智。非处智名诸法他相他行不可得则知非此法如是相如是行。是名非处智。是佛十智。初无畏亦十智等正受故。余此中差别者是处非处力差别有十力。初无畏差别有四无所畏。处非处智是境界差别故十种分别。初无畏亦境界差别故四种分别。
问。四辩亦智性所有。此亦应当分别。一一几智。答。

147 法辩辞辩一 应义辩俱十
愿智是七智 智最胜所说

法辩辞辩一者法辩名觉诸法名。是等智。非以无漏智受名。世欲中名是假号。无漏智不以此行。辞辩名觉正说。此亦等是俗中假智号。应义辩俱十者应辩名观及现无所挂碍方便智。是十智。义辩名觉诸法真实。彼亦十智受真实相故。[其人云辞应二辩应一等智法义二辩十智] 。问。愿智有几智。答。愿智是七智智最胜所说愿智有七智除他心智尽智无生智。愿智者利捷疾境界于三世受一切诸法。是七智性所有。[其人云一等智] 。

# CHAPTER VII. CONCENTRATION[1]

Question: So we know all knowledges. How must these knowledges be?

Answer: (148) Depending on the concentrations, knowledge goes its unhindered course. [823b] So, reflect on concentration and seek for its truth!

Depending on the concentrations, knowledge goes its unhindered course: just as a lantern depends on oil and, far from a windy place, its light shines very bright, thus knowledge depends on a concentrated mind and, far from all disturbance, the light of knowledge is very bright. Most certainly and without any doubt it will proceed within its object. So, reflect on concentration and seek for its truth!

> (149) The Certain One has expounded four trances and (four) formless attainments. Every one of them is said to be mixed with relishing, clean, or pure.

The Certain One[2] has expounded four trances and (four) formless attainments[3]: there are eight concentrations: four trances and four formless attainments.

Every one of them is said to be mixed with relishing[4], clean[5], or pure[6]: the first trance is threefold: associated with relishing, clean, or pure. The same applies to all concentrations.

Question: What does associated with relishing[7] mean? What does clean[8] mean? What does pure[9] mean?

---

1 *samādhivarga.*
2 *niścita.*
3 *dhyāna* and *ārūpyasamāpatti.*
4 *āsvādana* (saṃprayukta).
5 *śuddhaka.*
6 *anāsrava.*
7 See note 4.
8 See note 5.
9 See note 6.

Answer: (150) One that is wholesome and impure, is clean. One without feverishness is called pure. One with relishing is associated with craving. In the supreme (stage) there is no pure one.

One that is wholesome and impure[10], is clean[11]: i.e. because the wholesome one[12] is clean, it is called clean.

One without feverishness[13] is called pure[14]: another term for affliction[15] is feverishness. A concentration without affliction is namely pure.

One with relishing[16] is associated with craving[17]: i.e. when a trance or a formless attainment[18] is associated with craving[19], it is[20] associated with all[21] and all proceed within it. It is said to be associated with relishing.

In the supreme (stage) there is no pure one[22]: the supreme (stage) is the sphere of neither-perception-nor-non-perception[23]. In it there is no pure one. Because it is not swiftly[24] proceeded in, it is twofold[25], while the others are all threefold.
Question: What nature do the trances have?

---

10 *kuśala sāsrava*.
11 See note 5.
12 *kuśala*.
13 *nirjvara*.
14 See note 6.
15 *kleśa*.
16 See note 4.
17 *tṛṣṇā*.
18 See note 3.
19 See note 17.
20 We do not follow the 3 editions: 是以. The Ms. II 19 agrees with the *taishō* edition.
21 Scil. *kleśas*. This concentration is *kliṣṭa*.
22 See note 6.
23 *naivasaṃjñānāsaṃjñāyatana*.
24 捷疾: prompt, swift. Cf. note 305 of the previous chapter. AH2 856b adds: "The noble (*ārya*) path (*mārga*) is swift, prompt."
In the *bhavāgra* there is no *anāsrava* concentration.
cf. *Kośa* VI 292 and VIII 175.
25 The 3 editions and the MS. II 20: 二.

Answer: (151) The one with five members, with adjusted and discursive thinking, and also with three feelings, different classes and four thoughts, they call it the first trance.

Five members[26]: i.e. in a combination[27] of five members one experiences the first trance so that it is firm, and with these one obtains it. They are called: adjusted thinking, discursive thinking, joy, happiness, and undivided attention. The term adjusted thinking[28]: when, at the moment of engaging in concentration, one begins[29] to produce wholesome qualities[30], one first reflects with coarse thoughts[31]. The term discursive thinking[32] is used when one connects and links thoughts with subtlety[33]. Joy[34] is called the contentment in concentration. Happiness[35] is called the happiness which is peace[36] in body and in mind after contentment[37]. Undivided attention[38] is called the fact that one's thoughts are concentrated on their object[39], not scattered. These elements are the members when dwelling in concentration, and also when engaging in it and when abandoning it. And so, five members are the first trance.

With adjusted and discursive thinking[40]: the one with adjusted thinking and with discursive thinking is the first trance.

Question: Since[41] we know the five members, what need is there now for adjusted and discursive thoughts?

---

[26] *aṅga*.
[27] Usual translation for *saṃgṛh*°.
[28] *vitarka*.
[29] The 3 editions and Ms. III 3: 初生.
[30] *guṇa*.
[31] *sthūlacitta*.
[32] *vicāra*.
[33] *sūkṣmatā*.
[34] *prīti*.
[35] *sukha*.
[36] Seems to translate *praśrabdhi*.
[37] May translate *prāmodya*.
[38] *cittaikāgratā*.
[39] *ālambana*.
[40] *savitarka savicāra*.
[41] Ms. III 6: 已.

Answer: As for the members, the so-called wholesome ones are among the five members. They say that a defiled (trance) and an indeterminate one [823c] also have adjusted thoughts and discursive thoughts, but not the wholesome ones'

Also with three feelings[42]: in the first trance there are three feelings: the faculty happiness, the faculty gladness, and the faculty evenmindedness. Among the feelings, the faculty happiness[43] is bodily feeling[44]. The faculty gladness[45] is in the stage of the mind[46]. The faculty evenmindedness[47] is in four consciousnesses[48].

Different classes[49]: in the brahma-world[50] there are different classes. There is an upper one and there is a lower one[51]. It is explained as having places for birth.

Four thoughts: in the first trance there are four thoughts: eye-consciousness, ear-consciousness, body-consciousness, and mind-consciousness[52].

They call it the first trance: all these factors are namely the first trance.

We have explained the first trance. The second one will now be explained.

---

[42] *vedanā*.
[43] *sukhendriya*.
[44] *kāyikī vedanā*.
[45] *saumanasyendriya*.
[46] *manas* (*manovijñāna*).
[47] *upekṣendriya*.
[48] *vijñāna*. In verse c the 4 are called 四心: four thoughts. cf. supra note 168 in chapter IV.
[49] 若干种 translates such words as *nānāprakāra, nānābhāva, nānāvidha*. What are meant are classes of celestial bodies.
[50] *Brahmaloka*, the first *dhyāna*.
[51] AH2 856b adds: "They are born through the power of *vitarka* and *vicāra*". According to stanza 177 there are 2 classes in the stage of the first dhyāna or brahma-world: 1. *brahmakāyika;* 2. *brahmapurohita*.
[52] *cakṣur*°, *śrotra*°, *kāyavijñāna*, and *manovijñāna*.

(152) With two feelings and different classes, the second trance has four members. The third one has five members. This trance is said to be of two feelings.

Two feelings[53]: in the second trance there are two feelings: the faculty gladness and the faculty evenmindedness[54].

Different classes: in it there are different classes of bodies[55], and, having left adjusted and discursive thoughts[56], there are different thoughts. At one moment one may engage in the faculty gladness, and another moment one engages in the faculty evenmindedness [57]. The faculty [58] gladness rests in the fundamental one, and in the adjacent one[59] there is the faculty evenmindedness[60].

The second trance has four members[61]: in the second trance there are four members: serenity, joy, happiness, and undivided attention. The term serenity[62] is the faith[63] one produces when believing in renouncement. Having left the first trance, one has

---

[53] See note 43.
[54] *saumanasya* and *upekṣā*.
[55] Instead of 有, AH2 856b and MAH 924c have the negation 无: there are not. Indeed, in the second *dhyāna* there are different gods (*parīttābha, apramāṇābha, ābhāsvara.* cf. stanza 177), but they do not have different bodies (*nānātvakāya*). They have different notions (*nānātvasaṃjñin*). See also *Kośa* III 19, explaining the third of 7 *vijñānasthitis* (cf. stanza 178). The Ms. III 13 has 有.
[56] *vitarka* and *vicāra*.
[57] i.e.: at one moment one engages in the trance with *saumanasyendriya* (i.e. the fundamental second trance), at another moment one engages in the trance with *upekṣendriya* (i.e. the *sāmantaka* of the second *dhyāna*). See note 61.
[58] Ms. III 14 has the expected 喜根: *saumanasyendriya.*
[59] 边: *anta*, stands for *sāmantaka*: near, neighbouring. The *sāmantaka* meant here is the trance through which one enters the fundamental (*maula*) second trance. MAH 924c has another translation for *sāmantaka*: 眷属: related. Cf. infra note 310.
The *sāmantaka* of the first *dhyāna* is called *anāgamya*. The *sāmantaka* of the second *dhyāna* (*avitarka* and *avicāra*) must not be confused with the *dhyānāntara* (having only *vicāra*). See *Kośa* VIII 178f.
[60] *saumanasyendriya* in the *maula* second *dhyāna*, and *upekṣendriya* in its *sāmantaka*.
[61] *aṅga*.
[62] *adhyātmasaṃprasāda*. Chinese: inner purity. cf. *Kośa* VIII 158.
[63] *śraddhā*.

this thought: "All can be left". The other members are as previously explained[64]. These elements are the members in relation to the second trance.

The third one has five members: in the third trance there are five members: happiness, evenmindedness, mindfulness, full awareness, and undivided attention. Happiness is the faculty happiness[65] in the stage of mind-consciousnesses[66].

Evenmindedness [67]: being happy, not seeking for more happiness[68].
[[69]Some say that, even though evenmindedness makes sense, it should not be called a member.]
Mindfulness[70] guards one's application and does not abandon it. Full awareness[71] does not cause happiness. Undivided attention[72] is concentration[73]. These elements are the members in relation to the third trance.

This trance is said to be of two feelings[74]: in the third trance there are two feelings: the faculty happiness and the faculty evenmindedness[75]. The faculty happiness is of the fundamental one, and the faculty evenmindedness is of the adjacent one[76].

> (153) Free from breathing in and breathing out[77], in the fourth one there are four members. These members are said to be wholesome. We have also distinctly established their kinds.

---

[64] i.e. *prīti, sukha*, and *cittaikāgratā*. See stanza 151.
[65] *sukhendriya*.
[66] *manovijñāna*. cf. stanzas 151-152: *sukha* in the 2 first trances.
[67] *upekṣā*.
[68] MAH 924c calls this *saṃskāropekṣā*.
[69] Not in Ms. III 18. cf. note 300 of chapter VI.
[70] *smṛti*.
[71] *saṃprajanya*. Chinese: knowledge.
[72] *cittaikāgratā*.
[73] *samādhi*.
[74] See note 43.
[75] See note 55.
[76] *sukhendriya* is in the *maula*, fundamental, third *dhyāna*, and *upekṣendriya* is in the *sāmantaka* of the third *dhyāna*. cf. supra note 61.
[77] *ānāpāna*.

Free from breathing in and breathing out: breathing in is a coming, and breathing out is a going. They do not exist in the fourth trance. Why? Through the power of concentration there, the pores of the body are closed.

In the fourth one there are four members[78]: in the fourth trance there are four members: neither-suffering-nor-happiness, evenmindedness, pure mindfulness, and undivided attention[79]. Forever[80] free from suffering and happiness one does not suffer and one is not happy. The rest are as explained before[81].
Question: Which trances are associated with the members[82]?

Answer: These members are said to be wholesome[83]. A wholesome trance is associated with the members. The members are neither defiled nor indeterminate[84].

We have also distinctly established their kinds: [824a] i.e. their kinds are explained according to their places. One should know that they will not exist in other places, e.g. in the first trance there is adjusted thinking and there is discursive thinking and four thoughts[85]. This means that these kinds do not exist in any other stage. The fourth trance is without breathing in and breathing out[86]. It goes without saying that this is not so in the three[87].

We have spoken about the four trances and the four formless attainments[88]. That is to say, the rest will now be explained.

---

[78] See note 62.
[79] *aduḥkhāsukha*, *upekṣā*, *smṛtipariśuddhi*, *cittaikāgratā*.
[80] The 3 editions and Ms. IV 5: 永.
[81] Stanza 152.
[82] See note 62.
[83] *kuśala*.
[84] Neither *kliṣṭa* nor *avyākṛta*.
[85] Stanza 151.
[86] See note 78.
[87] First, second and third *dhyānas*.
[88] 4 *dhyānas* and 4 *ārūpyasamāpattis*.

Question: As the World-Honored One has said: "They have a fundamental base." When one has not yet renounced desire[89], one does not yet have a fundamental base. However, having pure qualities[90], within what stage are these pure qualities comprised?

Answer: They are comprised within the pre-trance[91]. Furthermore, in the World-Honored One's expositions[92] there are three concentrations: one with adjusted thinking and with discursive thinking, one without adjusted thinking, only with discursive thinking, and one without adjusted thinking and without discursive thinking[93]. Among them, the first trance is the one with adjusted thinking and with discursive thinking. The second trance is the one without adjusted thinking and without discursive thinking. Namely within which stage is the concentration without adjusted thinking, only with discursive thinking comprised?

Answer: It is comprised within the intermediate trance[94]. The characteristics of this pre-trance[95] and of this intermediate trance[96] will now be explained.

> (154) When in an associated one there is adjusted thinking and discursive thinking, both are in the pre-trance. The wise have expounded that the one associated with discursive thinking is intermediate.

When in an associated one[97] there is adjusted thinking and discursive thinking[98], both are in the pre-trance[99]: in the pre-trance there is adjusted thinking and there is discursive thinking.

---

[89] Scil. the desire of the *kāmadhātu*.
[90] Pure, *anāsrava*; quality, *guṇa*.
[91] *anāgamya*.
[92] cf. *Kośa* VIII 183 note 1.
[93] 1. *savitarka savicāra*; 2. *avitarka vicāramātra* (Chinese: with little vicāra); 3. *avitarkāvicāra*.
[94] *dhyānāntara*.
[95] See note 92.
[96] See note 95.
[97] i.e. associated with *vitarka* and *vicāra*, or only with *vicāra*, as is the case in c of this stanza.

The wise have expounded that the one associated with discursive thinking[100] is intermediate: in the intermediate trance[101] there is only discursive thinking[102] and no adjusted thinking[103]. There, little by little one's thoughts are appeased[104].

> (155) Being without base, it is twofold, subtracting the one associated with relishing. The intermediate trance is threefold. Both are said to have one feeling.

Being without base[105], it is twofold, subtracting the one associated with relishing[106]: the pre-trance[107] only is wholesome and impure[108], and pure[109]. The so-called impure one is clean[110]. The one without impurity is the pure one[111].

The intermediate trance[112] is threefold: the intermediate trance is threefold: with relishing, clean, and pure[113], because one abides in birth and death[114].

Both are said to have one feeling[115]: both in the pre-trancc and in the intermediate trance[116] there is one feeling: the faculty evenmindedness[117], because they are not fundamental[118] stages.

---

98 *vitarka* and *vicāra*.
99 See note 92.
100 *vicāramātra*.
101 See note 95.
102 See note 101.
103 *avitarka*.
104 *śam°*.
105 i.e. without a fundamental base.
106 *āsvādanasaṃprayukta*.
107 See note 92.
108 *kuśala sāsrava*. The *śuddhaka* is meant. See stanza 150a.
109 *anāsrava*.
110 *śuddha*.
111 See note 110.
112 See note 95.
113 *āsvādana* (*saṃprayukta*), *śuddhaka*, and *anāsrava*. See stanza 150.
114 See the explanation of *āsvādanasaṃprayukta* in stanza 150c. Such a concentration is associated with *tṛṣṇā*, craving.
115 *vedanā*.
116 *anāgamya* and *dhyānāntara*.
117 *upekṣendriya*.
118 *maula*.

We have explained the concentrations. The remaining qualities[119] comprised within them, will now be explained.

> (156) The *samādhis*, all superknowledges, the immeasurables, the all-bases which are developed, the spheres of mastery, the knowledges and the deliverances arise within them.

The *samādhis*: the three *samādhis*: of emptiness, of aimlessness, and of the signless[120], because one's thoughts are tied to that which is pure[121].

All superknowledges[122]: there are six superknowledges: the knowledge of the base of psychic power, the knowledge of heavenly ear, the superknowledge of the mental make-up of others, the knowledge which is recollection of the former lives, the knowledge of birth and death, and the superknowledge of the extinction of the outflows[123].

The immeasurables[124]: four immeasurables: friendliness, compassion, sympathetic joy, and evenmindedness[125]. Because immeasurable beings are their range, they are called immeasurables.

[824b] The all-bases which are developed: ten all-bases[126]: the all-basis earth, the all-bases water, fire, wind, blue, yellow, red, and white, the all-basis of the sphere of unlimited space, and the all-basis of the sphere of unlimited consciousness[127]. Because one has complete understanding they are all-bases.

---

119 *guṇa*.

120 *śūnyatā, apraṇihita, ānimitta* (*samādhi*). cf. Kośa VIII 184ff.

121 See note 110.

122 (所) 有通, *abhijñā*.

123 *ṛddhipāda, divyaśrotrajñāna, cetaḥparyāyajñāna, pūrvanivāsānusmṛtijñāna, cyutyupapādajñāna, āsravakśayajñāna*.

124 *apramāṇa*.

125 *maitrī, karuṇā, muditā, upekṣā*.

126 *kṛtsnāyatana*. Chinese: 一切 (totality); 入 (entering, basis).

127 *pṛthivī°, ap°, tejas°, vāyu°, nīla°, pīta°, lohita°, avadāta°, ākāśānantyāyatana°, vijñānānantyāyatanakṛtsnāyatana*.

The spheres of mastery[128]: eight spheres of mastery: 1. internally not yet having removed the notion of form[129] and contemplating its impurity[130], it has few ranges; 2. immeasurable ranges; 3. having removed the notion of one's form[131] it has few ranges; 4. immeasurable ranges. Furthermore, the spheres of mastery in which that which is blue, yellow, red, and white[132] are contemplated, having removed the notion of one's form. Because[133] of the removal and purification of their range, they are called spheres of mastery.

The knowledges: there are ten knowledges, as previously explained[134].

The deliverances[135]: eight deliverances: 1. not yet having removed the notion of form, one reflects on its impurity[136]; 2. having removed the notion of one's form, one reflects on that which is impure[137]; 3. pure reflection[138]; the four formlessnesses and the attainment of cessation[139]. Because one turns one's back on the ranges and does not turn towards them, they are called deliverances.

They arise within them: all these qualities[140] can be obtained in nine stages[141], and they arise within them.
[[142]Some say it should be ten stages[143].]

---

[128] *abhibhvāyatana*. Chinese: 除 (renouncing); 入(entering, basis, sphere). See *Kośa* VIII 212.
[129] *rūpasaṃjñā*. The 3 editions and Ms. V6: 想.
[130] *aśubha*.
[131] See note 130.
[132] *nīlapītalohitāvadāta*.
[133] Ms. V 8 has 故 only once.
[134] Stanzas 124-125-126.
[135] *vimokṣa*.
[136] cf. the explanation of the first of the 8 *abhibhvāyatanas*. Reflection on (or contemplation of) impurity, *aśubhabhāvanā*. cf. *Kośa* VIII 204.
[137] i.e. internally having removed the notion of one's form, one reflects on the impurity of the *rūpa* outside.
[138] *śubhabhāvanā*.
[139] The 4 *ārūpya* (*samāpattis*) and *nirodhasamāpatti*.
[140] See note 120.
[141] Probably *kāmadhātu*, 4 *dhyānas*, 4 *ārūpyasamāpattis*. cf. stanzas 157-160.

We have explained all qualities. Their possible attainment according to the stages will now be explained.

> (157) One wisdom, compassion, evenmindedness, friendliness, and all five superknowledges are said to reside in all four trances. In six there is knowledge of the visible.

One wisdom, compassion, evenmindedness, friendliness, and all five superknowledges[144] are said to reside in all four trances: the one wisdom, namely knowledge of the thoughts of others[145], three immeasurables[146], and five superknowledges[147], all these qualities only reside in the fundamental four trances.

In six there is knowledge of the visible[148]: knowledge of the visible is knowledge of the law[149]. Among the six stages there are the fundamental four trances, the pre-trance, and the intermediate trance[150].

> (158) The qualities among which are namely four spheres of mastery, and among which there is sympathetic joy, the first deliverance and also the second (deliverance)[151] reside in the first and in the second trances.

The first four spheres of mastery and sympathetic joy agree with the first and second deliverances. These qualities only reside in the first and in the second trances.

---

[142] Not in Ms. V 10. cf. note 300 of chapter VI.
[143] *anāgamyadhyāna* and *dhyānāntara*, 4 *dhyānas* and 4 *ārūpyasamāpattis*.
[144] *prajñā*, *karuṇā*, *upekṣā*, *maitrī*, *abhijñā*.
[145] *paracittajñāna*.
[146] See note 125.
[147] *abhijñā* 1-5.
[148] *dṛṣṭa*. cf. supra stanza 124.
[149] *dharmajñāna*.
[150] Four *mauladhyānas*, *anāgamya*, *dhyānāntara*.
[151] *abhibhvāyatanas* 1-4, *muditā*, *vimokṣas* 1-2.

(159) That is to say, the rest of the spheres of mastery, and also one of the deliverances, and eight all-bases reside in the highest trance, Buddha says.

The last four spheres of mastery, the pure deliverance, and the first eight all-bases[152], these qualities reside only in the fourth trance.

(160) Other deliverances are explained by their names. The same applies to the two all-bases. Cessation (resides in) the final (stage). The rest, that is to say the pure ones, reside in nine (stages).

Other deliverances are explained by their names. The same applies to the two all-bases[153]: four other deliverances are explained by their own names, [824c] and the same applies to the two all-bases. The deliverance of the sphere of unlimited space[154] and the all-basis of the sphere of unlimited space[155] are comprised within the sphere of unlimited space, and so on until the sphere of neither-perception-nor-non-perception[156].

Cessation (resides in) the final (stage): the attainment of cessation[157] is comprised within the sphere of neither-perception-nor-non-perception[158]. Why? That is to say, not yet having renounced the desire there, one still engages in it[159].

The rest, that is to say the pure ones, reside in nine (stages): i.e. the remaining pure factors[160] are comprised within nine stages. The three *samādhis*, seven knowledges, and the superknowledge

---

[152] *abhibhvāyatanas* 5-8, *vimokṣa* 3 ( *śubha*), *kṛtsnāyatanas* 1-8.

[153] *vimokṣa* 4-7: *ākāśānantya*°, *vijñānāntya*°, *ākiṃcanya*°, *naivasaṃjñānāsaṃjñāyatana*.
*kṛtsnāyatana* 9-10: *ākāśānantya*°, *vijñānānantyāyatana*.

[154] *ākāśānantyāyatana*.

[155] See note 155.

[156] *naivasaṃjñānāsaṃjñāyatana* (*bhavāgra*).

[157] *nirodhasamāpatti*, the last of the *vimokṣas*.

[158] See note 157.

[159] Scil. in the *nirodhasamāpatti*.

[160] The remaining (cf. stanzas 157-158-159) *anāsrava dharmas*.

of the extinction of the outflows[161] are comprised within nine stages: the four trances, three formlessnesses, the pre-trance and the intermediate one[162]. Conventional knowledge[163] is comprised within ten stages. This can also be obtained in the sphere of neither-perception-nor-non-perception [164], because it has the nature of the attainment[165].

Question: How many of these qualities are impure, and how many are pure?

Answer: (161) Let it be known that three deliverances are impure or pure. Concentrations and knowledges are already distinctly established. That is to say, the rest are all impure.

Let it be known that three deliverances are impure or pure: the deliverances of the sphere of unlimited space, of the sphere of unlimited consciousness, and of the sphere of nothingness[166], are impure or pure[167].

Concentrations and knowledges are already distinctly established: the concentrations are as will be explained in the chapter: Scriptural Texts[168]. Pure knowledges and the superknowledges are as explained in the chapter: Knowledge[169].

That is to say, the rest are all impure: all other qualities are only impure[170]: three superknowledges[171], because one is a factor

---

[161] The 3 *samādhis*, i.e. *śūnyatā*°, *apraṇihita*°, *ānimittasamādhi*; 7 *jñānas* (the 10 minus *paracitta*°, *dharma*°, *saṃvṛtijñāna*); *āsravakṣayābhijñā*.

[162] 4 *dhyānas*, 3 *ārūpyasamāpattis* (not *bhavāgra*), *anāgamya*, *dhyānāntara*.

[163] *saṃvṛtijñāna*.

[164] *naivasaṃjñānāsaṃjñāyatana* (bhavāgra).

[165] i.e. both *bhavāgra* (see stanza 150d) and *saṃvṛtijñāna* are *sāsrava*. 数: calculated as...often translates a *vṛddhi*

[166] *Ākāśānantya*°, *vijñānānantya*, *ākiṃcanyāyatana*.

[167] *Sāsrava* and *anāsrava*.

[168] Chapter 8: *Sūtravarga*. See e.g. stanza 187. See also stanzas 149, 150, and 155.

[169] Chapter VI: *jñānavarga*. See stanzas 124 et seq. for *jñāna*, and stanzas 144-145 for the *abhijñās*.

[170] The other *guṇas* are *sāsrava*.

relating to deportment[172], and because they are characterized by their experiencing of form and of sound[173]; the immeasurables[174], because the beings are their objects; the all-bases[175], because of the attention through resolve[176]. The same applies to three deliverances[177]: the sphere of neither-perception-nor-non-perception[178], because the going is not swift[179]; the cessation of perception and feeling[180], because it is free from insight[181]; the spheres of mastery[182], also because of the attention through resolve[183].

We have explained the characteristics of all qualities. Their accomplishing will now be explained.

> (162) Still unable to pass beyond desire, one accomplishes that which is associated with relishing. When one has passed beyond the lower one but has not yet reached the higher one, one accomplishes clean concentrations.

---

[171] The *abhijñās*: *ṛddhipāda*, *divyacakṣus*, *divyaśrotra*.
[172] *Airyāpathika*. *Ṛddhipāda* is meant. AH2 858a also has *airyāpathika*, but MAH 928c has *śailpasthānika*, relating to craftmanship.
[173] See AH2 858a and MAH 928c.
Form, *rūpa*; sound, *śabda*.
[174] See note 125.
[175] See note 127.
[176] *Adhimuktimanasikāra*. See *Kośa* VIII 214 note 1: "acte d'attention imaginative" and 200: "jugement arbitraire ou volontier, non pas un jugement exact (*tattvamanasikāra*)". See also *Kośa* II 325-6.
AH: 意解 (*adhimukti*) 希望 (*manasikāra*): expectations after understanding; AH2 858a: 信解念处; MAH 928c: 得解思惟.
[177] See note 167.
[178] See note 157.
[179] See note 24.
[180] *Saṃjñāveditanirodha* (*samapātti*). *Vedita* is translated as 智: knowledge, instead of 受: feeling.
See *Kośa* II 203ff.
[181] The MS. VI 8 reads: 离观故. 观 may translate *vipaśyanā*. The *Taishō* edition: "free from *vitarka* (觉) and *vicāra* (观)" does not make sense to us. Possibly 觉 is added because it is often combined with 观.
AH2 858a: "because it is without wisdom (慧)".
MAH 928c: "because it is opposed to thought". cf. *Kośa* II 203.
[182] See note 129.
[183] See note 177.

Still unable to pass beyond desire, one accomplishes that which is associated with relishing[184]: i.e. when one has not yet renounced desire in a stage, one accomplishes that which is associated with relishing in that stage.

When one has passed beyond the lower one but has not yet reached the higher one, one accomplishes clean[185] concentrations: i.e. when one has renounced desire in the realm of desire, but when one is not yet born in the stage above the brahma-world[186], one accomplishes the clean[187] first trance and the impure[188] qualities of the stage of the first trance. All must be understood thus[189].

> (163) Let it be known that, dwelling in a higher (stage), one accomplishes a trance without impurity. Know that the qualities obtained after seeking, do not rest in desirelessness!

[825a] Let it be known that, dwelling in a higher (stage), one accomplishes a trance without impurity: i.e. when one has renounced the desire of the lower stage, one dwells in a higher stage and accomplishes that which is pure[190] of the lower stage, e.g. when someone who views the truths[191] has renounced desire and dwells in the stage above the brahma-world[192], he accomplishes the pure[193] first trance and the pure qualities: concentrations, etc[194] of the stage of the first trance. Thus all

---

[184] *Āsvādanasaṃprayukta.*
Stanzas 162 and 163 deal with the accomplishing of the concentrations and their qualities. Three kinds are distinguished: 162ab *upapattiuābhika* (*āsvādanasaṃprayukta*) 162cd and 163ab *vairāgyalābhika* (*śuddhaka* and *anāsrava*) 163cd *prayogalābhika*.

[185] *Śuddhaka.*

[186] i.e. second *dhyāna*. The *brahmaloka* is the first *dhyāna*.

[187] *Śuddhaka.*

[188] *Sāsrava*, i.e. *kuśala sāsrava*.

[189] i.e. all *bhūmis*, stages.

[190] *Anāsrava.*

[191] i.e. the *ārya*.

[192] See note 187.

[193] See note 191.

[194] See stanza 160d.

must be understood[195]. The worldly qualities are tied to the places according to one's birth, but the pure ones[196] rest in the (places) which are abandoned. Therefore, leaving a place of birth, one abandons the impure qualities but does not abandon the pure ones.

Know that the qualities obtained after seeking[197], do not rest in desirelessness![198]: we have explained the qualities in a higher stage, accomplished after renouncing desire in the lower one. Let it be known that it is not the case that all qualities are obtained when renouncing desire, such as the knowledge of the base of psychic power, the knowledge of heavenly eye, and the knowledge of heavenly ear[199], because[200] they have an indeterminate nature[201], and also the attainment of cessation[202]. These qualities[203] are obtained after seeking. They are not obtained when renouncing the desire of the lower stage.

We have explained how they are accomplished. (How they are) conditions as causes[204] will now be explained. There are twenty-three kinds of concentration: eight associated with relishing, eight clean ones, and seven pure ones[205].

Question: For how many kinds is each one of these kinds the cause[206]?

---

[195] See note 190.
[196] See note 191.
[197] AH2 858b and MAH 929a: 方便生: *prayogaja.*
[198] The *guṇas* or qualities which are *prayogaja,* produced through application, are not *vairāgyalābhika*, obtained through renouncement.
[199] *ṛddhipāda, divyacakṣus, divyaśrotra.*
[200] The 3 editions and the Ms. VI 17: 故.
[201] AH2 858b and MAH 929a only mention *divyacakṣus* and *divyaśrotra* as *avyākṛta*, indeterminate. cf. *Kośa* VII 107. Did AH add 如意足 because of the 如 in the text? The MS. VI 17 has 如 only once.
[202] *nirodhasamāpatti.*
[203] The 3 editions and the Ms. VI 17: 此功德.
[204] *hetupratyaya*. See stanza 30.
[205] In 4 *dhyānas* and 4 *ārūpyas*: *āsvādanasaṃprayukta* and *śuddhaka*. In 7 (subtracting the last *ārūpya*): *anāsrava*. See stanzas 149-150.
[206] hetu.

Answer: (164) They call the wonderfully pure and stainless one a cause for seven kinds. Let it be known that that which is caused by a clean trance and a trance which is associated with relishing, is one.

They call the wonderfully pure and stainless one[207] a cause for seven kinds: each one of the pure ones is similar cause[208] for the seven kinds, and associated cause and concomitant cause[209] for its particular stage[210].

Let it be known that that which is caused by a clean trance and a trance which is associated with relishing[211], is one: the first trance which is associated with relishing is cause only for the first trance which is associated with relishing. It is neither cause for the wholesome one[212], because it is not like it, nor cause for the defiled ones in the other stages[213], because it is opposed to their proceeding[214]. The clean[215] first trance is cause for the clean first trance. It is neither cause for the defiled one[216], because it is not like it, nor cause for the pure one[217], because it is not like it either, nor cause for the clean ones in the other stages, because its retribution is in its particular stage[218] and because it is tied to its particular stage. Thus all must be understood[219].

---

207 染: *rañj*°.

208 *sabhāgahetu*. See stanza 25.

209 *saṃprayuktakahetu* and *sahabhūhetu*. See stanza 25.

210 E.g the *anāsrava* concentration in the stage of the first *dhyāna* is *sabhāgahetu* for the 7 *anāsrava* concentrations from the first *ādhyāna* to the *ākiṃcanyāyatana*, and also *saṃprayuktaka*° and *sahabhūhetu* for the first *dhyāna*.

211 *śuddhaka* and *āsvādanasaṃprayukta*.

212 *kuśala* (sāsrava): *śuddhaka*.

213 *āsvādanasaṃprayukta* (i.e. *kliṣṭa*, defiled) in the other *bhūmis*.

214 MAH 929b says: of *āsvādanasaṃprayuktas* there are 5 kinds (*prakāra*), i.e. *duḥkhadarśanaheya* ...*bhāvanāheya*. One that is *duḥkhadarśanaprahātavya* is cause for one that is *duḥkhadarśanaprahātavya*.

215 *śuddhaka*.

216 *kliṣṭa*, i.e. *āsvādanasaṃprayukta*.

217 *anāsrava*.

218 *svabhūmi*.

219 See note 190.

We have explained the conditions as causes[220]. The conditions as immediate antecedents[221] will now be explained.

Question: How many kinds does each one produce in succession[222]?

Answer: (165) After a pure trance one produces six kinds of trance. One has seven, eight, nine, or ten, when producing trances and concentrations of emptiness.

After the pure[223] first trance one produces six kinds: the clean one[224] and the pure one of the own stage, and likewise of the second and of the third trances. After the pure sphere of nothingness[225] one produces seven: two of that particular stage, four of the lower stages, and one of the higher stage[226]. After the pure second[227] trance one produces eight: two of that particular stage, two of the lower stage, and four of the higher stages. After the pure sphere of unlimited consciousness[228] one produces nine: two of that particular stage, four of the lower stages, and three of the higher stages[229]. After the remaining pure ones one produces ten: [825b] two of their particular stage, four of the lower stages, and four of the higher stages.

(166) To a clean (concentration) there are six, seven, eight, nine, or ten, or one produces eleven. The trances which are associated with relishing produce from two to[230] ten.

To a clean[231] (concentration) there are six, seven, eight, nine, or ten, or one produces eleven: after the clean sphere of neither-

---

[220] See note 205.
[221] *samanantarapratyaya.*
[222] See *Kośa* VIII 167-168.
[223] See note 218.
[224] See note 216.
[225] *anāsrava ākiṃcanyāyatana.*
[226] No *anāsrava naivasaṃjñānāsaṃjñāyatana*. cf. stanza 161d.
[227] The Ms. VII 6: 二.
[228] *anāsrava vijñānānantyāyatana.*
[229] See note 227.
[230] The Ms. VII 8: 以.
[231] See note 216.

perception-nor-non-perception[232] one produces six: the one associated with relishing[233] and the clean one of that particular stage, and four of the lower stages: the clean and the pure[234] spheres of nothingness and spheres of unlimited consciousness[235], not the ones associated with relishing, because one has renounced their desire. All must be understood thus[236]. All have the one associated with relishing of their particular stage.

The trances which are associated with relishing[237] produce from two to ten: after a trance which is associated with relishing one produces two: the one associated with relishing and the clean one of that particular stage. One does not produce the other one, because each one is opposed to it. Thus all have two of their particular stage, and of the lower stage only the clean one.
[Some say the one clean one of the lower stage should not be there. [238]]

All the ones associated with relishing are produced at the moment of death[239].

We have explained the conditions as immediate antecedents. The conditions as objects[240] will now be explained.

---

232 *śuddhaka naivasaṃjñānāsaṃjñāyatana*.
233 *āsvādanasaṃprayukta*.
234 See note 218.
235 *ākiṃcanyāyatana* and *vijñānānantyāyatana*.
236 *śuddhaka naivasaṃjñānāsaṃjñāyatana*: own stage 2, lower 4:6
*śuddhaka ākiṃcanyāyatana:* own stage 3, lower 4, higher 1 (no *anāsrava*): 8
*śuddhaka vijñānānantyāyatana*: own stage 3, lower 4, higher 3:10
*śuddhaka ākāśānantyāyatana*: own stage 3, lower 4, higher 4:11
*śuddhaka* fourth, and third *dhyāna*: own stage 3, lower 4, higher 4:11
*śuddhaka* second *dhyāna*: own stage 3, lower 2, higher 4:9
*śuddhaka* first *dhyāna*: own stage 3, higher 4:7
See AH2 858c.
237 See note 234.
238 Not in the Ms. VII 12. cf. note 300 of chapter VI.
239 *maraṇa*. cf. *Kośa* VIII 171.
*āsvādanasaṃprayukta* first dhyāna: own stage 2 (āsvādanasaṃprayukta and *śuddhaka*); *bhavāgra*: 3 (own stage 2, and the *śuddhaka* of the stage below it) + the *āsvādanasaṃprayuktas* of the 7 stages below it (at death).
240 *ālambanapratyaya*. See stanza 30.
We follow the 3 editions and the Ms. VII 12. The *Taishō* edition has 缘 only twice.

Question: How many kinds does each one have as objects[241]?

Answer: (167) A clean and a pure trance certainly take all stages as their objects. A defiled associated trance only takes its particular stage as its object.

A clean and a pure[242] trance certainly take all stages as their objects: a clean and a pure trance take all elements[243] in all stages as their objects.

A defiled associated trance only takes its particular stage as its object: a trance which is associated with relishing takes the trance which is associated with relishing and the clean one of its particular stage as its objects, not the pure one[244]. Craving[245] does not have a pure object and it does not find happiness in another stage.

> (168) Formless ones do not have the power to take a lower impure stage as their object, when they are wholesome in a fundamental stage. The defiled ones are just like the trances with relishing.

Formless ones do not have the power to take a lower impure stage as their object: a formless attainment[246] cannot take the impure[247] factors of a lower stage as its objects, because it is very quiet[248].

Question: Which are the formless ones that cannot take the impure factors of a lower stage as their objects?

---

[241] *ālambana*.
[242] *śuddhaka* and *anāsrava*.
[243] AH2 858c: 一切事 (*vastu*): all elements, everything. cf. *Kośa* VIII 176-177.
[244] See note 218.
[245] *tṛṣṇā*.
[246] *ārūpyasamāpatti*.
[247] *sāsrava*.
[248] May translate *śānta*.

Answer: When they are wholesome in a fundamental stage[249]. A clean and also a pure[250] fundamental formless one take their particular stage and also a higher stage as their objects, but they do not take a lower stage as their object.

The defiled ones[251] are just like the trances with relishing[252]: the explanation of the trances[253] which are associated with relishing also applies to the formless ones[254].

> (169) The World-Honored One has expounded that so-called other qualities in the realm of form: the immeasurables, etc., certainly have the realm of desire as their object.

So-called other qualities[255] in the realm of form, such as[256] all-bases, spheres of mastery, and deliverances[257], only have the realm of desire as their object. They take the forms of the immeasurable suffering beings, blue, etc., as their objects. These are [825c] in the realm of desire. Why[258]? Because the superknowledges[259] take two realms as their object[260].

Question: What about the mixed trances[261], expounded by the World-Honored One?

---

[249] i.e. *kuśala* (*śuddhaka* or *anāsrava*) in a fundamental (*maula*)*bhūmi*(*samāpatti*).

[250] See note 243.

[251] *kliṣṭa*, i.e. *āsvādanasaṃprayukta*(*samāpatti*).

[252] *āsvādana*.

[253] The 3 editions add 禅. cf. Ms. VII 18.

[254] Stanza 167cd.

[255] i.e. not the *abhijñās*.

[256] Ms. VII 19-20: 如是等: *evamādi*, not 如无量等.

[257] *kṛtsnāyatana* (8), *abhibhvāyatana* (all 8), *vimokṣa* (3). Also the 4 *apramāṇas*.
cf. stanza 156. See also MAH 926a and bc.

[258] i.e. why the other qualities, immeasurables etc., but not the *abhijñās*?

[259] *abhijñā*.

[260] i.e. *kāma*° and *rūpadhātu*. AH2 859a.

[261] *vyavakīrṇa*. cf. *Kośa* VI 221-222.
熏: to fumigate, make fragrant. The commentator in MAH 930b explains this term as follows: "that which is *anāsrava*, is scattered over a *caitya* (shrine)".

Answer: The pure ones in all four mixed trances are mixed with the impure ones[262]. Through the power of that which is pure, one experiences a retribution in a pure abode[263].

Question: When all four trances are mixed, why does one not have the retribution in a pure abode in the lower three trances?

Answer: (170) When one mixes the trances, one relies on the fourth trance. Because the craving of three stages has ended, one dwells in the pure abodes among the ones having great fruition.

When one has obtained the fourth trance, one can mix the trances. The fourth trance is first mixed and later the other ones. That is to say, one obtains the fourth trance when one has renounced the desire of three trances. Therefore in the lower stages there is no pure abiding in the existences among the ones having great fruition[264].

Question: The World-Honored One has said there is a knowledge resulting from resolve[265]. What about this?

Answer:[266] (171) When one without attachment[267] is by nature immovable[268], he achieves all concentrations. Through his power of concentration he can give rise to the uppermost[269] fourth trance.

When he produces qualities in his mind here[270], they are the qualities: knowledge resulting from resolve, absence of strife, analytical knowledges, etc. Knowledge resulting from resolve[271]: having engaged in concentration according to his resolve, past, future, or present, formed or unformed[272], he knows them all

---

[262] *sāsrava*, i.e. *kuśala sāsrava*, meaning *śuddhaka*, according to MAH 930a.
[263] *śuddhāvāsa*, the last 5 gods of the fourth *dhyāna*, according to AH2 859a. cf. infra stanza 177.
[264] *bṛhatphala*. cf. stanza 177. These gods seem to mean: the fourth *dhyāna*.
[265] *praṇidhijñāna*. cf. stanza 147.
[266] 谓 does not occur in the 3 editions, but it occurs in the Ms. VIII 6.
[267] arhat.
[268] *akopya*. cf. stanza 114.
[269] *prāntakoṭika*. cf. *Kośa* VII 95-96.
[270] In the *prāntakoṭika* fourth *dhyāna*. cf. *Kośa* VII 95.
[271] *praṇidhijñāna*.
[272] *saṃskṛta* or *asaṃskṛta*.

completely. Absence of strife[273]: when he wants to arrange that strife does not arise in someone else's mind, it does not arise. Analytical knowledge[274]: when the meanings and the *vyañjanas*[275] of all factors are certain and beyond doubt, he is unhindered and fearless.

Question: Within which stages are the knowledge resulting from resolve, absence of strife and the analytical knowledges comprised[276]?

Answer: (172) In three stages there is knowledge resulting from resolve. Absence of strife relies on five stages. Analytical knowledge of factors and of expression rely on two (stages). Two analytical knowledges rely on nine.

In three stages there is knowledge resulting from resolve[277]: knowledge resulting from resolve is comprised within three stages: the fourth trance, the first trance, and the realm of desire. Having engaged in the fourth trance, one knows the first trance and also the realm of desire.

They say that absence of strife[278] relies on five stages: absence of strife can be obtained in five stages: the four of the fundamental four trances, and the realm of desire, when one wishes to ensure that no one knows strife.

Analytical knowledge of factors and of the expression rely on two (stages): the term analytical knowledge of factors[279] is used

---

[273] *araṇa*.
[274] *pratisaṃvid*. cf. stanza 147. The Ms. VIII 9 adds 谓 after 者.
[275] Meaning: *artha* (*arthapratisaṃvid*).
味 *wei:* *vy* (*añjana*): syllable, as explained in the commentary in MAH 943a
(cf. *dharmapratisaṃvid*).
[276] The 3 editions and the Ms. VIII 10, add 所 before 摄: *saṃghṛita*.
[277] See note 272.
[278] See note 274.
[279] *dharmapratisaṃvid*.

when one takes the *vyañjanas*[280] as object. It is in the realm of desire and in the world of the brahma-gods[281], but not in the higher stages, because they have renounced adjusted and discursive thinking[282]. The term analytical knowledge of expression[283] means the knowledge in which the *vyañjanas*[284] are selected. It can also be obtained in two stages: the realm of desire and the world of the brahma-gods[285].

Two analytical knowledges rely on nine: analytical knowledge of the meaning[286] and analytical knowledge of inspired speech[287] can be obtained in nine stages: the four trances, the four formless ones, and the realm of desire. When we mentioned the first trance, we should point out that we also mentioned the pre-trance and the intermediate one[288], because these are related to the first trance.

Question: How does one obtain these concentrations?

Answer: [826a] (173) By abandoning desire and also by birth one obtains the clean trance. The defiled one by falling away and by birth. The pure one only by abandoning desire.

By abandoning desire[289] and also by birth[290] one obtains the clean[291] trance: the clean first trance is obtained at two moments: at the moment of renouncing desire[292], and when, having

---

[280] *vyañjana*, syllable.
[281] First *dhyāna*.
[282] *vitarka and vicāra.*
[283] *niruktipratisaṃvid.*
[284] See note 281.
[285] See note 282.
[286] *arthapratisaṃvid.*
[287] *pratibhānapratisaṃvid.* cf. supra chapter VI, note 295.
[288] *anāgamya* and *dhyānāntara.*
[289] *vairāgya.* 断 actually means *prahā°.*
[290] *upapatti.*
[291] *śuddhaka.*
[292] *vairāgya.*

perished in a higher stage, one is born in the world of the brahma-gods. All must be understood thus[293].

The defiled one[294] by falling away[295] and by birth[296]: the defiled one, associated with relishing, is obtained at the moment of falling away. When one falls away to the ties of the realm of desire and of the world of the brahma-gods, at that moment one obtains the first trance which is associated with relishing. Obtainment at the moment of birth: when life in a higher stage has ended and when one is born in the realm of desire and in the world of the brahma-gods, at that moment one obtains the first trance which is associated with relishing. All must be understood thus[297].

The pure one[298] only by abandoning desire[299]: the pure one is obtained only at the moment of abandoning desire: i.e. when the noble one[300] has renounced desire[301], at that moment he obtains the pure first trance. All must be understood thus[302].

Question: Can[303] any of these qualities[304] remove affliction[305]?

Answer: (174) The pure one removes affliction, and so do the adjacent concentrations. All adjacent concentrations are associated with the faculty evenmindedness.

The pure one[306] removes affliction: the pure first trance removes affliction for eight stages[307]. All must be understood thus[308].

---

[293] i.e. all *bhūmis*, stages.
[294] *kliṣṭa*, i.e. *āsvādanasaṃprayukta*.
[295] *parihāṇi*.
[296] See note 291.
[297] See note 294.
[298] *anāsrava*.
[299] See note 290.
[300] *ārya*.
[301] Scil. of the *kāmadhātu*.
[302] See note 294.
[303] Ms. IX 3 also has 能. The 3 editions have 除.
[304] *guṇa*.
[305] *kleśa*.
[306] See note 299.
[307] 4 *dhyānas*, 4 *ārūpyas*.

So do the adjacent concentrations[309]: that which is called the adjacent concentration namely removes the desire of the lower stage. Because it is a preparatory path[310], one never obtains the fundamental stage as long as[311] one has not renounced desire. The other (concentrations) cannot remove it[312].

All adjacent concentrations[313] are associated with the faculty evenmindedness[314]: all adjacent concentrations are associated with the faculty evenmindedness. One never obtains gladness[315] as long as one has not obtained that which is meaningful[316].

Question: How many magical creations[317] are produced by one's thoughts, that is to say when one who has the base of psychic power[318] makes magical creations?

Answer: Eight[319]. The four trances have a fruition in the realm of desire, and the four trances have a fruition in the stage of the first trance[320].

Question: By whom are they[321] accomplished?

---

[308] i.e. all *bhūmis*. The last *anāsrava* one, i.e. of the *ākiṃcanyāyatana*, removes affliction for 2 stages: *ākiṃcanyāyatana* and *naivasaṃjñānāsaṃjñāyatana*.

[309] *sāmantaka*. Chinese: 定中间: between concentrations, i.e. intermediate concentration. cf. stanza 152, note 60, where we find another translation for *sāmantaka*.

[310] *prayogamārga*.

[311] The Ming edition and the Ms. IX 5 do not have 生, but 地至. 至未 means *yāvan na*.

[312] The other concentrations cannot remove affliction.

[313] See note 310.

[314] *upekṣendriya*.

[315] *saumanasya*. cf. note 59.

[316] *artha*. i.e. the fundamental concentration. AH2 859c: 所求: that which one strives for.

[317] *nirmāṇa*.

[318] *ṛddhipāda*.

[319] i.e. 8 *nirmāṇas*, magical creations. cf. *Kośa* VII 114-115; MAH 931a.

[320] The *dhyānas* produce *nirmāṇacittas*, magically transforming thoughts. These number 14. The first *dhyāna* produces *cittas* of 2 *bhūmis* (*kāmadhātu* and first *dhyāna*), the second *dhyāna* of 3 *bhūmis* (*kāmadhātu*, first and second *dhyāna*), etc. Finally, the fourth *dhyāna* produces *cittas* of 5 *bhūmis*. This all adds up to 14 thoughts. cf. AH2 859c and MAH 951ab.
The *nirmāṇacittas* bring about the magical creations, *nirmāṇas*.

Answer: (175) As for the magically transforming thoughts of the lower stages, one accomplishes those kinds of fruition. The higher stages may be mentioned when they are combined with three kinds of thoughts.

As for the magically transforming thoughts[322] of the lower stages, one accomplishes those kinds of fruition: i.e. when one accomplishes a trance, it accomplishes its fruition and the magically transforming thoughts of the lower stages[323].

Question: As explained, in the first trance there are four thoughts[324]. When one who dwells in a higher stage[325] wants to hear or see, how will he see or hear[326]?
Answer: The consciousnesses of the stage of the brahma-world[327] are then present[328].

Question: At how many moments are they[329] accomplished?

Answer: The higher stages[330] may be mentioned when they are combined with three kinds of thoughts[331]. When[332] these consciousnesses[333] are present[334]: eye-consciousness, ear-consciousness, and body-consciousness[335], at that moment they

---

321 The magical creations.
322 *nirmāṇacittas.*
323 cf. note 321.
324 *cakṣur°*, *śrotra°*, *kāya°*, *manovijñāna*. See stanza 151c.
325 i.e. higher than the first *dhyāna*.
326 In those higher *bhūmis* there is neither *cakṣur°* nor *śrotravijñāna*. cf. explanation of stanza 153c.
327 i.e. first *dhyāna*.
328 *saṃmukhībhūta*.
329 See note 322.
330 See note 326.
331 *citta*, i.e. *vijñāna*.
332 Ms. IX 11: 得, not 时.
333 *vijñāna*.
334 See note 329.
335 *cakṣur°*, *śrotra°*, *kāyavijñāna*: 3.
*jihvāvijñāna*, which is mentioned in the *Taishō* edition, does not occur in the Ms. IX 12. *Jihvāvijñāna* is obviously mentioned by mistake in the *Taishō* edition. It does not exist in the first *dhyāna*.

are accomplished. When these consciousnesses [826b] are not present, when they are extinct, at that moment they are not accomplished.

Treatise on the Essence of Scholasticism. Vol.III.

**定品第七**

问如是知诸智。此智当云何。答

148 智依于诸定 行无挂碍行
是以思惟定 欲求其真实

智依于诸定行无挂碍行者如灯依油离风处光焰甚明如是智依于定意离诸乱智光甚明。必定无疑行于缘。是以思惟定欲求其真实。

149 决定说四禅 及与无色定
此中一一说 杂味净无漏

决定说四禅及与无色定者有八定四禅及四无色定。此中一一说杂味净无漏者初禅有三种味相应净无漏。如是一切诸定。
问。云何味相应。云何净。云何无漏。答。

150 善有漏是净 无热谓无漏
气味爱相应 最上无无漏

善有漏是净者谓善是净故说净。无热谓无漏者烦恼假名热。谓定无烦恼是无漏。气味爱相应者谓禅无色定爱相应是具足共相应共行。是说味相应。最上无无漏者最上非想非非想处。彼中无无漏。不捷疾行故是有二种。余各三种。
问。禅何性所有。答。

151 五枝有觉观 亦复有三痛
若干种四心 谓之是初禅

五枝者谓五枝摄受初禅令坚固亦从此得。名觉观喜乐一心。觉名当入定时初生善功德始粗心思惟。观名令心细相续相连。喜名于定中悦。乐名已悦于身心中安隐快乐。一心名于缘中心专不散。此种住定时是枝及入时舍时。是故五枝初禅。有觉观者有觉有观即是初禅。问。已受五枝今觉观何用。答。枝者谓善是于五枝中。说秽污及无记亦有觉有观而不是善。亦复有三痛者初禅有三痛乐根喜根护根。于痛中乐根是身痛。喜根是意地。护根在四识。若干种者梵世中若干种。有上有下。是说具足生处。四心者初禅有四心眼识耳识身识意识。谓之是初禅者此一切诸法谓是初禅。
已说初禅。第二禅今当说。

152 二痛若干种 二禅有四枝
五枝是第三 此禅说二痛

二痛者第二禅有二痛喜根及护根。若干种者于中身有若干种。已离觉观有若干心。或时入喜根或时入护根。喜根是根本。边有护根。二禅有四枝者第二禅有四枝内净喜乐一心。内净名是信于离中生信。已得初禅离便作是念一切可离。余枝如前说。此种于第二禅是枝。 五枝是第三者第三禅有五枝乐护念智一心。乐者意识地中乐根。护者已乐于乐不求余[其人云护虽有义不应立枝也]念者是护方便不舍智者不令乐。一心者定。此种于第三禅中是枝。此禅说二痛者第三禅有二痛乐根及护根。乐根是根本。护根是边。

153 离息入息出 第四有四枝
此枝谓说善 亦复分别种。

离息入息出者息入者来息出者去。是第四禅中无。所以者何。彼由定力故身诸毛孔合。第四有四枝者第四禅有四枝不苦不乐护净念一心永离苦乐不苦不乐。余如前说。问。何禅是枝相应。答。此枝谓说善。善禅枝相应。枝非秽污亦非无记。亦复分别种者谓种随处已说。当知是余处不应有。如初禅有觉有观四心。说此种余一切地无。第四禅离息入息出。是三中无不应说。已说四禅四无色定。谓余今当说。问。如世尊言有根本依。若未离欲未有根本依而有无漏功德是无漏功德何地所摄。答。未来禅所摄。又世尊所说有三定有觉有观无觉少观无觉无观。于中初禅是有觉有观。第二禅是无觉无观。谓无觉少观定是何地所摄。答。是中间所摄。
是未来禅中间禅相今当说。

154 相应有觉观 俱在未来禅。
观相应中间 明智之所说

相应有觉观俱在未来禅者未来禅中有觉有观。观相应中间明知之所说者中间禅少有观而无觉。彼渐渐心息止。

155 无依而二种 除其味相应
中禅有三种 俱为说一痛

无依而二种除其味相应者未来禅一向善有漏及无漏。有漏者净。无漏即无漏。中禅有三种者中间禅有三种味净无漏生死居故。俱为说一痛者未来禅及中间禅俱有一痛护根非根本地故。已说诸定。余功德于中摄今当说。

156 三摩提有通 无量修一切
除入及诸智 解脱于中起

三摩提者三三摩提空无愿无相无漏心系缚故。有通者有六通如意足智天耳智他心通智忆宿命智生死智漏尽通智。无量者四无量慈悲喜护。无量众生境界故日无量。修一切者十一切入地一切入水火风青黄赤白一切入无量空处一切入无量识处一切入。尽具解故一切入。除入者八除入内未除色想不净观少境界一无量境界。二除色想少境界三无量境界四。复除色想青黄赤白观除入。除净境界故故日除入。及诸智者诸智有十如前说。解脱者八解脱未除色想不净思惟一除色想不净思惟二净思惟三四无色及灭尽定。境界背不向故说解脱。于中起者此诸功德九地中可得及于中起。[其入云应十地]。
已说诸功德。随地可得今当说。

157 一慧悲及护 慈亦有五通
说遍四禅中 六中有现智

一慧悲及护慈亦有五通说遍四禅中者一慧谓他心智三无量及五通是一切功德根本四禅中非余。六中有现智者现智是法智。六地中有根本四禅未来禅中间禅。

158 除入中说四 于中亦有喜
初解脱及二 功德初二禅。

前四除入喜等初第二解脱。此功德初第二禅中非余。

159 除入谓有余 及与解脱一
亦八一切入 佛说最上禅

后四除入净解脱前八一切入是功德第四禅中非余。

160 余脱即名说 二一切亦然
灭尽最在后 余九谓无漏

余脱即名说二一切亦然者余四解脱自名所说。及二一切入亦如是。无量空处解脱无量空处一切入于无量空处中所摄。如是至非想非非想处。灭尽最在后者灭尽定非想非非想处所摄。所以者何。谓未离彼欲亦入。余九谓无漏者谓余无漏法九地所摄。如三三摩提七智漏尽通是九地所摄四禅三无色未来及中间。等智是十地所摄。此亦非想非非想处可得以定数故。
问。此功德几有漏几无漏。答。

161 三解脱当知 有漏及无漏
定智已分别 谓余尽有漏

三解脱当知有漏及无漏者无量空处无量识处无所有处解脱是有漏无漏。定智已分别者定如契经品说。无漏智及诸通如智品说。谓余尽有漏者余一切功德一向有漏。如三通威仪法故色声受相故。无量众生缘故。一切入意解希望故。三解脱亦如是非想非非想处非捷疾行故。想智灭离观故。除入亦意解希望故。
已说诸功德。相成就今当说。

162 未能度于欲 成就味相应
度下未至上 成就净诸定

未能度于欲成就味相应者谓地若未离欲于彼地成就味相应。度下未至上成就净诸定者谓离欲界欲若未生梵世上地彼成就净初禅及初禅地有漏功德。如是一切尽当知。

163 住上应当知 无漏成就禅
求得诸功德 知非无欲中

住上应当知无漏成就禅者谓离下地欲彼住上地亦成就下地无漏。如见谛离欲住梵世上地成就无漏初禅及初禅地定等诸无漏功德。如是一切尽当知。世俗功德系在随生处。无漏在断中。是以离生处舍有漏功德不舍无漏。求得诸功德知非无欲中者已说离下地欲成就上功德。当知非一切功德离欲时得如如意足智天眼智天耳智无记性所有故及灭尽定。此功德求得。非离下地欲时得。已说成就。因缘今当说。定种有二十三八味相应八净七无漏。问。此
一 一种几种因。答。

164 妙无漏无染 七种谓之因
净味相应禅 当知因有一

妙无漏无染七种谓之因者一一无漏七种自然因自地相应因共因。净味相应禅。
当知因有一者味相应初禅于味相应初禅因非余。非善因不相似故。非余地秽污因行相违故。
净初禅于净初禅因。非秽污因不相似故。非无漏因亦不相似故。非余地净因自地果报故及自地系缚故。如是一切尽当知。
已说因缘。次第缘今当说。问。一 一次第生几种。答。

165 无漏禅次第 兴起六种禅
七八九有十 起禅亦空定

无漏初禅次第生六种自地净及无漏。如是第二第三禅。无漏无所有处次第生七自地二下地四上地一。无漏第二禅次第生八自地二下地二上地四。无漏无量识处次第生九自地二下地四上地三。余无漏次第生十自地二下地四上地四。

166 净六有七八 九十生十一
味相应诸禅 兴二乃以十

净六有七八九十生十一者净非想非非想处次第生六自地味相应及净下地四净无漏无所有处无量识处非味相应离欲故。如是一切尽当知。一切自地味相应。味相应诸禅兴二乃以十者味相应禅次第生二自地味相应及净。不生余各各相违故。如是一切自地二下地一净。[其人云不应有下地一净]一切味相应死时生。
已说次第缘。缘缘今当说。问。一一几种缘。答。

167 净以无漏禅 必缘一切地
秽污相应禅 独缘于已地

净以无漏禅必缘一切地者净及无漏禅一切地缘一切种。秽污相应禅独缘于已地者味相应禅缘于自地味相应禅及净非无漏。爱无无漏缘亦不乐于他地。

168 无色无有力 缘下有漏地
善有根本地 秽污如味禅

无色无有力缘下有漏地者无色定不能缘下地有漏法极寂静故。问。何谓无色不能缘下地有漏法。答。善有根本地。净及无漏根本无色是自地缘及上地非下地缘。秽污如味禅者如味相应禅说无色亦然。

169 谓余于色界 无量等功德。
是必欲界缘 世尊之所说

谓色界余功德如是等一切入除入及解脱唯缘欲界缘无量苦众生青等诸色。此则欲界。所以者何。神通二界缘故。问。世尊所说熏禅是云何。答。熏一切四禅无漏者熏有漏。是无漏力故受净居果报。
问。若一切四禅熏者以何等故下三禅中无净居果。答。

170 若能熏诸禅 是依第四禅
三地爱尽故 净居果实中

若得第四禅是能熏禅。第四禅者先熏余者后。谓得第四禅离三禅欲。以是故下地无有净居果实中有。
问。世尊言有愿智。是云何。答。

171 无着性不熏 是得一切定
彼由定力故 能起顶四禅

于中若彼意生功德愿智不诤辩首诸功德。愿智者如所原入定。或过去或未来或现在或有为或无为是一切尽知。不诤者欲令他意不起诤便不起。辩者诸法义及味决定无疑不挂碍无所畏。
问。是愿智不诤及辩何地所摄。答。

172 三地有愿智 无诤依五地
法辞辩依二 二辩依于九

三地有愿智者愿智三地所摄第四禅初禅及欲界。入第四禅知初禅及欲界。说无诤依五地者无诤五地可得根本四禅四及欲界欲令一切不诤。法辞辩依二者法辩名缘味。是欲界及梵天世非上地离觉观故。辞辩名是味撰智。彼亦二地中可得欲界及梵天世。二辩依于九者义辩及应辩九地中可得四禅四无色及欲界。
已说初禅。当知已说未来及中间此是初禅眷属故。
问。云何得此定。答。

173 断欲亦复生 而得于净禅
秽污退及生 无漏唯断欲

断欲亦复生而得于净禅者净初禅二时得离欲时及上地没生梵天世。如是一切尽当知。秽污退及生者秽污味相应是退时得。若欲界及梵天世缠退于尔时得味相应初禅。生时得者若上地命终生欲界及梵天世于尔时得味相应初禅。如是一切尽当知。无漏唯断欲者无漏唯断欲时得。谓圣得离欲于尔时得无漏初禅。如是一切尽当知。
问。此功德谁能断烦恼。答。

174　　无漏除烦恼　　亦复定中间
　　　一切定中间　　相应于护根

无漏除烦恼者无漏初禅八地除烦恼。如是一切尽当知。亦复定中间者定中间名谓下地除欲。以方便道故终不得根本地至未得离欲。余不能除。一切定中间相应于护根者一切定中间护根相应。终不得喜至不得义。问。变化心有几谓有如意足能变化。答。八。四禅果欲界。四禅果初禅地。问。彼谁成就。答。

175　　下地变化意　　成就彼种果
　　　若合三种心　　上地应当说

下地变化意成就彼种果者谓若成就禅是成就彼果下地变化心。问。如说初禅有四心。住于上地欲闻欲见彼云何见闻。答。梵世地识现在前。问。彼几时成就。答。若合三种心上地应当说。若得彼识现在前若眼识若耳识若身识尔时成就。彼识若不现在前即灭尔时不成就。

阿毗昙心论卷第三

Treatise on the Essence of Scholasticism. Vol. IV, composed by Bhadanta Dharmaśreṣṭhin, translated on Mount Lu by Saṃghadeva of the Eastern Jin, with Huiyuan.

## Chapter VIII. Scriptural Texts[1]

We have expounded the chapter: Concentration. The chapter: Scriptural Texts will now be expounded.

> (176) The subtle meanings in the scriptural texts, expounded by the All-Knower[2], those I[3] will explain now. Listen with suitable thoughts!

Although all *abhidharma* is the meaning of the scriptural texts, yet the scriptural texts must be fully known. They will now be explained.

The World-Honored One has expounded three realms: the realm of desire, the realm of form, and the realm of formlessness[4].

Question: What about these?

Answer: (177) In the realm of desire there are ten abodes. The realm of form is said to have seventeen. In formlessness there are four. The same applies to the three existences.

In the realm of desire there are ten abodes: in this realm of desire there are ten abodes: hell, animal birth, hungry ghost, man, and the six desiring gods: the gods of the four celestial

---

1 *sūtravarga*.
The Ms. IX 13 does not mention a new 卷 Volume. It only says: "Chapter 5 (mistake for 8): *Sūtravarga*, of the Essence of Scholasticism." cf. Ms. II 10: "Chapter 7: *Samādhivarga*, of the Essence of Scholasticism".

2 *sarvajña*, i.e. Buddha.

3 Ms. IX 14: 品, not 吾 "...will now be explained in this chapter."

4 *kāmadhātu*, *rūpadhātu*, *ārūpyadhātu*.

kings, the thirty-three gods, the *yāma*-gods, the *tuṣita*-gods[5], the gods who enjoy magical creations, and the gods controlling (enjoyments) magically created by others[6]. These beings produce desirous notions. Now, the things one can obtain in these places are all in the grasp of desire[7]. Therefore they are said to be of the realm of desire.

Question: What about the realm of form?

Answer: The realm of form is said to have seventeen. The realm of form is said to have seventeen[8]: abodes among brahma's group, the *brahmapurohitas*[9], the ones of limited radiance[10], the ones of unlimited radiance, the shining ones[11], the ones of limited magnificence, the ones of unlimited magnificence, the entirely magnificent ones[12], the unclouded[13] ones, the ones having increase of merit[14], the ones having great fruition, the beings without perception, the ones not troubled, the ones not distressed, the clearly-visible ones, the clear-visioned ones, and the highest[15] ones[16]. In these places one does not produce desirous notions. One only assumes the very subtle form neither male nor female in shape. Therefore they are said to be[17] of the realm of form.

In formlessness there are four: four abodes in the realm of formlessness: the sphere of unlimited space, the sphere of unlimited consciousness, the sphere of nothingness, and the

---

[5] Ms. IX 17: 斗师多.

[6] *naraka*, *tiryagyoni*, *preta*, *manuṣya*.
6 *kāmadevas*: *caturmahārājika*, *trāyastriṃśa*, *yāma*, *tuṣita*, *nirmāṇarati*, *paranirmitavaśavartin*.

[7] Ms. IX 17: 淫, not 婬.

[8] 17: this view is held by *bahirdeśakas*. See *Kośa* III, 3 note 1d.

[9] *dhyāna* 1: *brahmakāyika*, *brahmapurohita*.

[10] The Ms. IX 18 does not have 光 before 少.

[11] *dhyāna* 2: *parīttābha*, *apramāṇābha*, *ābhāsvara*.

[12] dhyāna 3: *parīttaśubha*, *apramāṇaśubha*, *śubhakṛtsna*.

[13] Chinese: unhindered.

[14] Chinese: experiencing merit.

[15] Chinese: *aghaniṣtha*: the final ones in form.

[16] *dhyāna* 4: *anabhraka*, *puṇyaprasava*, *bṛhatphala*, *asaṃjñisattva*, *avṛha*, *atapa*, *sudṛśa*, *sudarśana*, *akaniṣṭha*.

[17] Ms. IX 20, adds 说. Idem 3 editions.

sphere of neither-perception-nor-non-perception[18]. In these places there is no form. They are free from [826c] desire for form. Therefore they are said to be of the realm of formlessness.

Question: The World-Honored One has expounded three existences[19]: the existence of desire, the existence of form, and the existence of formlessness. What about these?

Answer: The same applies to the three existences. I.e. the distinctions of the realms mentioned earlier, are the three existences.

Question: The seven abodes of consciousness[20] as expounded by the World-Honored One, what about these?

Answer: (178) When the wholesome courses[21] are of the realm of desire and also of three stages in the realm of form - the same applies to formlessness-, wisdom knows them as the abodes of consciousness.

When in this realm of desire one's course is of a wholesome nature, i.e. man and the six desiring gods[22], the first three stages of the realm of form, and the first three stages of formlessness[23] - two in the stage of the first trance[24], three in the stage of the second trance above the stage of the first trance, three in the stage of the third trance above the stage of the second trance, nine in the stage of the fourth trance above the stage of the third trance[25]: the first three stages among them, and also the first three stages of formlessness[26]- these are called the seven abodes of consciousness[27]. Why? Because they do not ruin

---

[18] *ākāśānantya*°, *vijñānānantya*°, *ākiṃcanya*°, *naivasaṃjñānāsaṃjñāyatana.*
[19] *tribhava.*
[20] *vijñānasthiti.*
[21] *sugati.*
[22] *manuṣya* and the 6 *kāmadevas.* See note 6.
[23] i.e. the gods of *dhyāna* 1-2-3, and stages 1-2-3 in the *ārūpyadhātu.*
[24] Ms. X 5: 初禅地二. These words do not occur in the *Taishō* edition.
[25] The *devas* in the 4 trances: see notes 9-11-12-16.
[26] See note 23.
[27] See note 20.

consciousness [28]. Because (consciousness) is ruined by unpleasant feeling[29] in the woeful courses[30], one cannot establish an abode of consciousness. Because in the fourth trance it is ruined by the attainment without perception [31], one cannot establish an abode of consciousness either. Because in the sphere of neither-perception-nor-non-perception[32] it is ruined by the attainment of cessation[33], one cannot establish an abode of consciousness. For these reasons they are not mentioned.

> (179) With the summit of existence and the (beings) without perception, the abodes of the beings are said to be nine. The impure four aggregates are called the four abodes of consciousness.

With the summit of existence [34] and the (beings) without perception[35], the abodes of the beings[36] are said to be nine: these seven abodes of consciousness[37], the beings without perception[38], and the sphere of neither-perception-nor-non-perception [39] are called the nine abodes of the beings[40]. Because the beings abide in them, they are called abodes of the beings.
The impure[41] four aggregates [42] are called the four abodes of consciousness [43]: impure form, feeling, perception, and formation[44]: when consciousness[45] forms a series[46] (with them),

---

[28] *vijñāna*.
[29] *duḥkhavedanā*.
[30] *durgati*.
[31] *asaṃjñisamāpatti*.
[32] *naivasaṃjñānāsaṃjñāyatana*.
[33] *nirodhasamāpatti*.
[34] *bhavāgra*.
[35] *asaṃjñisattva*.
[36] *sattvāvāsa*. See *Kośa* III 22.
[37] See note 20.
[38] See note 35.
[39] See note 32.
[40] See note 36.
[41] *sāsrava*.
[42] *skandha*.
[43] See note 20.
[44] *rūpa*, vedanā, saṃjñā, saṃskāra.
[45] See note 28.
[46] *saṃtati*.

they are accompanied by it. Therefore they are called abodes of consciousness.

Question: The World-Honored One has expounded the conditioned co-production [47] with twelve members. Its characteristics will also be explained now.

Answer: (180) The afflictions and actions together with the entities[48] are gradually produced. They are said to contain the members. The beings are produced by all.

Among them, the afflictions consist of ignorance, craving, and grasping[49]. That which is called action consists of the formations and existence[50]. That which is called entity consists of the remaining members[51]. They are gradually produced by all beings. On the basis of the entities they establish affliction, actions caused by the affliction, and entities caused by the actions. And so twelve elements are distinctly established.

Question: Do these members proceed in one moment, or gradually?

Answer: They are not twelve in one moment. The aggregates[52] are said to have twelve members: ignorance[53], etc.

> [827a] (181) They are gradually established, experienced in birth and death. Past are two[54], and future (are two). That which is in between is explained by eight.

---

[47] *pratītyasamutpāda*.
[48] *kleśa*, *karman*, and *vastu*.
Together with: 有: *sa°*.
[49] *avidyā, tṛṣṇā, upādāna* (Chinese: experiencing); var. lec. grasping: 取.
[50] *saṃskāra*, *bhava*.
[51] Scil. *vijñāna*, *nāmarūpa*, *ṣaḍāyatana*, *sparśa*, *vedanā*, *jāti*, *jarāmaraṇa*.
陰: *skandha*. cf. *Kośa* III 70 and 88. AH has 苦 *duḥkha°*. Ms. X 13 has 者, i.e. 十二者.
[53] *avidyā*.
[54] Ms. X 14: 二. The old Song edition (1104-1148) also reads 一.

The (elements) with the members[55] are gradually established. Amongst them, the common existence and companionship of all afflictions in the former life is called ignorance[56]. Because of it one performs actions[57], and the results produced by actions are formations[58]. The thoughts[59] produced by them are consciousness[60]. Its connection[61] with four aggregates[62] at birth is name-and-form[63]. Amongst them[64], the eyes, etc.[65] on which one relies, are called[66] the six bases[67]. The combination of the faculty, its range, and the thought[68], is contact[69]. The experiencing produced by contact[70] is feeling[71]. Attachment through feeling is craving[72]. The being troubled by the possession of feeling, is grasping[73]. The actions[74] performed by the one who is troubled, are existence[75]. The fruition again experienced here, is birth[76]. The immeasurable calamities which arise in relation to birth, are old age and death[77]. Thus these (elements) with the members[78] are in all lives: two are comprised within the past world, and two within the future one[79]. Eight[80] are comprised within the present life.

---

[55] i.e. the 3 elements explained in stanza 180.
[56] See note 53.
[57] *karman*.
[58] *saṃskāra*.
[59] Ms. X 15: 种种.
[60] *vijñāna*.
[61] *pratisaṃdhi*.
[62] *skandha*.
[63] *nāmarūpa*.
[64] i.e. among the 12 members.
[65] The indriyas: *cakṣus*, etc.
[66] Ms. X 16 has 说, not 诸根.
[67] *ṣaḍāyatana*.
[68] *indriya*, *viṣaya*, *citta*, i.e. the *vijñāna*.
[69] *sparśa*.
[70] See note 69.
[71] *vedanā*.
[72] *tṛṣṇā*.
[73] *upādāna*.
[74] See note 57.
[75] *bhava*.
[76] *jāti*.
[77] *jarāmaraṇa*.
[78] See note 55.
[79] Past: *avidyā*, *saṃskāra*.
Future: *jāti*, *jarāmaraṇa*.
[80] The remaining 8 of the 12.

Question:The World-Honored One has expounded six elements[81]. What about them?

Answer: (182) There are namely four great elements, in addition to impure consciousness and to that which may be known as connected with form. These elements are said to be the fundaments of birth.

There are namely four great elements[82], in addition to impure consciousness[83] and to that which may be known as connected with form[84]: the great elements: earth, water, fire, and wind[85], impure consciousness, and that which may be known as connected with form[86], i.e. that which the eye experiences, these six factors[87] are called elements[88].
Question: Why among the many factors[89] do they mention six elements[90]?

Answer: These elements are said to be the fundaments of birth. These six factors are the fundaments of birth and of death[91]. In relation to them one has the concept of a man. Among them, earth produces the body, water moistens it, fire makes it mature, and, but for its stench when rotten, its wind[92] raises it. In its empty space it is fed. Because wind[93] leaves and enters, it is established with consciousness. In relation to them one produces the concept of a man. Because it is their nature to be born and to die, they are called his elements[94].

---

81 *dhātu*.
82 *mahābhūtāni*: *pṛthivī*, *āpas*, *tejas*, *vāyu*.
83 *sāsrava vijñāna*.
84 The *ākāśadhātu*, the element space, is meant. 色中间: that which is within form, a translation of *aghasāmantaka*. cf. *Kośa* I 50.
85 See note 82.
86 See note 84.
87 *dharma*.
88 See note 81.
89 i.e. the 18 *dhātus*, according to AH2 860c and MAH 936b. cf. stanza 8c.
90 See note 81.
91 cf. *Kośa* I 50.
92 i.e. the breath.
93 See note 92.
94 See note 81.

Question: The World-Honored One has expounded four noble truths[95]. What about their characteristics?

Answer: (183) All formations which are a fruition and impure, are said to imply suffering, and all which are a cause imply origination. The end of suffering is called cessation.

All[96] formations[97] which are a fruition and impure[98], are said to imply suffering[99]: all impure formations are produced by[100] a cause, and bring about all hardship. Therefore all formations are said to imply the truth of suffering.
All which are a cause imply origination[101]: all impure formations are a cause for something else. Therefore all formations are said to imply the truth of origination. Just as a woman is either called mother or woman because of what has happened or what will happen, thus impure formations are either said to imply the truth of suffering[102] or they are said to imply the truth of origination[103], because they have produced or will produce.

The end[104] of suffering is called cessation[105]: the fact that all impure formations are extinguished and appeased, implies namely the [827b] truth of cessation.

(184) All pure formations are said to imply the truth of the path. They are so for two reasons. When one's vision is clear, one perceives that which is subtle.

All pure[106] formations[107] are said to imply the truth of the path[108]: all pure formations are said to imply the truth of the path. Why?

---

95 *āryasatyāni*.
96 若有, cf. chapter III, note 132.
97 *saṃskāra*.
98 *sāsrava*.
99 *duḥkha*.
100 Ms. XI 3, and the 3 editions: 行从.
101 *samudaya*.
102 See note 99.
103 *samudaya*.
104 *kṣaya*.
105 *nirodha*.

Because one is completely endowed with them when appeasing suffering.

Question: Why do they call them truths[109]?

Answer: They are so for two reasons. For two reasons they are called truths: their particular characteristic[110] is truth, not error[111], and, when viewing them, one obtains a mind free from[112] error.
Question: When the cause is first and the effect is later, why did the World-Honored One first expound the effect and later expound the cause[113]?

Answer: When one's vision is clear, one perceives that which is subtle[114]. Although in the noble truths one has first origination[115] and later suffering[116], although one first develops the path[117] and later obtains cessation[118], still one must first view the truth of suffering and afterwards one views the truth of origination. In this way one must first view the truth of cessation and afterwards one views the truth of the path. Why? Suffering is coarse and origination is subtle[119]. Cessation is coarse and the path is subtle. Therefore the World-Honored One has first expounded the truth of suffering and expounded the truth of origination later. (Therefore) he has first expounded the truth of cessation and expounded the truth of the path later.

---

[106] *anāsrava*.
[107] *saṃskāra*.
[108] *mārga*.
[109] *satya*.
[110] *svalakṣaṇa*.
[111] *viparīta*.
[112] Ms. XI 9: 不.
[113] *samudaya* (2) is the cause, and *duḥkha* (1) is the effect. *Mārga* (4) is the cause, and *nirodha* (3) is the effect.
[114] Meaning: 细: *sūkṣma*.
[115] See note 103.
[116] See note 99.
[117] See note 108.
[118] See note 105.
[119] See note 114.

Question: The World-Honored One has expounded four fruitions of *śramaṇaship*[120]. How many elements do they have?

Answer: (185) The noble fruitions have six elements. The most excellent one is in nine stages. The third one is in six stages. Two both rely on the pre-(trance).

The noble fruitions[121] have six elements[122]: the four fruitions of *śramaṇaship* have six elements: the pure five aggregates[123], and cessation as a result of careful consideration[124].

Question: Within which stages are the four fruitions of *śramaṇaship* comprised?

Answer: The most excellent one is in nine stages. The most excellent one is the fruition of being without attachment[125]. It is comprised within nine stages: the fundamental four trances, three formlessnesses, the pre-trance and the intermediate one[126].

The third one is in six stages: the fruition of not returning[127] is comprised within six stages. One has it in the four trances, in the pre-trance, and in the intermediate one[128], not in formlessness[129], because it is without the knowledge of the law[130].

---

120 *śrāmaṇyaphala*. The Ms. XI 13 does not have 圣: *ārya*.

121 The noble (*ārya*) or pure (*anāsrava*) path (*mārga*) means *śramaṇaship* (*śrāmaṇya*). See MAH 936c. For the 4 fruitions of *śramaṇaship* (*śrāmaṇyaphala*): see stanzas 107 et seq. The noble path: see stanzas 104 et seq.

122 AH2 861b and MAH 936c have *vastu:* 事, although *prakāra* and *vidhāna* are not impossible. AH: 种 translates such words as *prakāra, vastu, bīja, vidhā, vidhāna*.

123 *skandha*. *Anāsravaskandhas*. cf. Kośa VI 297 note 2.

124 *pratisaṃkhyānirodha*.

125 *arhattvaphala*.

126 *maula* 4 *dhyānas*; 3 *ārūpyas*; *anāgamya*; (*dhyāna*)*antara*.

127 *anāgāmiphala*.

128 4 *dhyānas*; *anāgamya*; (*dhyāna*)*antara*.

129 *ārāpya*.

130 *dharmajñāna*.

Two both rely on the pre-(trance): the *srotaāpatti*-fruition and the *sakṛdāgāmi* one are comprised within the pre-trance[131], because they have not yet renounced desire.

Question: The World-Honored One has expounded four paths of progress[132]: unpleasant and with slow comprehension, unpleasant and with quick comprehension, pleasant and with slow[133] comprehension, pleasant and with quick comprehension[134]. Which are their characteristics?

Answer: (186) The factors of the faith-follower are without affliction and slowly perceived. The factors of the law-follower are without affliction and quickly perçeived.

The factors of the faith-follower[135] are without affliction and slowly[136] perceived: the pure[137] factors[138] of the faith-follower are not quick. In the grasp of his weak faculties[139], they are slow. As he experiences them, let it be known that one given to faith and one who is temporarily released[140] also experiences the same, because of their weak faculties[141].

The factors of the law-follower[142] are without affliction [827c] and quickly[143] perceived: the pure[144] factors[145] of the law-

131 *anāgamyadhyāna*. Ms. XI 17 has 地: *bhūmi*, not 禅: *dhyāna*.
132 *pratipad*.
133 Ms. XI 18: 非, not 不速.
134 Unpleasant path: *duḥkhāpratipad*.
Pleasant path: *sukhāpratipad*.
With quick comprehension: *kṣiprābhijñā*.
135 *śraddhānusārin*. cf. stanza 106.
136 *dhandha*.
137 *anāsrava*.
138 *dharmāḥ*.
139 *mṛdvindriya*.
140 *śraddhādhimukta* and *samayavimukta*. See stanza 108 and 114.
141 See note 139.
142 *dharmānusārin*. See stanza 106.
143 *kṣipra*.
144 See note 137.
145 See note 138.

follower[146], in the grasp of his keen faculties[147], are quick. As he experiences them, let it be known that one who has attained correct views and one who is finally released[148] also experience the same, because of their keen faculties[149].

> (187) Let it be known that in the stages of the fundamental trances another term used for them is pleasant perceptions. Because they are small and hard to obtain, the rest are all unpleasant perceptions.

Let it be known that in the stages of the fundamental trances[150] another term used for them is pleasant perceptions: the factors of the keen faculties [151] and of the weak faculties [152] in the fundamental four trances are called the pleasant path. Why? Because of the well-balanced path[153] of quietude and insight[154], and because of the pleasant going.

Because they are small and hard to obtain, the rest are all unpleasant perceptions: that which is pure[155], comprised within the other stages, are unpleasant perceptions. Why? Because they are small. The path of quietude[156] in the pre-trance and in the intermediate trance[157] is narrow. In formlessness, insight[158] is shallow. Therefore they are very unpleasant. Because they are very hard to obtain and small, they are called unpleasant.

Question: The World-Honored One has expounded four perfect faiths[159]: perfect faith in Buddha, perfect faith in the law, in the *saṃgha*, and in noble morality[160]. What about these?

---

[146] See note 142.
[147] *tīkṣṇendriya*.
[148] *dṛṣṭiprāpta* and *asamayavimukta*. See stanzas 108 and 115.
[149] See note 147.
[150] *mauladhyāna*.
[151] See note 147.
[152] See note 139.
[153] Ms. XII 6, and the 3 editions: 等道.
[154] *śamatha* and *vipaśyanā*.
[155] See note 137.
[156] *śamatha*.
[157] *anāgamyadhyāna* and *dhyànāntara*.
[158] *vipaśyanā*.
[159] *avetyaprasāda*. Chinese: unspoilt purity. 不坏: *abhedya*.
[160] *avetyaprasāda* in: *Buddha*, *dharma*, *saṃgha* and *āryaśīla*.

Answer: (188) Pure and stainless faith in the factors of the self-awakened and of the disciple, in deliverance and in the remaining causality, and noble morality have attained certainty.

Pure and stainless faith[161] in the factors[162] of the self-awakened and of the disciple[163], in deliverance and in the remaining causality: self-awakened is the Buddha. That buddhahood is comprised within the fruition of being without attachment[164]. The qualities[165] of one who has no more training to do[166] are the factors[167] of a Buddha. When one has pure[168] faith[169] in these factors[170], it is called perfect faith in Buddha[171]. Having taken up the realization of that which is right[172], one is a disciple[173]. The qualities[174] of one in training[175] and of one who has no more training to do[176] are said to be the factors[177] of a disciple. When one has pure faith in these factors, it is called perfect faith in the *saṃgha*[178]. Pure faith in *nirvāṇa*[179] and faith in the remaining formed factors, such as the truth of suffering and the truth of origination[180], faith in the pure qualities[181] of the bodhisattva, and faith in the factors[182] of the *pratyekabuddha* who is in training[183]

---

161 *śraddhā*.
162 See note 138.
163 *śrāvaka*.
164 *arhattvaphala*.
165 *guṇa*.
166 *aśaikṣa*.
167 See note 138.
168 See note 137.
169 See note 161.
170 See note 138.
171 *buddhe'vetyaprasāda*.
172 正证. AH2 861c has 正决定, a translation for *samyaktvaniyāma*. cf. chapter V, note 96.
173 See note 163.
174 See note 165.
175 *śaikṣa*.
176 See note 166.
177 See note 138.
178 *saṃghe'vetyaprasāda*.
179 i.e. nirodhasatya.
180 *duḥkhe*° and *samudayasatya*.
181 See note 165.
182 See note 138.

or who has no more training to do[184], this is called perfect faith in the law[185].

Noble morality[186] is pure[187] morality. This is called perfect faith in morality[188].

Question: Why are the perfect faiths only pure[189], not impure?

Answer: They have attained certainty[190]. They are certain because they are produced by right vision. Pure[191] faith and pure morality are sure to be pure, but impure faith is spoilt by disbelief, and impure morality is spoilt by immorality[192]. Therefore they are not certain. That which is pure[193] reaches the later life unspoilt. Because[194] they are certain, the perfect faiths are exclusively pure.

Question: The World-Honored One has said that there are four ways of developing concentration[195]. There is the developing of concentration which obtains a happy state[196] in the visible world[197]. There is the developing of concentration which obtains knowledge and vision[198]. There is the developing of concentration which distinguishes wisdom[199]. There is the developing of concentration which obtains extinction of the outflows[200]. Which are their characteristics?

---

[183] *śaikṣa.*
[184] See note 166.
[185] *dharme'vetyaprasāda.*
[186] *āryaśīla.*
[187] See note 137.
[188] *śīle'vetyaprasāda.*
[189] See note 137.
[190] *niyata.*
[191] See note 137.
[192] *duḥśīla.*
[193] *anāsrava.*
[194] Ms. XII 18-19 reads: 是决定故.
[195] *samādhibhāvanā.*
[196] *sukhavihāra.*
[197] *dṛṣṭadharma.*
[198] *jñānadarśana.* Ms.XII 20 reads 智: *jñāna.*
[199] *prajñāprabheda.*
[200] *āsravakṣaya.* The Ms. XII 20 does not have 得. It reads: "…the *samādhibhāvanā* through which the *āsravas* are extinguished."

Answer: (189) When the first trance is wholesome, they say the visible world is happy. [828a] When one knows birth and death, this is called knowledge[201] and vision.

When the first trance is wholesome[202], they say the visible world[203] is happy: in the clean and in the pure first trance[204] one can obtain a happy state[205] in the visible world.

When one knows birth and death, this is called knowledge[206] and vision: the superknowledge which is knowledge of birth and death[207] is said to be the knowledge[208] and vision of the developing of concentration. Together[209] they rely on the five aggregates[210].

> (190) Let it be known that the distinctions of wisdom are the qualities obtained after seeking. The diamond-like fourth trance is called extinction of the outflows.

Let it be known that the distinctions of wisdom[211] are the qualities[212] obtained after seeking[213]: qualities produced by application[214] are called: the restraint of the realm of desire[215], the qualities through learning, reflection, and development[216], all wholesome factors in the realms of form and of formlessness,

---

[201] Ms. XII 21: 智.
[202] *kuśala.*
[203] See note 197.
[204] *śuddhaka* and *anāsrava* first *dhyāna.*
[205] See note 196.
[206] Ms. XIII 3: 智.
[207] *cyutyupapādajñāna* (智); *abhijñā* (通), also called *divyacakṣus.* See stanza 156; *Kośa* VII 100.
[208] See note 206.
[209] i.e. both *samādhibhāvanās*, developing concentration.
[210] *skandha.*
[211] See note 199.
[212] See note 165.
[213] *prayoga.* See stanza 163c.
[214] See note 213.
[215] See stanza 40d.
[216] *śrutamaya, cintāmaya, bhāvanāmaya.*

and all pure formed[217] factors. They are all wisdom distinguished through the developing of concentration.

The diamond-like[218] fourth trance is called extinction of the outflows[219]: diamond-like is called that which is associated with and exists with the last thought of one in training[220]. Comprised within the fourth trance, it is called extinction of the outflows through the developing of concentration. What does this[221] mean? This is explained by the Tathāgata himself[222].

Question: The World-Honored One has explained four bases of psychic power, four right rejections, and four applications of mindfulness[223]. Their characteristics must also be explained.

Answer: (191) The wholesome formed factors which are produced by application, Buddha calls them bases of psychic power. They are also seen as right mental rejections.

The wholesome formed factors[224] which are produced[225] by application[226], Buddha calls them bases of psychic power[227]: that which is produced by application agrees with the previous explanation of wisdom distinguished through the developing of concentration[228]. They are all bases of psychic power, because they are capacities reached as one wishes.

---

[217] Pure: *anāsrava*; formed: *saṃskṛta*.
[218] *vajropama*. cf. stanza 113.
[219] *āsravakṣaya*.
[220] *śaikṣacitta*.
[221] Ms. XIII 8 has 此.
[222] i.e. the Buddha, a *bodhisattva* at the time, obtained *āsravakṣaya* in the *vajropamasamādhi* on the basis of the fourth *dhyāna*. See *Kośa* VI 177, II 206 and VII 195.
[223] *ṛddhipāda*, *samyakprahāṇa*, *smṛtyupasthāna*.
[224] Wholesome (*kuśala*) formed (*saṃskṛta*) *dharmas*.
[225] 等: *sam*°.
[226] *prayoga*.
[227] *ṛddhipāda*.
[228] Stanza 190ab.

They are also seen as right mental rejections[229]: i.e. all these qualities[230] are called right rejections.

> (192) They are also applications of mindfulness. The same applies to the four noble attitudes. It is explained by the noble that they are namely produced by a power to which they are indebted.

They are also applications of mindfulness[231]: i.e. these factors are also called applications of mindfulness.

Question: The World-Honored One has expounded four noble attitudes[232]. What about these?

Answer: The same applies to the four noble attitudes. I.e. these factors are also called four noble attitudes.

Question: Why are all these qualities called applications of mindfulness, right rejection, bases of psychic power, and noble attitudes[233]?

Answer: It is explained by the noble that they are namely produced by a power to which they are indebted. I.e. because these factors are produced by the power to which they are indebted, viz. concentration, because one dwells [234] in concentration [235], they are called bases of psychic power [236]. Because they are produced by the power to which they are indebted, viz. vigorous pursuit [237], they are called right rejections[238]. Because they are produced by the power to which they are indebted, viz. mindfulness [239], they are called

---

[229] *samyakprahāṇa*.
[230] See note 228.
[231] *smṛtyupasthāna*.
[232] *āryavaṃśa*. Chinese: noble seed.
[233] *smṛtyupasthāna*, *samyakprahāṇa*, *ṛddhipāda*, *āryavaṃśa*.
[234] Ms. XIII 16: 住故.
[235] *samādhi*.
[236] See note 227.
[237] *vīrya*.
[238] See note 229.
[239] *smṛti*.

applications of mindfulness[240]. Because they are produced by the power to which they are indebted, viz. little desire and contentment[241], they are called noble attitudes[242].

We have distinctly established the elements which collectively contribute to awakenment[243]. Their particular characteristics will now be explained.

> [828b] (193) These factors are called the elements which contribute to awakenment: pure faith, vigorous pursuit, mindfulness, joy, wisdom, the (member of) enlightenment repose [244], evenmindedness, intention, morality, and concentration.

Only these ten factors are called elements which contribute to awakenment[245]. Among them, faith is the faculty faith and the power faith[246]. Vigorous pursuit is the four right rejections, the faculty vigorous pursuit, the power vigorous pursuit, the member of enlightenment vigorous pursuit, and right exertion [247]. Mindfulness is the faculty mindfulness, the power mindfulness, the member of enlightenment mindfulness, and right mindfulness[248]. Joy is the member of enlightenment joy[249]. Wisdom is the four applications of mindfulness, the faculty wisdom, the power wisdom, the member of enlightenment investigation of the factors, and the right view[250]. Repose is the member of enlightenment repose[251]. Evenmindedness is the

---

[240] See note 231.
[241] *alpecchatā* and *saṃtuṣṭi*.
[242] See note 232.
[243] *bodhipākṣika*.
AH2 862b: 助菩提分 confuses *pakkhiya* and *bhāgīya*.
[244] Ms. XIII 19: 猗.
[245] See note 243.
[246] *śraddhā*: *śraddhendriya*, *śraddhābala*.
[247] vīrya: 4 *samyakprahāṇas*, *vīryendriya*, *vīryabala*, *vīryasaṃbodhyaṅga*, *samyagvyāyāma*.
[248] *smṛti*: *smṛtīndriya*, *smṛtibala*, *smṛtisaṃbodhyaṅga*, *samyaksmṛti*.
[249] *prīti*: *prītisaṃbodhyaṅga*.
[250] *prajñā*: 4 *smṛtyupasthānas*, *prajñendriya*, *prajñābala*, *dharmapravicayasaṃbodhyaṅga*, *samyagdṛṣṭi*.
[251] *praśrabdhi*: *praśrabdhisaṃbodhyaṅga*.

member of enlightenment evenmindedness[252]. Intention is right intention[253]. Morality is right speech, right action, and right livelihood[254]. Concentration is the four bases of psychic power, the faculty concentration, the power concentration, the member of enlightenment concentration, and right concentration[255].

Question: Why are these factors distinguished into so many kinds?

Answer: (194) (Because of) application, exertion, undivided attention, weak and keen faculties, the path of vision, and the path of development, Buddha has mentioned thirty-seven.

Application[256]: because right mindfulness[257] is established in relation to an object[258], he has mentioned the applications of mindfulness[259].
Exertion[260]: because of right exertion[261] he has mentioned right rejections[262].

Undivided attention[263]: because one has established undivided attention, he has mentioned the bases of psychic power[264].

Weak[265]: because a weak mind is obtained, he has mentioned the faculties[266].

---

252 *upekṣā*: *upekṣāsaṃbodhyaṅga*.
253 *saṃkalpa*: *samyaksaṃkalpa*.
254 *śīla*: *samyagvāc*, *samyakkarmānta*, *samygājīva*.
255 *samādhi*: 4 *ṛddhipādas*, *samādhīndriya*, *samādhibala*, *samādhisaṃbodhyaṅga*, *samyaksamādhi*.
256 *upasthāna*.
257 *samyaksmṛti*.
258 *ālambana*.
259 *smṛtyupasthāna*.
260 *vyāyāma*.
261 *samyagvyāyāma*.
262 *samyakprahāṇa*.
263 *cittaikāgratā*, *samādhi*.
264 *ṛddhipāda*.
265 The Ms. XIV 7: 濡钝者 (*mṛdu*).
266 *indriya*.

Keen faculties[267]: because a mind with keen faculties is obtained, he has mentioned the powers[268].

Path of vision[269]: because the path of vision is obtained, he has mentioned the members of the path[270].

Path of development[271]: because the path of development is obtained, he has mentioned the members of enlightenment[272].

It is namely because he has distinguished their effectiveness[273] that Buddha has mentioned thirty-seven. Because of their effectiveness these ten factors are said by Buddha to be thirty-seven.

Question: Within which stages are these elements contributing to awakenment comprised?

Answer: (195) The second trance and the pre-trance are said to contain thirty-six. The third one and the fourth one contain thirty-five. The same applies to the intermediate trance.

The second trance and the pre-trance[274] are said to contain thirty-six: in the second trance there is no right intention[275], and in the pre-trance there is no member of enlightenment joy[276], but the rest are there.

The third one and the fourth one contain thirty-five. The same applies to the intermediate trance[277]: in the third and in the fourth trances, and in the intermediate trance there is no member

---

[267] *tīkṣṇendriya.*
[268] *bala.*
[269] *darśanamārga.*
[270] *mārgāṅga.*
[271] *bhāvanāmārga.*
[272] *saṃbodhyaṅga.*
[273] cf. AH2 862c: 业 may translate *karaṇa.*
[274] *anāgamya.*
[275] *samyaksaṃkalpa.*
[276] *prītisaṃbodhyaṅga.*
[277] *dhyānāntara.*

of enlightenment joy[278], and there is no right intention[279], but the rest are there.

> (196) The first (trance) is said to contain all. Three emptinesses contain thirty-one. The supreme (stage) contains twenty-one. The realm of desire contains twenty-two.

The first (trance) is said to contain all: the first trance has all thirty-seven.

Three emptinesses[280] contain thirty-one: in three emptinesses there are thirty-one. Joy, right intention, right speech, right action, right livelihood, [828c] and application of mindfulness to the body[281] are not there, but the rest are there.

The supreme (stage) contains twenty-one: in the sphere of neither-perception-nor-non-perception[282] these are absent: the seven (members of) enlightenment, the eight (members of the) path, and application of mindfulness to the body[283].

The realm of desire contains twenty-two: they are all there except for the members of enlightenment and the members of the path[284].

Question: The World-Honored One has expounded four foods[285]: solid food, the food of contact, the food of volition, and the food of consciousness[286]. Which are their characteristics[287]?

---

[278] See note 276.
[279] See note 275.
[280] i.e. 3 *ārūpyas*.
[281] *prīti* (saṃbodhyaṅga), *samyaksaṃkalpa*, *samyagvāc*, *samyakkarmānta*, *samyagājīva*, *kāyasmṛtyupasthāna*.
[282] *naivasaṃjñānāsaṃjñāyatana*.
[283] 7 *saṃbodhyaṅgas*, 8 *mārgāṅgas*, *kāyasmṛtyupasthāna*.
[284] 7 *saṃbodhyaṅgas*, 8 *mārgāṅgas*.
[285] *āhāra*.
[286] *kavaḍīkārāhāra*,*sparśāhāra*,*manaḥsaṃcetanāhāra*,*vijñānāhāra*.
[287] Ms. XIV 18: 相.

Answer: (197) Among the foods, solid food is of three kinds in the realm of desire. When consciousness, volition, and contact are namely impure, they are foods.

Among the foods, solid food[288] is of three kinds in the realm of desire: solid food in the realm of desire is of three kinds: smell, taste, and the tactile[289]. Because they do away with hunger and thirst, they are called food.

When consciousness, volition, and contact[290] are namely impure[291], they are foods: impure consciousness, impure volition, and impure contact are called foods.

What does this mean? Because the series of later lives is not interrupted, they are called foods.

Question: The World-Honored One has expounded three *samādhis*: of emptiness, of aimlessness, and of the signless[292]. How do these *samādhis* proceed, and in how many aspects[293]?

Answer: (198) The one of aimlessness has ten aspects. The concentration of emptiness has two aspects. The concentration of the signless[294] is said to have four aspects from among the noble aspects.

The one of aimlessness[295] has ten aspects: the *samādhi* of aimlessness proceeds within ten aspects: the aspect impermanence, the aspect suffering, the four aspects of the truth of origination, and the four aspects of the truth of the path[296].

---

[288] *kavaḍīkārāhāra*.
[289] *gandha*, *rasa*, *spraṣṭavya*.
[290] *vijñāna*, *saṃcetanā*, *sparśa*.
[291] *sāsrava*.
[292] *śūnyatā*°, *apraṇihita*°, *ānimittasamādhi*.
[293] *ākāra*. The 16 *ākāras*: see stanza 101, and chapter V, note 29.
[294] The 3 editions: 相.
[295] *apraṇihita*.
[296] *anitya*; *duḥkha*; 4 of the *samudayasatya*; 4 of the *mārgasatya*.

The concentration of emptiness[297] has two aspects: the *samādhi* of emptiness[298] has two aspects: the aspects emptiness and selflessness[299].

The concentration of the signless[300] is said to have four aspects from among the noble aspects: the *samādhi* of the signless has the four aspects of the truth of cessation[301].

Question: The World-Honored One has expounded four perversities[302]: perversity of thought, perversity of notion and perversity of view[303], having the notion of permanence[304] in relation to that which is impermanent; perversity of thought, perversity of notion, and perversity of view, having the notion of happiness[305] in relation to that which is painful, having the notion of purity[306] in relation to that which is impure, and having the notion of a self[307] in relation to that which is selfless. By means of which vision are they abandoned? What is their nature?

Answer: (199) Know that four kinds, which are to be abandoned through the vision of suffering[308], are the perversities! They have the nature of three views. It is said that the rejection of the views is brought about through the right view.

Know that four kinds, which are to be abandoned through the vision of suffering[309], are the perversities!: all four perversities are to be abandoned through the vision of suffering, because they proceed within that in which suffering dwells.

---

297 *śūnyatāsamādhi*.
298 *śūnyatāsamādhi*.
299 *śūnya; anātmaka*.
300 *ānimittasamādhi*.
301 4 of the *nirodhasatya*.
302 *viparyāsa*.
303 *citta°*, *saṃjñā°*, *dṛṣṭiviparyāsa*.
304 *nitya°*.
305 *sukha°*.
306 *śubha°*.
307 *ātma°*.
308 *duḥkhadarśanaheya*.
309 See note 308.

They have the nature of three views[310]. It is said that the rejection of the views is brought about through the right view[311]: the perversities are views by nature. That which is supreme in three views is called perversity. The view of individuality[312] is said to be a view of a self[313], because one sees a self. In the view of extremes[314], one sees eternity and annihilation[315]. In evil adherence to wrong views[316], that which is not pure[317] is seen as pure. They all proceed within that in which suffering dwells, and they have the nature of views. Because the thoughts, notions, and views create confusion, they are called perversity of thought, perversity of notion, and perversity of view[318], [829a] but it is not the case that they are perversities by nature.

Question: The World-Honored One has mentioned many views: sixty-two [319] views [320], etc. Within which views are they comprised?

---

[310] *dṛṣṭi*. For the *dṛṣṭis*: see stanza 71.
[311] *samyagdṛṣṭi*.
[312] *satkāyadṛṣṭi*.
[313] *ātmadṛṣṭi*.
[314] *antagrāhadṛṣṭi*.
[315] *śāśvata* and *uccheda*.
[316] *dṛṣṭiparāmarśa*.
[317] *aśubha*.
[318] See note 303.
[319] *dvāṣaṣṭidṛṣṭi*. Also mentioned in AH2 863b. Not in MAH 939b.
The *Brahmajālasuttanta*, the first text of the *Dīghanikāya*, and the *pañcattayasutta* of the *Majjhimanikāya*, are expositions of the 62 heretical views. These views are concerned with the question of the personality. Some (44) are concerned with the future, and some (18) with the past. The *Majjhimanikāya*, ed. R. Chalmers, II, London 1951, pp. 228 and 233, says: "*Santi...eke sāmaṇabrāhmaṇā aparantakappikā aparantānudiṭṭhino... Santi...eke sāmaṇabrāhmaṇā pubbantakappikā pubbantānudiṭṭhino...*". I.B. Horner, *The Middle Length Sayings*, III, London 1959, pp. 15 and 19, translates: "There are...some recluses and brahmans who, conjecturing about the future, speculating about the future,...There are...some recluses and brahmans who, conjecturing about the past, speculating about the past...". The Chinese *Dīrghāgama* 长阿含经 *Chang'ehanjing*, T. 1, 21 梵动经 *fandongjing* p. 89c, uses the words 本劫 (kalpa) 本见 and 末劫末見.
See also *Kośa* IX 265 note 1, and T. 21: 佛说梵纲六十二见.
Foshuofanwang (Brahmajāla) liushierjian (*dvāṣaṣṭidṛṣṭi*)jing translated by Zhi Qian: 支谦.
[320] Ms. XV 15 adds 见为 after 二.

Answer: All views are comprised within the five views[321]: the view of individuality[322], etc.
Question: How is it that one may know this?

Answer: (200) Denying that which is real, this is said to be the wrong view. Although it is not real, yet seeing it as real, this is two views and a knowledge.

Denying[323] that which is real, this is said to be the wrong view[324]: i.e. when a view denies a real factor, (saying) that it does not exist, e.g. saying that there is no giving, no fasting[325], and no holy writ[326], all this is called the wrong view.

Although it is not real, yet seeing it as real, this is two views and a knowledge: the self, which is not real in the five aggregates[327], is seen as self. When seeing it as real[328], this view is called the view of individuality[329]. Seeing happiness and purity[330] which are not real as happy and pure, this view is evil adherence to wrong views[331], and the rest is wrong knowledge[332], to be abandoned through development[333], e.g. seeing something at night and thinking it is a thief, or a standing tree which has the appearance of a man.

(201) The view of purity, i.e. attachment to mere rules and ritual, sees that which is not a cause as a cause. It is said that the view of holding on to extremes is based on annihilation and eternity.

---

321 See note 310.
322 See note 312.
323 *apavad°*.
324 *mithyādṛṣṭi*.
325 The Ms. XV 18 and the 3 editions: 斋.
326 *dāna*; *poṣadha*; *pravacana*.
327 *skandha*.
328 The Ms. XV 20 and the 3 editions read: 有实是.
329 See note 312.
330 *śubha*.
331 See note 316.
332 *mithyājñāna*.
333 *bhāvanāheya*.

The view of purity[334], i.e. attachment to mere rules and ritual[335], sees that which is not a cause as a cause[336]: i.e. when one factor is not a cause for another factor, but is seen as its cause, this view is attachment to mere rules and ritual[337], e.g. when trying to reach deliverance through ascetic practice[338].

It is said that the view of holding on to extremes[339] is based on annihilation and eternity[340]: i.e. when, seeing impermanent things, one sees them as permanent, this is called the view of eternity[341]. When one is unaware of the continuity of causes and conditions[342], and[343] sees annihilation, this is called the view of annihilation[344]. They are called the view of extremes[345].

> (202) When the ones which establish and the ones which deny, the one in causality and the one which is based on two extremes proceed within something, they are to be abandoned through right vision.

The ones which establish[346] and the ones which deny[347]: it is said that when the wrong view[348] denies suffering[349], it is to be abandoned through the vision of suffering. When it denies origination, it is to be abandoned through the vision of origination. When it denies cessation, it is to be abandoned through the vision of cessation. When it denies the path, it is to be abandoned through the vision of the path[350]. The view of

---

[334] *śuddhidṛṣṭi.*
[335] *śīlavrataparāmarśa.*
[336] *hetu.*
[337] See note 335.
[338] 苦行 may translate *tapas.*
[339] *antagrāha.*
[340] *uccheda* and *śāśvata.*
[341] *śāśvatadṛṣṭi.*
[342] *hetupratyaya.*
[343] Ms. XVI 5: 以, not 已.
[344] *ucchedadṛṣṭi.*
[345] See note 314.
[346] *satkāyadṛṣṭi* and *dṛṣṭiparāmarśa.* See stanza 200cd.
[347] *mithyādṛṣṭi.* See stanza 200ab.
[348] See note 324.
[349] duḥkha°.
[350] i.e. *duḥkha°*, *samudaya°*, *nirodha°*, *mārgadarśanaheya.*

individuality[351] establishes in relation to a painful self that it is a self. It is to be abandoned through the vision of suffering. Evil adherence to wrong views [352] establishes suffering to be happiness. It is to be abandoned through the vision of suffering. In the case of origination, it is to be abandoned through the vision of origination. In the case of cessation, it is to be abandoned through the vision of cessation. Because it does not experience that which is right, it is to be abandoned through the vision of cessation, and the same applies to the path[353].

When attachment to mere rules and ritual[354] proceeds within something impure[355], it is to be abandoned through the vision of suffering. When it proceeds within something pure[356], it is to be abandoned through the vision of the path[357].

The one which sees annihilation and believes in eternity[358], this one also is to be abandoned through the vision of suffering. In relation to the five aggregates, which are visible[359], one holds (the view of) annihilation and believes in eternity, not in relation to that which is invisible.

Here we have distinctly established all views.

Question: The World-Honored One has expounded twenty-two faculties[360]. What about these?

Answer: [829b] (203) The noble have explained that the elements in relation to the internal, the three of the body and the faculty life, that these faculties are the basis of birth and death.

---

[351] See note 312.
[352] *dṛṣṭiparāmarśa.*
[353] i.e. *duḥkha°*, *samudaya°*, *nirodha°*, *mārgadarśanaheya.*
[354] See note 335.
[355] *sāsrava.*
[356] *anāsrava.*
[357] i.e. *duḥkha°*, *mārgadarśanaheya.*
[358] See note 340.
[359] cf. stanza 73.
[360] *indriya.* See notes 283-284-285-290-292-295-296-298.

The elements in relation to the internal[361]: eye, ear, nose, tongue[362], and mind[363].

The three of the body: the three kinds of faculties of the body: the faculty body, the male faculty, and the female faculty[364].

And the faculty life[365]: the faculty life is the ninth.

The noble have explained that these faculties are the basis[366] of birth and death: because these nine faculties are the basis of birth and death, they are called faculties. It is the nature[357] of beings to be born and to die.

> (204) From the feelings come all afflictions. Faith, etc. are based on purity. Nine faculties, viz. the pure ones, number three and depend on a path.

From the feelings[368] come all afflictions[369]: the faculty happiness, the faculty suffering, the faculty gladness, the faculty sadness, and the faculty evenmindedness[370] are called[371] feelings. They are called faculties because all afflictions come from them.
Faith, etc. are based on purity: the faculty faith, and the faculties vigorous pursuit, mindfulness, concentration, and wisdom[372] are called faculties because one is delivered through them.

Nine faculties, viz. the pure ones, number three and depend on a path: the five faculties: faith, etc., the three feelings[373] and the

---

[361] *ādhyātmika*.
[362] The Ms. XVI 16 adds *kāya*, body, after *jihvā*, tongue. The Ms. is mistaken because *kāyendriya* is mentioned as one of the three faculties of the body. See note 364.
[363] *cakṣus*, *śrotra*, *ghrāṇa*, *jihvā*, *manas*.
[364] kāyendriya, *puruṣendriya*, *strīndriya*.
[365] *jīvitendriya*.
[366] *āśraya*.
[367] Ms. XVI 18: 相: *lakṣaṇa*.
[368] *vedanā*.
[369] *kleśa*.
[370] The *indriyas*: *sukha*, *duḥkha*, *saumanasya*, *daurmanasya*, *upekṣā*.
[371] The Ms. XVI 19: 说.
[372] The *indriyas*: *śraddhā*, *vīrya*, *smṛti*, *samādhi*, *prajñā*.
[373] See note 368.

faculty mind[374] are called faculties because, when pure[375], they depend on a path. The ones which are comprised within the path of the faith-follower and of the law-follower[376], are the faculty "I shall come to understand the not yet understood"[377]. The ones which are comprised within the path of development, are the faculty of understanding[378]. The ones which are comprised within the path without training[379], are the faculty of one who has fully understood[380].

Question: How many among them are tied to the realm of desire? How many are tied to the realm of form? How many are tied to the realm of formlessness?

Answer: (205) In the realm of desire there are four. Eight are wholesome. The material ones number seven by nature. The ones which constitute thought's concomitants number ten. The wise explain that one is thought.

In the realm of desire there are four: the male faculty, the female faculty, the faculty suffering, and the faculty sadness are tied only to the realm of desire[381]. The other faculties[382] are as explained in the chapter: Elements[383].

Eight are wholesome: the five faculties: faith, etc., and the three pure faculties[384].

---

[374] *śraddhā*, *vīrya*, *smṛti*, *samādhi*, *prajñā*; *sukha*, *saumanasya*, *upekṣā* (AH2 864a); *manas*.
[375] See note 356.
[376] *śraddhānusārin, dharmānusārin*. Their path is the *darśanamārga* (cf. stanza 106).
[377] anājñātam ājñāsyāmīndriya. cf. stanza 118.
[378] *ājñendriya*. cf. stanza 118.
[379] aśaikṣamārga.
[380] *ājñātāvīndriya*. cf. stanza 119.
[381] The *indriyas*: *puruṣa*°, *strī*°, *duḥkha*°, *daurmanasya*° are in the *kāmadhātu*.
[382] Ms. XVII 7: 根.
[383] Stanza 11.
[384] *kuśala*: *śraddhā*, *vīrya*, *smṛti*, *samādhi*, *prajñā*, and the 3 *anāsrava* ones: *anājñātam ājñāsyāmīndriya*, *ājñendriya*, and *ājñātāvīndriya*.
The Ms. XVII 7 reads: 无漏根.

The material ones number seven by nature: the material faculties number seven: the five faculties with form, the male faculty, and the female faculty[385]. The rest are not material.

Question: How many are thought by nature? How many constitute thought's concomitants[386] by nature? How many are neither thought by nature nor thought's concomitants by nature?

Answer: The ones which constitute thought's concomitants number ten: the five faculties: faith, etc., and the five feelings[387]. The wise explain that one is thought: the faculty mind[388].

The other faculties are neither thought by nature nor thought's concomitants by nature.

Question: How many are with retribution, and how many are without retribution[389]?

Answer: (206) It is explained by the wise that one and ten possess retribution. Those who see what is true, have distinctly established that thirteen are retribution.

One: the faculty sadness possesses retribution only[390], because it is only wholesome or unwholesome[391]. It is produced[392] through application [393] in the present. It is not produced through retribution [394]. It neither relates to deportment nor to craftsmanship[395]. Therefore, as it is not [829c] indeterminate, it possesses retribution only.

---

385 *cakṣus*, *śrotra*, *ghrāṇa*, *jihvā*, *kāya*, and also *puruṣa* and *strī*.
386 *caitasika*.
387 *śraddhā*, *vīrya*, *smṛti*, *samādhi*, *prajñā*, and also the 5 *vedanās*: *sukha*, *duḥkha*, *saumanasya*, *daurmanasya*, *upekṣā*.
388 *manas*.
389 *savipāka* and *avipāka*.
390 Ms. XVII 11: 一向. See also AH2 864b.
391 *daurmanasyendriya* is *savipāka*, because it is *kuśala* or *akuśala*, not *avyākṛta*.
392 Ms. XVII 11: 生, not 起.
393 *prayoga*.
394 *vipākaja*.
395 Neither *airyāpathika* nor *śailpasthānika*, which are *avyākṛta*.

It is explained by the wise that ten possess retribution: the five faculties: faith, etc., possess retribution when they are impure, and they do not possess retribution when they are pure[396]. The faculty mind and the three feelings[397] do not possess retribution when they are indeterminate and when they are pure. Otherwise, when they are wholesome or unwholesome, they possess retribution. The faculty suffering[398] does not possess retribution when it is indeterminate. Otherwise it possesses retribution.

Question: How many are retribution, and how many are not retribution?

Answer: Those who see what is true, have distinctly established that thirteen are retribution: thirteen faculties are either retribution by nature or not. Because the indeterminate factors: the seven material faculties, the faculty life, the faculty mind, and the four feelings[399], are produced by that which is wholesome or unwholesome, they are retribution.

Question: How many faculties soon at birth are obtained as retribution?

Answer: (207) Scil. two or six, seven, or eight can be obtained at the first moment. In desire they are characterized by retribution. Further on six and higher-up one (can be obtained).

Scil. two or six, seven, or eight can be obtained at the first moment: i.e. one achieves the (other) faculties gradually. When egg-born, moisture-born, or born from the womb[400], it is the case

---

[396] *śraddhā*, *vīrya*, *smṛti*, *samādhi*, *prajñā*: *savipāka* when *sāsrava*, *avipāka* when *anāsrava*.
[397] *manas*, and the 3 *vedanās*: *sukha*, *saumanasya*, *upekṣā*.
[398] *duḥkhendriya*.
[399] 7 material faculties: *cakṣus*, *śrotra*, *ghrāna*, *jihvā*, *kāya*, *puruṣa*, *strī*; *jīvita*; *manas*; 4 *vedanās*: *sukha*, *saumanasya*, *duḥkha*, *upekṣā* (cf. AH2 864c). MAH 940c: *jīvitendriya* is always *vipāka*. The other 12 are either *vipāka* or not. The same in *Kośa* II 124 ff.
[400] *aṇḍaja*, *saṃsvedaja*, *jarāyuja*.

that in the first moment two faculties come into existence: the faculty body and the faculty life[401]. When they have no distinctive mark[402], the apparitionally born[403] obtain six faculties: five material faculties and the faculty life[404]. When they have one distinctive mark: seven[405], and when they have the two distinctive marks: eight[406].

In desire they are characterized[407] by retribution: they are said to be only for the beings in the realm of desire.

Further on six and higher-up one: in the realm of form one first obtains six faculties[408], and in formlessness one faculty[409].
The other (faculties) are at that moment only defiled[410] thoughts. Therefore they are only obtained after defilement. As factors which constitute thought and its concomitants, they are not retribution[411].

Question: How many faculties are finally lost when life ends?

Answer: (208) Four are lost, or one loses eight, nine, or ten, when at the moment of death one is gradually extinguished. When losing them in a wholesome way, all are increased with five.

Four are lost, or one loses eight, nine, or ten, when at the moment of death one is gradually extinguished[412]: at a gradual ending of life and with indeterminate thoughts one finally loses

---

[401] *kāya*, *jīvita*.
[402] *vyañjana*. i.e. when they are sexless.
[403] *upapāduka*, e.g. gods, the beings in hell, the beings of the intermediate existence (*antarābhava*). Cf. *Kośa* III 27-28.
[404] *cakṣus, śrotra, ghrāṇa, jihvā, kāya, and jīvita.*
[405] Plus *strī*, or *puruṣa*.
[406] The 6 plus *strī* and *puruṣa*.
[407] 相. See stanza c.
[408] cf. note 404.
[409] The 6 minus the 5 material faculties. Only *jīvita* remains. cf. note 404.
[410] *kliṣṭa*.
[411] cf. *Kośa* II 132 and III 118.
[412] In AH2 864c and in MAH 940c the third verse reads: "when dying gradually and when perishing suddenly."
See also *Kośa* II 133.

four faculties: the faculties body, mind, life, and evenmindedness[413]. When the life of one who has no distinctive mark[414] ends suddenly and with indeterminate thoughts, he loses eight faculties. One who has one distinctive mark (loses) nine, and one who has two distinctive marks (loses) ten[415].

When losing them in a wholesome way, all are increased with five: when they have wholesome thoughts, one must add the five faculties: faith, etc[416]. The same also applies to the realms of form and of formlessness, in accordance with the faculties which may be obtained[417].

Question: How many are to be abandoned through vision? How many are to be abandoned through development? How many are not the object of abandonment[418]?

Answer: (209) Four are to be abandoned through the two and are not the object of abandonment. There are six faculties of two kinds. The three subtle ones are not to be abandoned. It is thought that the rest are to be abandoned through development.

Four are to be abandoned through the two and are not the object of abandonment: four faculties are to be abandoned through

---

[413] *kāya, manas, jīvita, upekṣā.*
[414] See note 402.
[415] a. The sexless: *cakṣus, śrotra, ghrāṇa, jihvā, kāya, jīvita, manas, upekṣā.*
b. One sex: + *strī*, or *puruṣa*.
c. Both sexes: the 8+ *strī*, and *puruṣa*.
See AH2 864c.
[416] When dying with wholesome (*kuśala*) thoughts, 5 more faculties are lost, i.e. *śraddhā, vīrya, smṛti, samādhi, prajñā.*
[417] In the *rūpa*° and in the *ārūpyadhātu* there is only sudden death: see MAH 941a.
*rūpadhātu:* 8 *indriyas* lost when dying with indeterminate (*avyākṛta*) thoughts. Beings there have no distinctive mark. They are sexless. cf. note 415a. Five *indriyas* must be added when dying with wholesome thoughts. cf. note 416.
b. *ārūpyadhātu*: 3 *indriyas* lost, i.e. the 8 minus the 5 material ones. Five *indriyas* must be added when dying with wholesome thoughts. cf. note 416.
[418] *darśanaheya; bhāvanāheya;* litt. having nothing one should abandon.

vision, are to be abandoned through development, and are not the object of abandonment: the faculty mind and three feelings[419].

There are six faculties of two kinds: the five faculties: faith, etc., and the faculty sadness[420].

The three [830a] subtle ones are not to be abandoned: the three pure ones are not to be abandoned[421].
It is thought that the rest are to be abandoned through development: nine faculties are to be abandoned through development: eight: the faculties life, etc.[422], and also the faculty suffering[423].

We have explained the scriptural texts. Some categories will now be explained[424].

Question: The World-Honored One has expounded a group[425] of six consciousnesses: eye-consciousness, ear-, nose-, tongue-, body-, and mind-consciousness[426]. Which factors do these consciousnesses know?

Answer: (210) When they grasp that which is meaningful for the faculties, five kinds of thought-elements are involved. That which experiences all factors is namely the element mind-consciousness.

---

[419] *manas*; *sukha*, *saumanasya*, *upekṣā*. cf. MAH 941a.
[420] According to AH2 865a:
a. *śraddhā*, *vīrya*, *smṛti*, *samādhi*, *prajñā*: *bhāvanāheya*, and not the object of abandonment.
b. *daurmanasya*: *darśana*° and *bhāvanāheya*.
[421] The 3 *anāsrava* faculties (cfr. stanza 204cd) are not the object of abandonment.
[422] *cakṣus*, *śrotra*, *ghrāṇa*, *jihvā*, *kāya*, *puruṣa*, *strī*, *jīvita*.
[423] *duḥkha*.
[424] This sentence occurs only in AH. The different factors which are mentioned in the sūtras have already been explained. In the stanzas which follow, the 3 categories, *paryāya* (门): *vijñāna*, *jñāna*, *anuśaya*, will be explained, i.e. the objective ranges of *vijñāna*, etc.
[425] The Ms. XVIII 14 has 身: *kāya*. See also AH2 865a.
[426] *cakṣus*°, *śrotra*°, *ghrāṇa*°, *jihvā*, *kāya*°, *manovijñāna*.

When they grasp that which is meaningful[427] for the faculties, five kinds of thought-elements[428] are involved: that which is meaningful for the faculties[429] is said to be the five kinds of form. They are known by five consciousnesses. Eye-consciousness knows form, and so forth until body-consciousness which knows the tactile[430].

That which experiences all factors is namely the element mind-consciousness [431] : mind-consciousness knows all factors because[432] it takes all factors as its range.

Question: There are ten factors: the associated and the non-associated of the realm of desire, the associated and the non-associated of the realm of form, the associated and the non-associated of the realm of formlessness, the formed and pure associated and non-associated, and two unformed kinds: wholesome and indeterminate[433] . In relation to these, one must distinguish the knowledges. How many factors do the different knowledges take as their range?

Answer: (211) Let it be known that five factors constitute the range of the knowledge of the law. Subsequent knowledge takes seven, and (the knowledge of) the thoughts of others takes three as its range.

Let it be known that five factors constitute the range of the knowledge of the law[434]: five factors are taken as its range by the knowledge of the law: the associated and the non-associated of the realm of desire, the pure associated and non-associated, and the unformed wholesome ones.

---

[427] *artha*. The ranges, *viṣaya*, of the *indriyas* are meant.
[428] *citta* (i.e. *vijñāna*) *dhātu*.
[429] The Ms. XVIII 16 has 根.
[430] *cakṣurvijñāna* knows *rūpa*...*kāyavijñāna* knows *spraṣṭavya*.
[431] *manovijñāna*.
[432] The Ms. XVIII 18: 故.
[433] (Citta)*saṃprayukta* and *viprayukta* of the *kāmadhātu*, of the *rūpadhātu*, and of the *ārūpyadhātu*, the *anāsrava saṃskṛtadharmas*, both *saṃprayukta* and *viprayukta*, and the *kuśala* and *avyākṛta asaṃskṛtadharmas*. cfr. Kośa VII 44.
[434] *dharmajñāna*: 5 factors as object.

Subsequent knowledge takes seven (as its range)[435]: subsequent knowledge takes seven factors as its range: the associated and the non-associated of the realms of form and of formlessness, the pure associated and non-associated, and the unformed wholesome ones.

(The knowledge of) the thoughts of others takes three as its range[436]: the knowledge of the thoughts of others takes three factors as its range: the associated of (the realms of) desire and of form, and the pure associated.

Answer: (212) The impure knowledge has (all) ten factors. The one of the cause and the one of the effect take six as their ranges. The knowledge of deliverance (takes) one factor, and the one of the path (takes) two (as its range). The remaining ones have[437] nine[438].

The impure knowledge has (all) ten factors: the impure knowledge is conventional knowledge. It has all ten factors as its range, because all factors are its range.

The one of the cause and the one of the effect take six as their ranges: the knowledge of suffering and the knowledge of origination take six factors as their ranges: the associated and the non-associated of the three realms.

The knowledge of deliverance (takes) one factor (as its range): the knowledge of cessation takes one factor as its range: only the unformed wholesome one.

The one of the path (takes) two (as its range): the knowledge of the path takes two factors as its range: the formed and pure associated and non-associated.

---

[435] *anvayajñāna*: 7 factors as object.
[436] *paracittajñāna*: 3 factors as object.
[437] Ms. XIX 6 and 10 read: 余有九.
[438] *saṃvṛtijñāna*: 10; *duḥkha*° and *samudayajñāna*: 6; *nirodhajñāna*: 1; *mārgajñāna*: 2; *kṣaya*° and *anutpādajñāna*: 9.

The remaining ones have[439] nine: the remaining knowledges of extinction and of non-production (each) take nine factors as their ranges, subtracting the unformed indeterminate ones. These are understood by the knowledges.

> [830b] (213) [440] The (urges of a) particular stage are definitely developed by afflictions in their particular stage. The universal ones are (urges), the kinds of which are developed by other categories.

The (urges of a) particular stage are definitely developed[441] by afflictions in their particular stage: the afflictions of the realm of desire are developed by those in the realm of desire. The afflictions of the brahma-world[442] are developed by those in the brahma-world. It must be known that this is the case for all to the sphere of neither-perception-nor-non-perception[443].

The universal ones are (urges), the kinds [444] of which are developed by other categories: both universal [445] and non-universal ones are developed by the afflictions according to their kinds, but the universal ones by other kinds too, e.g. the view of individuality [446] is to be abandoned through the vision of suffering[447], and in this respect it is developed by all urges which are to be abandoned through (the vision of) the truth of suffering[448], but (it is) also (developed) by the universal ones which are to be abandoned through the vision of origination[449]. This is the case up to the faculty life[450], which is to be abandoned through development[451]. It is developed by all (urges[452]) which

---

[439] See note 437.
[440] cf. stanzas 77-78-79.
[441] *anuśerate*, to take *anuśayana*.
[442] i.e. the first *dhyāna*.
[443] *naivasaṃjñānāsaṃjñāyatana*.
[444] *prakāra*.
[445] *sarvatraga*.
[446] *satkāyadṛṣṭi* is *sarvatraga*. cf. stanza 74.
[447] *duḥkhadarśanaheya*.
[448] *duḥkhadarśanaheya*.
[449] *samudayadarśanaheya*.
[450] *jīvitendriya*.
[451] Not in the Ms. XIX 17.
cf. stanza 209d: *bhāvanāheya*.

are to be abandoned through development, and also by the universal (urges).

> (214) When an affliction of the three realms is fixed, it is fixed in the three realms. Let it be known that the same applies to two realms and to one realm.

When an affliction of the three realms is fixed, it is fixed in the three realms: i.e. the factors comprised within the three realms are fixed in the three realms, and are developed there by all urges of the three realms, e.g. the faculty mind[453] is fixed in the three realms and is developed there by all urges.

Let it be known that (the same applies to) two realms: i.e. the factors comprised within two realms are fixed in the two realms and are developed there by all urges of the two realms, according to the realms which may be obtained, e.g. adjusted thinking and discursive thinking[454] are fixed in the realms of desire and of form, and are developed there by all urges of the realms of desire and of form.

The same applies to one realm: i.e. when a factor is fixed in one realm, it is developed there by all urges of that one realm, e.g. the faculty sadness[455] is fixed in the realm of desire and is developed there by all urges of the realm of desire[456].

> (215) The scriptural texts, expounded by Buddha, show all factors. They distinctly establish the three categories: consciousness, knowledge, and the urges.

When it is expounded in the scriptural texts of Buddha that all factors belong to three categories, one must distinguish the category of consciousness, the category of knowledge, and the category of the urges,

---

[452] Not in the *Taishō* edition. Not in the Ms. XIX 17. The 3 editions have 使.
[453] *manas*.
[454] *vitarka* and *vicāra*.
[455] *daurmanasya*.
[456] The 3 editions and the Ms. XX 4 add: 此中欲界.

e.g. that which is meaningful[457] for the five faculties in the existence of desire[458], is known by the six consciousnesses, but in the realm of form by four consciousnesses, subtracting nose-consciousness and tongue-consciousness[459]. Because it is associated or non-associated, it is known by seven knowledges[460]. Because it is of five kinds[461], it is developed by the urges of the realms of desire and of form.

[457] *artha*, scil. the object or objective range: 境界.
cf. stanza 210.
[458] i.e. *cakṣus, śrotra, ghrāṇa, jihvā, kāya* in the *kāmabhava*.
[459] In the *rūpadhātu* 3 *indriyas*: i.e. the 5 minus *ghrāṇa* and *jihvā*.
The fourth consciousness is *manovijñāna*.
[460] i.e. the 10 minus *anvaya°*, *nirodha°*, *mārgajñāna*. See AH2 865bc and MAH 942b.
[461] i.e. the 5 *prakāras*; *duḥkhadarśanaheya*...*bhāvanāheya*.

**阿毗昙心论卷第四**

尊者法胜造
东晋僧伽提婆
共慧远于庐山译

**契经品第八**

已说定品。契经品今当说。

176 一切智所说 契经微妙义。
此吾今当说 宜应善心听

虽有一切阿毗昙契经义然诸契经应具分别。今当说。
世尊说三界欲界色界无色界。问。此云何。答。

177 欲界十居止 色界说十七
无色中有四 三有亦复然

欲界十居止者此欲界十居止地狱畜生饿鬼人六欲天四天王天三十三天炎摩天兜师哆天化乐天他化自在天。是众生起欲想。此处所中若可得物尽淫欲所有。是以说欲界。问。色界云何。答。色界说十七。色界说十七者居止梵身梵富楼少光无量光光曜少净无量净遍净无罣碍受福果实无想众生不烦不热善见善现色究竟。此处所不起欲想。但成极妙色非男非女形。是故说色界。无色中有四者无色界四居无量空处无量识处无所有处非想非 非想处。此处所无色。彼离色欲。是以说无色界。问。世尊说三有欲有色有无色有。此云何。答。三有亦复然。谓前三界分别即是三有。
问。如世尊所说七识住是云何。答。

178 善趣是欲界 及色界三地
无色亦如是 慧知诸识住

此欲界中若趣善数如人及六欲天色界前三地无色前三地初禅第二初禅地上二禅地三二禅地上三禅地三三禅地上四禅地九于中前三地及无色前三地是说七识住。何以故。不坏识故。恶趣中苦痛坏故不得立识住。第四禅无想定坏故亦不得立识住。非想非非想处灭尽定坏故不得立识住。是故不说。

179 第一有无想 众生居说九
诸有漏四阴 是说四识住

第一有无想众生居说九者此七识住及住及无想众生非想非非想处是说九众生居。于中众生居止是故说众生居。诸有漏四阴是说四识住者有漏色痛想行若识相续有此伴。是故说识住。
问。世尊说十二枝缘起。此亦应当说相。答。

180 诸烦恼及业 有体渐渐生
是名说有枝 众生一切生

于中烦恼是无明爱受。名说业者行及有。名说体者余枝。是一切众生渐渐生。依体立烦恼烦恼所作业业所作体。是故十二种分别。问。此枝为一时行为渐渐。答。非一时十二者。阴说十二枝无明为首。

181 彼是次第立 受于生死中
过二及未来 处中说于八

彼有枝次第立。于中前生时一切烦恼共有及伴说无明。由此故造业。业造果是行。彼生种种心是识。彼共生四阴相续是名色。于中所依眼为首。说是六入。根境界心和合是更乐。更乐所生受是痛。痛所著是爱痛具所烦劳是受。彼所劳造业是有。于中更受果是生。彼生中无量起灾害是老死。如是此有枝一切生中。二摄过去世二未来。八现在生中摄。
问。世尊说六界此云何答。

182 诸大谓有四 及与有漏识
亦色中间知 是界说生本

诸大谓有四及与有漏识亦色中间知者四大地水火风有漏识及色中间可知谓眼所受此六法说界。问。以何等故于众多法中说六界。答。是界说生本。是六法生死之本。此中有士夫想。于中身地所生水所润火成熟除烂腐臭风所起。空中间饮食。由风行出入识所立。此中起士夫想。是生死性故说界。
问。世尊说四圣谛。此相云何。答。

183 诸行若有果 有漏是说苦
若有因是习 苦尽谓之灭

诸行若有果有漏是说苦者一切有漏行从因中生亦作一切苦患。是故一切行说苦谛。若有因是习者一切有漏行他因。是以一切行说习谛。如一女亦说母亦说女前后故如是有漏行亦说苦谛亦说习谛。已生当生故。苦尽谓之灭者一切有漏行灭休息止谓之灭谛。

184 若有无漏行 是说为道谛
彼为二事故 见著则知微

若有无漏行是说为道谛者一切无漏行说道谛。何以故。休息苦时尽是具故。问。何以故说谛。答。彼为二事故。二事说谛。自相真实非颠倒及见彼得非颠倒意。问。如前因后果以何等故世尊前说果后说因。答。见著则知微。圣谛虽有前习后苦先修道后得灭但应前见苦谛后见习谛。如是应先见灭谛后见道谛。何以故。苦粗习细灭粗道细是故世尊先说苦谛后说习谛先说灭谛后说道谛。
问。世尊说四圣沙门果。此几种。答。

185 圣果有六种 最胜在九地
第三在六地 二俱依未来

圣果有六种者六种四沙门果无漏五阴及数缘灭。问。四沙门果何地所摄。答。最胜在九地。最胜是无著果。是九地所摄根本四禅三无色未来及中间。第三在六地者不还果六地所摄。具足四禅未来及中间非无色以无法智故。二俱依未来者须陀洹果及斯陀含未来禅所摄以未离欲故。
问。世尊说四道苦非速通苦速通乐不速通乐速通。此何相。答。

186 从信行诸法 无烦恼迟想
从法行诸法 无烦恼速想

从信行诸法无烦恼迟想者从信行无漏法是非速。钝根辈所摄是迟。若受此当知信解脱时解脱亦受同钝根故。从法行诸法无烦恼速想者从法行无漏法利根辈所摄是速。若受此当知见到不时解脱亦受同利根故。

187 根本禅地中 知假名乐想
小及难得故 余皆是苦想

根本禅地中知假名乐想者根本四禅中利根及钝根法说乐道。何以故。止观等导故及乐行故。小及难得故余皆是苦想者余地摄无漏是苦想。所以者何。以小故。未来禅中间禅止道小。无色中观小。是故极苦。一向难得及小故说苦。
问。世尊说四不坏净于佛不坏净于法僧圣戒不坏净。此云何。

188 自觉声闻法 解脱亦余因
清净无垢信 圣戒及决定

自觉声闻法解脱亦余因清净无垢信者自觉是佛。彼佛无著果所摄。无学功德是佛法。于此法若无漏信是说于佛不坏净。已取正证声闻。彼学无学功德是说声闻法。于此法若无漏信是说于僧不坏净。涅槃中无漏信及余有为法如苦谛习谛信菩萨无漏功德信学无学辟支佛法信是说于法不坏净。圣戒者无漏戒。是说于戒不坏净。问。以何等故不坏净一向无漏非有漏。答。及决定。此是决定从正见中生故。无漏信无漏戒定无漏。有漏信者为不信所坏。有漏戒者为非戒所坏。是以不决定。无漏不坏至后生。是决定故不坏净一向无漏。
问。世尊说修定有四。有修定于现法中得乐居。有修定得知见。有修定分别慧。有修定得漏尽。此何相。答。

189 初禅若有善 说现法是乐
若知于生死 是说名知见

初禅若有善说现法是乐者净及无漏初禅能得现法乐居。若知于生死是说名知见者生死智通是说修定知见。共依五阴。

190 慧分别当知 求得诸功德

金刚喻四禅 是名为漏尽

慧分别当知求得诸功德者方便生功德名欲界戒闻思修功德一切色无色界善法一切无漏有为法。是一切修定分别慧。金刚喻四禅是名为漏尽者金刚喻名最后学心共相应共有。第四禅所摄是说修定漏尽。此何义。此如来自己说。

问。世尊说四如意足四正断四意止。彼亦应当说相。答。

191 善有为诸法 求方便等起

佛说如意足 亦现正意断

善有为诸法求方便等起佛说如意足者求方便等起如前修定分别慧说。是一切如意足如意乘器故。亦现正意断者即此一切功德说正断。

192 彼亦是意止 四圣种亦然

谓有恩力生 彼圣之所说

彼亦是意止者即此法亦说意止。问。世尊说四圣种。此云何。答。四圣种亦然。即此法亦说四圣种。问。何以故此一切功德说意止正断如意足圣种。答。谓有恩力生彼圣之所说。此诸法谓定恩力生由定住故。是故说如意足。精进恩力生故说正断。念恩力生故说意止。少欲知足恩力生故说圣种。

已共分别道品。自相今当说。

193 净信精进念 喜慧及猗觉

护思惟戒定 是法谓道品

此十法说道品非余。于中信是信根信力。精进是四正断精进根精进力精进觉枝正方便。念是念根念力念觉枝正念。喜是喜觉枝。慧是四意止慧根慧力择法觉枝正见。猗是猗觉枝。护是护觉枝。思惟是正志。戒是正语正业正命。定是四如意足定根定力定觉枝正定。

问。何以此法如是多种分别。答。

194 处方便一意 濡钝及利根

见道思惟道 佛说三十七

处者正念立缘中故说意止。方便者正方便故说正断。一意者立一意故说如意足。濡钝者濡钝意得故说根。利根者利根意得故说力。见道者见道得故说道支。思惟道者思惟道得故说觉支。是谓分别事故佛说三十七。此十法事故佛说三十七。

问。此道品何地所摄。答。

195 禅第二未来 是说三十六

三四三十五 中间禅亦然

禅第二未来是说三十六者第二禅无正志。未来禅无喜觉枝余有。三四三十五中间禅亦然者第三第四禅中间禅无喜觉枝无正志余有。

| 196 | 第一说一切 | 三空三十一 |
| --- | --- | --- |
| | 最上二十一 | 欲界二十二 |

第一说一切者初禅具有三十七。三空三十一者三空中有三十一。喜正志正语正业正命身意止彼中无余有。最上二十一者非想非非想处无七觉八道及身意止。欲界二十二者除觉枝道枝余有。问。世尊说四食揣食更乐食意思食识食。是何相。答。

| 197 | 诸食中揣食 | 是欲界三种 |
| --- | --- | --- |
| | 识思及更乐 | 是食谓有漏 |

诸食中揣食是欲界三种者欲界揣食三种香味细滑。除饥渴故说食。识思及更乐是食谓有漏者有漏识有漏思有漏更乐是说食。有何义。后生相续不断故说食。
问。世尊说三三摩提空无愿无相。此三摩提云何行几行。答。

| 198 | 无愿有十行 | 二行是空定 |
| --- | --- | --- |
| | 圣行中四行 | 说是无相定 |

无愿有十行者无缘三摩提行十行无常行苦行习谛四行道谛四行。二行是空定者空三摩提二行空及无我行。圣行中四行说是无相定者无相三摩提灭谛四行。
问。世尊说四颠倒于无常有常想心颠倒想颠倒见颠倒苦有乐想不净有净想非我有我想心颠倒想颠倒见颠倒。此何见断。为何性。答。

| 199 | 晓了见苦断 | 四种是颠倒 |
| --- | --- | --- |
| | 三见性所有 | 舍见正见说 |

晓了见苦断四种是颠倒者一切四颠倒见苦断以行苦处故。三见性所有舍见正见说者颠倒是见性。三见中最上即是说颠倒。身见是说我见我是我见故。边见见有常及断。见盗不净见净。彼一切行苦处及见性所有。心想见作乱故说心颠倒想颠倒见颠倒但非性颠倒。问。世尊说多见六十二见为首。是何见所摄。答。一切见是五见所摄身见为首。
问。云何知。答。

| 200 | 诽谤于真实 | 此说为邪见 |
| --- | --- | --- |
| | 非实而见实 | 是二见及智 |

诽谤于真实此说为邪见者谓见诽谤真实法无此如说无施无齐无说如是一切说邪见。非实而见实是二见及智者五阴中不真实我见我。观有实是见说身见。非真实乐净观有乐净是见见盗。及余邪智思惟所断如夜有见谓是贼如竖木人像。

| 201 | 净见谓戒盗 | 是非因见因 |
| --- | --- | --- |
| | 受边说此见 | 依断灭有常 |

净见谓戒盗是非因见因者谓法于法非因见是因此见是戒盗如苦行至解脱。受边说此见依断灭有常者谓见无常事见常是谓有常见。谓因缘相续不识以见断是谓断见。谓之受见。

202 建立诸诽谤 因依于二边
若有事转行 是正见应断

建立诸诽谤者说邪见彼若诽谤苦是见苦断。若诽谤习是见习断。若诽谤灭是见灭断。若诽谤道是见道断。身见建立于苦我是我。是见苦断。见盗建立苦为乐。是见苦断。若习是见习断。若灭是见灭断。不受正法是故见灭断。道亦复然。戒盗若行有漏处是见苦断。若行无漏处是见道断。见断灭计常是亦见苦断。现五阴受断灭计常非不现。此中分别一切诸见。
问。世尊说二十二根。此云何。答。

203 诸界在于内 身三及命根
是根生死依 圣人之所说

诸界在于内者眼耳鼻舌意。身三者身根三种身根男根女根。及命根者命根第九。是根生死依圣人之所说者此九根生死依故说根。众生是生死相。

204 从痛诸烦恼 信首依清净
九根谓无漏 是三依于道

从痛诸烦恼者乐根苦根喜根忧根护根是说诸痛。从此诸烦恼故说根。信首依清净者信根精进念定慧根依此解脱故说根。九根谓无漏是三依于道者信道五根三痛及意根是若无漏依道故说根。谓从信行法行道所摄是未知根。谓思惟道所摄是已知根。谓无学道所摄是无知根。
问。此中几欲界系。几色界系。几无色界系。答。

205 欲界四善八 色种性有七
诸心数者十 一心慧所说

欲界四者男根女根苦根忧根是一向欲界系。余根如界品说。善八者信首五根及三无漏根色种性有七者色根有七五色根男根女根余者非色。问。几性心。几性心数。几非性心非性心数。答。诸心数者十信首五根及五痛。一心慧所说者意根。是余根非性心非性心数。
问。几有报。几无报。答。

206 一及十有报 是慧之所说
十三中是报 见实者分别

一者忧根一向有报一向善不善故。现在方便生是不从报生。非威仪非工巧。是以非无记故一向有报。及十有报是慧之所说者信首五根谓有漏是有报。谓无漏是无报。意根及三痛谓无记及无漏是无报。余善不善是有报。苦根谓无记是无报。余有报。问。几是报。几非是报。答。十三中是报见实者分别。十三根中或性是报或非。色根七命根意根及四痛无记法者善不善中生故报。问。生时几根最初得报。答。

207 二或六七八 谓初时可得
欲中有报相 亦六及上一

二或六七八谓初时可得者谓渐渐成根。如卵生湿生胎生是最初时二根生身根及命根。化生无形得六根五色根及命根。一形七二形八。欲中有报相者此说是一向欲界众生。亦六及上一者色界最初得六根无色一根。彼尔时一向秽污心。是以一向秽污得。心心数法非报。
问。命终时几根最后舍。答。

208 四舍八与九 或复舍于十
死时渐渐灭 善舍各增五

四舍八与九或复舍于十死时渐渐灭者无记心渐命终时最后舍四根身意命护根。无形一时无记心命终舍八根。一形九二形十。善舍各增五者即彼善心加增信首五根。如是色无色界随根可得亦如是。
问。几见断。几思惟断。几无断。答。

209 二断无断四 二种根有六
三微妙不断 谓余思惟断

二断无断四者四根见断思惟断无断意根及三痛。二种根有六者信首五根及忧根。三微妙不断者三无漏是不断。谓余思惟断者九根思惟断命根八及苦根。
已说诸经。门今当说。问。世尊说六识身眼识耳鼻舌身意识。此说识何法。答。

210 若取诸根义 是五种心界
受一切诸法 是谓意识界

若取诸根义是五种心界者根义名五种色。是五识识。眼识识色乃至身识识细滑。受一切诸法是谓意识界者意识识一切诸法。此境界一切诸法故。
问。有十法欲界相应不相应色界相应不相应无色界相应不相应有为无漏相应不相应无为二种善及无记。此中应分别智。一一智境界几法。答。

211 五法应当知 法智之境界
未知智为七 他心境界三

五法应当知法智之境界者五法法智境界欲界相应不相应无漏相应不相应无为善。未知智为七者。未知智境界七法色无色界及无漏相应不相应无为善。他心境界三者他心智境界三法欲色及无漏相应。

212 有漏智有十 因果境界六

解脱智一法　　道二余有九

有漏智有十者有漏智是等智。彼一切十法境界一切法境界故。因果境界六者苦智及习智是境界六法三界相应不相应。解脱智一法者灭智境界一法唯无为善。道二者道智境界二法有为无漏相应不相应。余有九者余尽智无生智是境界九法除其无为无记。是谓智解。

213　自地烦恼定　　所使于自地。
一切遍是种　　随在于彼类

自地烦恼定所使于自地者欲界诸烦恼所使于欲界。梵世诸烦恼所使于梵世。如是至非想非非想处尽当知。一切遍是种随在于彼类者通一切遍不通一切遍诸烦恼所使随种。通一切遍亦他种如身见见苦断。此中苦谛所断一切使所使及见习断通一切遍。如是至命根思惟断。此思惟所断一切所使及通一切。

214　三界烦恼定　　定在于三界
二界应当知　　一界亦复然

三界烦恼定定在于三界者谓法三界所摄是定在于三界此中三界一切使所使。如意根定在三界。此中一切使所使。二界应当知者谓法二界所摄是定于二界。此中二界一切使所使随界可得。如觉观定在欲色界此中欲色界一切使所使。一界亦复然者谓法定在一界此中一界一切使所使。如忧根定在欲界此中欲界一切使所使。

215　此佛说契经　　显示于诸法
识智及诸使　　分别此三门

此佛契经中若说诸法是三门应分别识门智门使门。如欲有中五根义是六识识色界四识除鼻识舌识。相应不相应故七智知。五种故欲色界使所使。

# CHAPTER IX. MISCELLANEOUS[1]

We have explained the chapter: Scriptural Texts. The chapter: Miscellaneous will now be explained.

> (216) We have explained that one distinctly establishes the various factors according to their correspondences. [830c] Various meanings of the above will now briefly be explained. Listen well!

> (217) Having an object and associated. Having an aspect and a basis. Thought and the factors which constitute thought's concomitants are meant by (these) same meanings.

For thought and the factors which constitute thought's concomitants[2], these terms are distinguished: because they all proceed within an object, they are said to have an object[3]. Because of their mutual correspondences[4], they are called associated[5]. Because of the aspects of their ranges, they are said (to have) an aspect[6]. Because they are produced depending on a basis, they are said (to have) a basis[7].

> (218) Let it be known that they are: produced by conditions; causes; having causes; formed; grounds of discourse; with time; having a fruition.

For the formed[8] factors these terms are distinguished: because they depend on conditions, they are said to be produced by conditions[9]. Because they produce other (factors), they are

---

1 *prakīrṇakavarga.*
2 *citta* and *caitasikadharma.*
3 *sālambana.*
4 About the mutual correspondence between thought and its concomitants: see AH2 865b and MAH 942c. See also *Kośa* II 178.
5 *samprayukta.*
6 *sākāra.* cf. *Kośa* II 177 note 5.
7 *sāśraya*, the *āśraya* being the *indriyas.* See AH2 865c.
8 *saṃskṛta.*
9 *pratyaya.*

called causes[10]. Because they depend on causes, they are said to have causes[11]. Because they depend on formed existence, they are called formed[12]. Because they are well revealed by many expedients[13], they are grounds of discourse[14]. Because they depend on the times[15]: past, future, and present, they are said to be with time. Because, as existence proceeds, they accomplish a fruition, they are said to have a fruition[16].

> (219) Faulty and obscure, defiled, inferior, and black. For the ones which are wholesome and formed, and which are to be practiced, one uses the term "to be developed".

Faulty and obscure, defiled, inferior, and black: for the unwholesome and the obscure indeterminate factors[17] these terms are distinguished: because they are established in a lifetime which is not worth mentioning, they are called faulty[18]. Because they are covered by affliction[19], they are called obscure[20]. Because they are tainted by the stains of affliction, they are called defiled[21]. Because of their vileness they are called inferior[22]. Because they are without knowledge and confused by darkness, they are called black[23].

The ones which are wholesome and formed, and which are to be practiced[24]: for the wholesome formed factors these terms are distinguished: because they are produced in wisdom, they are called wholesome[25]. Because, when proceeding within them,

---

[10] *hetu*.
[11] *sahetuka*.
[12] See note 8.
[13] AH2 865c has 因: cause, a translation for *vastu*. cf. *Kośa* I 13.
[14] *kathāvastu*.
[15] *adhvan*.
[16] *phala*.
[17] *akuśala* and *nivṛtāvyākṛta*.
[18] *sāvadya*.
[19] *kleśāchādita*.
[20] *nivṛta*.
[21] *kliṣṭa*.
[22] *hīna*.
[23] *kṛṣṇa*.
[24] *sevya*, *sevitavya*.
[25] *kuśala*.

one can obtain qualities[26], and because one may proceed within them[27], they are said to be practiced[28] and to be developed[29].

We have explained the formations which are associated with thought. The formations which are not associated with thought[30] will now be explained.

> (220) Absence of perception, two attainments, the likeness of beings, the collection of sentences, the collection of *vyañjanas* and of words, the faculty life, the obtainment of factors,
>
> (221) the state of being a common man, and the four characteristics of factors are immaterial and not associated. It is said that they are formed formations.

Absence of perception[31]: when one is born among the gods without perception[32], the factors which constitute thought and its concomitants do not arise.
Two attainments: the attainment without perception and the attainment of cessation[33]. The term attainment without perception is used when, disgusted with birth and death, and having the notion that it means deliverance, the series of thoughts is suddenly broken off on the basis of the fourth trance. The term attainment of cessation is used when, disgusted with hardship, and having the notion that it means tranquility, the series of thoughts is suddenly broken off on the basis of (the sphere of) neither-perception-nor-non-perception[34].

---

[26] *guṇa*.
cf. stanzas 132 et seq.: chapter VI note 85: *pratilambhabhāvanā*.
[27] cf. stanzas 132 et seq.: chapter VI note 86: *niṣevaṇabhāvanā*.
[28] See note 24.
[29] *bhāvitavya*.
[30] *cittaviprayuktasaṃskāra*.
[31] *āsaṃjñika*.
[32] *asaṃjñideva*.
[33] *āsaṃjñisamāpatti* and *nirodhasamāpatti*.
[34] *naivasaṃjñānāsaṃjñāyatana*.

[831a] The likeness of beings[35]: once born in a place of rebirth, the beings rely on this place, and their thoughts are alike.

Sentence[36]: that which is expressed by a combination of words[37], e.g. "The formations are impermanent. It is namely their nature to arise and to pass away"[38].

*Vyañjanas*[39]: the elements of a combination of sentences, etc., such as *gāthās* and scriptural texts.

Word[40]: the meaning expressed by a combination of letters, e.g. when saying: "permanence".

The faculty life[41]: when faculties, great elements[42], etc… are continuous, not interrupted.
Obtainment[43]: when, having accomplished[44] factors, one does not lose them.

The state of being a common man[45]: he who has not yet taken up the realization of that which is right[46], and who is far from the factors of the noble, possesses the state of being a common man.

---

35 *sattvasabhāgatā*.
36 *pada*.
37 *nāman*.
38 AH quotes the opening tetrasyllabic verses of the Chinese *Dharmapada* 法句经 *Fajüjing*, T. 210 p. 559a, *Anityavarga*. These words do not occur in the Pāli *Dhammapada*, but in the Sanskrit *Udānavarga*, the *sarvāstivāda dharmapada*, I *Anityavarga* 3: *anityā bata saṃskārā utpādavyayadharminaḥ*. See also Tha. 1159.
39 *vyañjana*. 味 *wei*, transcribes *vy*(*añjana*), syllable. See the commentary in MAH 943a. cf. supra chapter VII, note 276.
40 *nāman*.
41 *jīvitendriya*.
42 *indriyas* and *mahābhūtas*.
43 *prāpti*.
44 *samanvāgam*°.
45 *pṛthagjanatva*.
46 *samyaktvaniyāma*. cf. chapter V note 96, and chapter VIII note 172, and stanza 188.
i.e. he who has not yet entered the *darśanamārga*, the beginning of the *āryamārga*.

The four characteristics: birth, abiding, old age, and impermanence[47].

Immaterial: all these factors as mentioned above, are neither material nor comprised within form.

Not associated: because they are without object[48].

It is said that they are formed formations: because they are formed by the formed[49], they are called formed formations.

Question: How many among them are wholesome, how many are unwholesome, and how many are indeterminate?

Answer: (222) Two are wholesome. Five are of three kinds. Seven must be indeterminate. Let it be known that two are in form, and that one is in the stage of formlessness.

Two are wholesome: the attainment without perception and the attainment of cessation.

Five are of three kinds: obtainment, birth, old age, abiding, and impermanence. In relation to that which is wholesome they are wholesome, in relation to that which is unwholesome they are unwholesome, and in relation to that which is indeterminate they are indeterminate.

Seven must be indeterminate: seven are indeterminate: the gods without perception, the likeness of beings, sentences, *vyañjanas*, words, life, and the state of being a common man[50].

---

[47] The 4 *lakṣaṇas*: *jāti*, *sthiti*, *jarā*, *anityatā*. cf. stanza 24.
[48] *ālambana*.
[49] AH2 866a: because they are comprised within the *saṃskāraskandha*.
[50] a) *kuśala*: *asaṃjñi*°, *nirodhasamāpatti*.
b) *kuśala*, *akuśala*, or *avyākṛta*: *prāpti*, jāti, jarā, sthiti, anityatā.
c) *avyākṛta*: *āsaṃjñika*, *sattvasabhāgatā*, *pada*, *vyañjana*, *nāman*, *jīvita*, *pṛthagjanatva*.

Question: How many among them are tied to the realm of desire, how many are tied to the realm of form, and how many are tied to the realm of formlessness?

Answer: Let it be known that two are in form, and that one is in the stage of formlessness.

Let it be known that two are in form: the attainment without perception and the gods without perception are in the realm of form.

One is in the stage of formlessness: the attainment of cessation is in the realm of formlessness[51].

> (223) Two realms are mentioned in relation to three. The rest are namely in the three realms. Five are impure or pure. The rest are definitely impure.

Two realms are mentioned in relation to three: sentences, *vyañjanas*, and words are both in the realm of desire and in the realm of form. They are not in the realm of formlessness, because it is without speech.

The rest are namely in the three realms: the likeness of beings, life, obtainment, the state of being a common man, and the four characteristics are throughout the three realms[52].

Question: How many among them are impure, and how many are pure?

Answer:[53]Five are impure or pure. The rest are definitely impure.

---

[51] a) In *rūpadhātu*: *asaṃjñisamāpatti*, *āsaṃjñika*.
b) In *ārūpyadhātu*: *nirodhasamāpatti*.

[52] a) In *kāmadhātu* and in *rūpadhātu*: *pada*, *vyañjana*, *nāman*.
b) In the 3 *dhātus*: *sattvasabhāgatā*, *jīvita*, *prāpti*, *pṛthagjanatva*, the 4 *lakṣaṇas*.

[53] The Ms. XXII 8 does not have 曰.

Five: obtainment, birth, old age, abiding, and impermanence[54]. In relation to that which is impure they are impure, and in relation to that which is pure they are pure.

The rest are definitely impure: i.e. all the rest are[55] impure.

Question: Another term for the (state of) being without the factors of the noble, is (the state of being) a common man[56], indeterminate in the three realms. How is it lost and how is it abandoned?

> (224) In the first pure thought it is not accomplished but lost by the noble. [831b] The common man passes through the different realms, but when he has renounced desire, (his state) is extinguished.

In the first pure thought[57] it is not accomplished but lost by the noble: when the moment of the attaining of the factors of the noble is reached in the first pure thought, it is not accomplished but lost.

The common man passes through the different realms: i.e. if, when passing through the different realms, his life ends in a place, it is lost in that place, and if he is reborn in a place, it is obtained in that other place, as it is indeterminate.

When he has renounced desire, (his state) is extinguished: i.e. when someone who is in the state of being a common man in a stage, has renounced desire in that stage, at that moment he has obtained the extinction of the state of being a common man.

We have explained the formations which are not associated with thought. The unformed will now be explained.

The three unformed factors are: cessation as a result of careful consideration, cessation not as a result of careful consideration,

---

[54] *sāsrava* or *anāsrava*: *prāpti*, *jāti*, *sthiti*, *anityatā*.

[55] The Ms. XXII 10 has 是, not 定.

[56] *pṛthagjanatva*.

[57] The first *anāsrava citta*, i.e. *duḥkhe dharmakṣānti*. See stanza 104.

and space. Among them: cessation as a result of careful consideration[58] means disconnection[59] from the afflictions. By cessation as a result of careful consideration the impure[60] factors are disconnected from affliction. When the power of the several conditions[61] does not exist after careful consideration of the existence of things through the power of knowledge, this is called cessation as a result of careful consideration[62]. That which has the characteristic of being without obstruction[63], is called space[64]. i.e. that which does not obstruct form, is space.

> (225) The factors are produced by all their conditions, but also by a basis with an object. When (the conditions) are not complete, then (the factors) are not produced. This cessation is not (a result of) knowledge.

All formed factors are produced by all their conditions[65]. Lacking a condition, they do not come into existence, e.g. eye-consciousness[66] depends on the eye, it depends on form, it depends on empty space, it depends on light, it depends on a stage, and it depends on serene attention[67]. When all these are combined, it is produced, but when some remain incomplete, it is not produced, e.g. when the eyes are closed, the eyes[68]continue to be produced, but at that moment one does not have the other elements, and eye-consciousness is not produced. When the eye-consciousness should be produced but is not produced after the coming into existence of the eye, it will never be produced as these conditions do not exist. Its existence will not be produced in the future. When all things which bring into existence[69] are separated, not combined, this means cessation not as a result of careful consideration[70]. All formations must be understood thus.

---

58 *pratisaṃkhyānirodha*.
59 *visaṃyoga*.
60 *sāsrava*.
61 *pratisaṃkhyānabala* is meant.
cf. chapter I, note 45.
62 See note 58.
63 *āvaraṇa*.
64 *ākāśa*.
65 *pratyaya*.
66 *cakṣurvijñāna* depends on a combination of conditions.
67 *manaskāra*. cf. AH2 866c and MAH 944a.
68 眠...眼: Ms. XXIII 3-4.
69 i.e. the *pratyayas*.
70 *apratisaṃkhyānirodha*.

We have explained the unformed. The causes[71] will now be explained.

Question: The formed factors are said to be causes. In this respect, how are they causes and what are they causes for?

Answer: (226) The previous (factors) cause similarity or increase. Some are produced together with their basis. It is said that only two causes and one condition are already produced.

The previous factors cause similarity[72] or increase[73]: a previously produced factor causes the similarity or the increase of one produced later, not its decrease[74], e.g. that which is mildly wholesome causes that which is mildly wholesome in that particular stage, and it also causes that which is medium and it causes that which is strong[75]. That which is medium causes that which is medium, and it also causes that which is strong. That which is strong only causes that which is strong. Because, when developing[76] a factor, there is abiding or increase, never decrease, it does not cause that which is weaker.

Some are produced together with their basis: some, such as the associated cause and the concomitant cause[77], cause that which arises at the same time.

It is said that only two causes and one condition are [831c] already produced[78]: let it be said that the similar cause[79] is already produced. It is not the case that the cause is not produced. That which precedes causes that which comes later, and for that which is not yet produced nothing precedes and nothing comes later. Supposing there were[80], it would

---

[71] *hetu*.
[72] Similar, *sadṛśa*.
[73] *vṛddhi*.
[74] *parihāṇi*. Ms. XXIII 10: 非濡.
[75] *mṛdu, madhya, adhimātra*: weak, medium, strong.
[76] 行: AH2 866c: 修习; MAH 944.1: 修.
[77] *saṃprayuktakahetu* and *sahabhūhetu*.
[78] i.e. past.
[79] *sabhāgahetu*.
[80] Ms. XXIII 14: 若有者.

gradually[81] be produced, not by a cause. But this is not the case, and therefore for (the not yet produced) nothing (precedes and nothing comes later). The same applies to the universal cause, and also to the condition as immediate antecedent[82].

Question: Does the so-called retribution[83] belong to the beings[84], or does it not belong to the beings?

Answer: (227a) Retribution belongs to the beings[85].

It is said that retribution is among the factors which belong to the beings. It is not the case that it does not belong to the beings. Why? That which belongs to the beings is not possessed in common, but that which does not belong to the beings is possessed in common. Therefore it is not retribution.

Question: What about the factors of this fruition?

Answer: (227b) It is formed or it is a fruition of disconnection[86].

Fruitions are by nature all formed factors, because they depend on causes and conditions. The unformed disconnection may also be called fruition of the path[87].

Question: How do the factors with an object[88] proceed within their object?

Answer: (227c) (Factors) with an object (proceed) together.

The factors with an object are associated, and they proceed together within one object, not separately.

---

[81] Ms. XXIII 14: 淅淅: gradually.
[82] *sarvatragahetu* and *samanantarapratyaya*.
[83] *vipāka*.
[84] *sattvākhya*.
[85] Stanza 227 reads: "Retribution belongs to the beings. It is formed or it is a fruition of disconnection. (Factors) with an object proceed together within another range."
[86] *visaṃyogaphala*, i.e. *pratisaṃkhyānirodha*. cf. Kośa II 275 ff.
[87] *mārgaphala*. See *Kośa* VI 242 and II 276.
[88] *sālambana*. See stanza 12c.

Question: Where do they proceed?

Answer: (227d) They proceed within another range.
They proceed within another range, not within themselves, because they proceed away from themselves and take something different as their object.

Question: Do the factors which constitute thought and its concomitants[89] have a place[90], or do they not have a place?

Answer: (228a) They do not have a place in which they abide[91].

Why? Because of their complete cause. Their complete cause produces the factors which constitute thought and its concomitants. Because of the two eyes, one produces one consciousness. If it had a place in which it abides, it would abide in one eye, because it is one consciousness. If so, the second eye would not see form, though it does. Therefore it is not the case that it abides in one eye. They must all be understood thus. When they are like this, therefore they are without a place in which they abide.

Question: The World-Honored One has spoken about deliverance[92] of thought. How are thoughts delivered? When they are past, when they are future, or when they are present?

Answer: (228b) They are delivered when they arise[93].

When their path[94] arises, they are delivered. Why?
When their path arises, the afflictions are extinguished. Therefore they are delivered when they arise.

---

[89] *cittacaitasikā dharmāḥ.*
[90] *deśa.*
[91] Ms. XXIV 5 reads: 无有住处所. This is stanza 228a. The whole stanza reads: "They do not have a place in which they abide. They are delivered when they arise. The wise say that, when their path perishes, they cast off the fetters."
[92] *vimukti.*
[93] i.e. future. cf. *Kośa* VI 298.
[94] i.e. *vimuktimārga.*

Question: When their path arises, do they cut short affliction or not?

Answer: (228cd) The wise say that, when their path perishes[95], they cast off the fetters[96].

When their path[97] perishes, they cut short affliction, not when it arises. Why? When their path arises, it is future, and a future path cannot perform anything. Therefore[98], when the immediate path[99] perishes, they cut short affliction, and when the path of deliverance[100] arises, they are delivered.

Question: The World-Honored One has expounded craving for existence and craving for non-existence[101]. How many kinds of craving for existence are there? How many kinds of craving[102] for non-existence are there?

Answer: (229ab) Craving for existence is fivefold. The one for non-existence is characterized by being only of one (kind).

Craving for existence is fivefold: the term craving for existence is used when one craves for born or unborn things. This is called craving for existence. It is fivefold: to be abandoned through the vision[103] of suffering, to be abandoned through the visions of origination, of cessation, and of the path, and to be abandoned through development[104].

---

[95] i.e. present. Cfr. *Kośa* VI 300.
[96] *saṃyojana*.
[97] i.e. *ānantaryamārga*.
[98] Ms. XXIV 13 does not have 故.
[99] See note 97.
[100] See note 94.
[101] *bhavatṛṣṇā* and *vibhavatṛṣṇā*.
[102] Ms. XXIV 15 and the 3 editions add: 爱.
[103] Ms. XXIV 17 and the 3 editions have: 见: *darśana*.
[104] *duḥkha°*, *samudaya°*, *nirodha°*, *mārgadarśanaheya*, and *bhāvanāheya*.

[832a] The one for non-existence is characterized by being only of one (kind): the term craving for non-existence is used when, having seen annihilation[105], one rejoices in annihilation. This is called craving for non-existence. This is to be abandoned through development[106] only. Why? Craving which follows a wrong view, is to be abandoned through development. Because it is a craving not to proceed in continuation[107], not a wrong view about craving, it is to be abandoned through development.

Question: The World-Honored One has expounded three elements: the element abandonment, the element renunciation, and the element cessation[108]. What are their characteristics?

Answer: (229cd) The destructions of desire, of objects, and of the other afflictions are the three elements.

The abandonment of desire[109] is the element renunciation.
The abandonment of objects[110] is the element cessation.
The abandonment of the other afflictions is the element abandonment.

Question: Of the ten thoughts[111]: wholesome, defiled, and indeterminate in the realm of desire; wholesome, defiled, and indeterminate in the realm of form; wholesome, defiled, and indeterminate in the realm of formlessness; and also pure thought[112], how many of these thoughts can be obtained in relation to a defiled thought? How many (can be obtained[113]) in

---

[105] *uccheda.*
[106] *bhāvanāheya.*
[107] 相续 may translate *pratisaṃdhi.*
[108] *prahāṇa*°, *virāga*°, *nirodhadhātu.* cf. Kośa VI 301.
[109] *rāga.*
[110] *vastu.* AH translates: 'place'. AH2 867b and MAH 944c both have 事: thing, entity.
[111] AH2 867b and MAH 945a: 12 thoughts. cf. *Kośa* II 315f. AH: 10 thoughts: *kuśala, kliṣṭa,* and *avyākṛta* in *kāma*°, *rūpa*°, and *ārūpyadhātu*, and also *anāsrava.*
For the explanation which follows: cf. *Kośa* II 328ff., especially 330.
[112] Ms. XXV 3 adds 心.
[113] Ms. XXV 4 does not have 可得 here.

relation to a wholesome thought, and how many (can be obtained) in relation to an indeterminate thought?

Answer: (230) The fully awakened say that a defiled thought obtains the ten. In relation to a wholesome thought one obtains six, and (in relation to) an indeterminate one, (one obtains) the indeterminate one.

The fully awakened[114] say that a defiled[115] thought obtains the ten: in relation to a defiled thought one obtains all ten thoughts. When returning from a realm[116] and from a stage, the wholesome, the defiled, and the indeterminate thoughts of the three realms are all obtained. When falling away[117], one obtains the pure one. In relation to a wholesome[118] thought one obtains six: in relation to a wholesome thought one obtains six thoughts: the wholesome one of the realm of desire, which is obtained through application and which is practiced in thought[119] and in speech, and the indeterminate one, viz. the magically transforming thought[120]; the wholesome one of the realm of form, and the indeterminate one, viz. the magically transforming thought; the wholesome thought of the realm of formlessness, and also the pure one.

In (relation to) an indeterminate [121] one, (one obtains) the indeterminate one: with an indeterminate thought one only obtains[122] the indeterminate one, because it is weak.

Question: The ten factors which contribute to awakenment [123] were explained earlier. How many among them possess the nature of faculties[124], and how many are not faculties?

---

114 *samyaksaṃbuddha*.
115 *kliṣṭa*.
116 *dhātupratyāgamana*.
e.g. when life has ended in a higher realm, and one is reborn in the *kāmadhātu*.
117 *parihāṇi*, e.g. from *aśaikṣa* to *śaikṣa*.
118 *kuśala*.
119 Ms. XXV 8: 心: thought.
120 *nirmāṇacitta*.
121 *avyākṛta*.
122 Ms. XXV 9 and the 3 editions add: 得.
123 *bodhipākṣika*. See stanza 193.
124 *indriya*.

Answer: (231ab) Among that which contributes to awakenment there are six factors which must be called[125] faculties.

Among them, six factors have the nature of faculties: the five faculties: faith, etc[126], and joy[127]. The rest do not have the nature of faculties.

Question: Are the factors associated with something of their own nature, or with something of another nature?

Answer: (231cd) Anything which is associated with the factors, is said to be different.

The factors are associated with something of another nature, not with something of their own nature. It is not the case that something of a particular nature accompanies something of its own nature.

Question: Now, what about the disconnections[128]?

Answer: (232ab) The Great Seer[129] says that one disconnects the tie to an object.

The afflictions are delusions in relation to an object[130]. When (the beings)[131] are not deluded, the tie to the object is then disconnected, but it is impossible to disconnect the association from the associated[132]. Why?

Because it is useless.

[832b] Question: Is the case of abandonment[133] also disconnection, or is it different?

---

[125] Ms. XXV 11: 说, not 知.
[126] *śraddhā, vīrya, smṛti, samādhi, prajñā.*
[127] *prīti.*
[128] *visaṃyoga.*
[129] *maharṣi.*
[130] *ālambana.*
[131] cf. AH2 867c.
[132] cf. stanza 79.
[133] *prahāṇa.*

Answer: It is thus: disconnection is namely abandonment.

Question: [134]Abandonment does not mean disconnection, does it?

Answer: Indeed!

> (232cd) After a measure of abandonment one is (still) tied to the old, in (the path[135] of) vision and in the (path) of development.

When the knowledge of suffering is produced but when the knowledge of origination[136] is not yet produced, the afflictions which are to be abandoned through the vision of suffering are abandoned, but one is tied (to them) by the afflictions which are to be abandoned through the vision of origination. The same applies to all kinds [137] which are to be abandoned through development, because they are mutually connected.

Question: How does one obtain the perfect faiths [138] when [139] viewing the four noble truths?

Answer: (233) One raises pure faith in two when one understands three truths, and in the four when one relies on the vision of the right path. One develops (factors) in two periods[140].

Two when one understands three truths: having intuitively realized [141] suffering, origination, and cessation, one obtains perfect faith in the law[142]. The faith which is associated with the

---

[134] 颇: see chapter VI, note 237.
[135] Ms. XXV 17 reads 或见, not 见道.
[136] *duḥkhajñāna* and *samudayajñāna*.
[137] cf. stanza 107. See *Kośa* V 67.
[138] *avetyaprasāda*. cf. stanza 188.
[139] Ms. XXV 19 adds 时 after 谛.
[140] This last verse does not occur in the Ms. XXVI 2.
[141] *abhisameti*.
[142] *dharme'vetyaprasāda*.

knowledges of suffering, of origination, and of cessation[143], is called perfect faith. One obtains this and also noble morality[144].

One raises pure faith in the four when one relies on the vision of the right path: when viewing the path[145], one obtains all four[146].

Question: In how many periods does one develop (factors)[147]?

Answer: One develops (factors) in two periods.

The factors are developed in two periods: present[148]: development which involves practice[149]; future: development which means acquisition[150].
Question: What about the factors which are companions of thought[151]?

Answer: (234) All factors which constitute thought's concomitants are said to be companions of thought[152]. The characteristics (of thought), those of the remaining factors, and an activity, must also be understood (thus).

All factors which constitute thought's concomitants[153] are said to be companions of thought[154]: all factors which constitute thought's concomitants are called companions of thought, because of their proximity to thought.

The characteristics (of thought): the thoughts have four characteristics: birth, abiding, old age, and impermanence[155].

---

[143] *duḥkha°*, *samudaya°*, *nirodhajñāna*. The Ms. XXVI 3 places 智 after 灭.
[144] *āryaśīla*.
[145] *mārgadarśana*.
[146] i.e. the 4 *avetyaprasādas*. See stanza 188.
[147] cf. AH2 867c. See stanza 132.
[148] Ms. XXVI 5 adds 者.
[149] *niṣevaṇabhāvanā*. The Ms. XXVI 5, and the 3 editions have the expected 行修.
[150] *pratilambhabhāvanā*.
[151] *cittānuparivartin*. cf. stanza 39 and *Kośa* II 249. The Ms. XXVI 6 reads: 心共回.
[152] Ms. XXVI 6 and 7: 共心行: *cittānuparivartin*.
[153] *caitasikadharma*.
[154] See note 152.
[155] The 4 *lakṣaṇas*: *jāti*, *sthiti*, *jarā*, *anityatā*. See stanza 24.

(These are companions), also because of their proximity to thought.

Those of the remaining factors: the characteristics of the remaining factors which constitute thought's concomitants, are also companions of thought.

And an activity must also be understood (thus): restraint which is non-information[156], as explained earlier[157].

Question: What about the factors which are to be abandoned[158]?

Answer: (235a) All impure factors are to be abandoned.[159]
All impure[160] factors are to be abandoned, because of their various evil.

Question: What about the cognizable[161] factors?

Answer: (235b) (These factors and) also the stainless ones[162] are cognizable.

Impure[163] and pure[164], these are all cognizable[165] factors, because all are ranges of knowledge.

Question: What about the far[166] factors?

Answer: (235c) The past and the future ones are far[167].

---

[156] I.e the *avijñapti saṃvara* (*dhyānaja* and *anāsrava*).
[157] See stanza 39.
[158] heya.
[159] Stanza 235: "All impure factors are to be abandoned. (These factors and) also the stainless ones are cognizable. The past and the future ones are far, and the rest are said to be near."
cf. AH2 868a and MAH 945b.
[160] *sāsrava*.
[161] *jñeya*.
[162] *amala*.
The Ms. XXVI 11 reads: 知彼诸法及无垢.
[163] See note 160.
[164] *anāsrava*.
[165] Ms. XXVI 11: 是一切法知.
[166] *vidūra*.

The past and the future ones are called far, because they do not perform anything[168].

Question: What about the near[169] factors?

Answer: (235d) The rest are said to be near[170].
The present ones are near because of their activity[171]. The unformed ones[172] are near because they are swiftly obtained.

Question: What about the destined[173] factors?

Answer: (236abc) The deadly and irredeemable sins, and also walking in all that is pure[174], the wise say that these are destined.

The five deadly sins[175] are destined, because one is sure to reach hell[176]. Pure conduct is also destined, because one is sure to reach the fruition of disconnection[177]. The rest are not destined.

Question: What about the places of the views[178]?

Answer: (236d) The places of the views [832c] are decidedly impure.

---

167 Ms. XXVI 12 has the verse: 过去未来远.
168 *kāritra*: activity, cf. stanza 228cd. See *Kośa* V 55. AH2 868a mentions 4 *dūratās: kāritra (kāla)*°, *deśa*°, *lakṣaṇa*°, *vipakṣa*°. MAH 945b refers to 882c, where the 4 *dūratās* are explained: *kāla*°, *deśa*°, *lakṣaṇa*°, *vipakṣa*°. cf. *Kośa* V 107.
169 *āsanna*.
170 Ms. XXVI 13: 谓余说于近.
171 See note 168.
172 *asaṃskṛta*.
173 *niyata*.
174 Ms. XXVI 15: 及行诸无漏.
175 *ānantaryakarman*. cf. *Kośa* IV 201. See also supra stanza 63.
176 *naraka*. AH2 868a speaks here of *mithyātvaniyata*, destined for perdition.
177 *visaṃyogaphala*. AH2 868a speaks of *samyaktvaniyata*, destined for salvation.
178 *dṛṣṭisthāna*. cf. *Kośa* I 14.

All impure factors are places of the views, because they are places of the five views[179].

Question: When one has accomplished the faculties, how many faculties does one have?

Answer: (237) They say that, when one has nineteen faculties, one has accomplished the highest number. Those who know the faculties say that the smallest number one accomplishes is eight.

They say that, when one has nineteen faculties, one has accomplished the highest number: nineteen faculties are the highest number accomplished, i.e. by one who has the two distinctive marks[180], and also by those who have all the faculties when viewing the truths, not yet having renounced desire[181].

Those who know the faculties say that the smallest number one accomplishes is eight: he accomplishes eight faculties, i.e. he who does not have all corporal faculties, having cut his wholesome roots[182], and also the common man who is born in formlessness[183].

Question: How many kinds of contact[184]?

---

179 5 *dṛṣṭis*: stanza 71.

180 i.e. one who has both the male and the female faculty or organ. In this case the 3 *anāsrava* faculties are lacking. See AH2 868b and *Kośa* II 143.

181 i.e. the *āryas* who are *śaikṣas*, still in training, not *arhats*. They are in the *darśana*° and in the *bhāvanāmārga*. AH2 868b says they lack 1 organ, i.e. the male or the female faculty, and the 2 *anāsrava* faculties. These 2 are explained in MAH 945c: in darśanamārga: ājñātāvīndriya, ājñendriya.
in *bhāvanāmārga*: *ājñātāvīndriya, anājñātam* ājñāsyāmīndriya.
See also *Kośa* II 143.

182 Wholesome root: *kuśalamūla*.
Such a one has the faculties: *kāya, manas, jīvita*, and 5 *vedanās*, according to AH2 868b and to MAH 946a. He does not have the male or the female faculty, and he does not have the faculties eye, ear, etc...

183 The *pṛthagjana* born in the *ārūpyadhātu*. AH2 868b and MAH 946a say he has the faculties: *manas, jīvita, upekṣā*, and the 5 moral faculties: *śraddhā*, etc...
See also *Kośa* II 142.

184 *sparśa*.

Answer: Five kinds.

> (238) Contacts of designation, with resistance, of ignorance, situated in the middle, and of wisdom. In the noble path there are the two (paths) together which can raise and accomplish a fruition.

The contact which is associated with mind-consciousness is called contact of designation [185]. The contacts which are associated with five consciousnesses, are called[186] contacts with resistance [187]. Defiled [188] contacts are called contacts of ignorance[189]. Pure[190] contacts are called contacts of wisdom[191]. Impure undefiled contacts are called contacts of neither-wisdom-nor ignorance[192].

Question: With which path does one obtain[193] a fruition? With the immediate path[194] or with the path of deliverance[195]?

Answer: In the noble path there are the two (paths) together which can raise and accomplish a fruition.

With the two paths together[196] one obtains a fruition. The one casts off the fetters, and with the other (path) one takes

---

[185] *adhivacanasaṃsparśa*. 增: *adhi*°, predominant, stands for 增语: *adhivacana*.
This *sparśa* is associated with *manovijñāna*.

[186] 说: Ms. XXVII 4.

[187] The contacts associated with the 6 *vijñānas* minus *manovijñāna*, are called *pratighasaṃsparśa*. They are called "with resistance" because of their *āśrayas*, bases, ie. the faculties or organs which are *sapratigha*, with resistance. See AH2 868b.

[188] *kliṣṭa*.

[189] *avidyāsparśa*.

[190] *anāsrava*.

[191] *vidyāsparśa*.

[192] *naivavidyānāvidyāsparśa*, i.e. the *sparśa* situated in the middle. It is *sāsrava*, impure, and not *kliṣṭa*, meaning *akuśala*, unwholesome.

[193] Ms. XXVII 6 and the 3 editions: 得.

[194] *ānantaryamārga*.

[195] *vimuktimārga*.

[196] Ms. XXVII: 7 俱.

possession of the disconnection. These two paths accomplish a fruition.

Question: Dwelling in which thought does one without attachment[197] obtain *nirvāṇa*[198]?

Answer: (239ab) One without attachment obtains the unformed *nirvāṇa* in a thought which is retribution[199].

In all things there is nothing which one without attachment brings about[200]. He seeks no abode. In a thought which is retribution[201] he obtains[202] *nirvāṇa*.

Question: How many existences[203]?

Answer: (239cd) Existence at birth and existence at death, the (existence) properly speaking, and also the intermediate one.

Existence at birth[204]: the aggregates[205] immediately at the moment of birth, are said to constitute existence at birth.

Existence at death[206]: the aggregates at the moment of death, are said to constitute existence at death.

Existence properly speaking[207]: neither the existence at birth nor the existence at death, but the aggregates in between are said to constitute existence properly speaking.

---

[197] *arhat*.
[198] The Ms. XXVII 8: 取涅槃.
[199] Ms. XXVII 8, and the 3 editions: 报心.
[200] The 3 editions read: 无所作无所为. The Ms. XXVII 9: 无所作为.
[201] i.e. a thought produced by the cause of retribution, *vipākaja*°. According to AH2 868c and MAH 946b, the *arhat* also enters *nirvāṇa* in an *airyāpathika* thought, a thought relating to deportment. See also *Kośa* III 133, note 2.
[202] Ms. XXVII 9. See note 199.
[203] *bhava*.
[204] *upapattibhava*. The Ms. XXVII 10 adds 者.
[205] *skandha*.
[206] *maraṇabhava*.

Intermediate existence[208]: the aggregates which are reached by the existing, are said to constitute intermediate existence.

Question: The World-Honored One [209] has said that there is disgust[210], and that there is renunciation of desire[211]. How is one disgusted, and how does one renounce desire?

Answer: (240) The knowledges in relation to suffering and its cause, and the (corresponding) patient acceptances develop disgust. The attainment of dispassion after the extinction of desire, is said to be in all four (truths).

The knowledges in relation to suffering and its cause, and the (corresponding) patient acceptances develop disgust: when knowledge and patient acceptance [212] take suffering and origination[213] as their objects, this is called disgust, because they proceed within objects[214] of disgust.

The attainment of dispassion[215] after the extinction of desire, is said to be in all [833a] four (truths): the knowledges and patient acceptances in relation to the four truths, are called renunciation of desire[216], because they can do away with desire.

---

[207] *pūrvakāla* (former time) *bhava*. MAH 946b explains this term: "because that which is sown by the former actions (*pūrvakarman*) dwells for a long time."

[208] *antarābhava*, the existence between death and rebirth.

[209] Ms. XXVII 13: 世尊.

[210] *nirveda*.

[211] *virāga*.

[212] *jñāna* and *kṣānti*.

[213] *duḥkha* and *samudaya*.

[214] *vastu*. AH translates: place, field. AH2 868c: 事: thing.

[215] *virāga*.

[216] Ms. XXVII 17: 无欲: dispassion.

**杂品第九**

已说契经品。杂品今当说。

216　已说随相应　一一分别法
　　于上众杂义　今略说善听

217　有缘亦相应　有行或与依
　　心及心数法　是同一义说

心及心数法此名差别。一切行一缘是故说有缘。更互相应故说相应。境界行故说行。由依生故说依。

218　是缘生亦因　有因及有为
　　说处有道路　有果应当知

有为法中此名差别。由依缘故说缘。生他故说因。由依因故说有因。由依造有故说有为。多方便善显现故说处。依过去未来现在道路故说道路。有转成果说有果。

219　有恶亦隐没　秽污下贱黑
　　善有为及习　亦复名修学

有恶亦隐没秽污下贱黑者不善及隐没无记法此名差别。不可说辈中立故说有恶。烦恼所覆故说隐没。烦恼垢污故说秽污。凡鄙故说下贱。无智闇乱故说黑。善有为及习者善有为法此名差别。慧中生故说善。行时能得功德及可行故说习及修。
已说心相应行。心不相应行今当说。

220　无思想二定　亦众生种类
　　句身味名身　命根与法得

221　凡夫性所有　及诸法四相
　　非色不相应　说是有为行

无思想者生无想天心心数法不起。二定者无想定灭尽定。无想定名厌于生死解脱想由第四禅心相续一时断。灭尽定名厌于劳务息止想由非想非非想心相续一时断。亦众生种类者生处已生于此处众生依及心相似。句者名会所说如所行非常谓兴衰法。味者句会事广说如偈及契经。名者字会说义如说常。命根者根及大等相续不断。得者成就诸法不舍。凡夫性者未取正证离圣法是凡夫性所有。四相者生住老无常。非色者此一切诸法如上所说非色非色所摄。不相应者无缘故。说是有为行者有为造故说有为行。
问。此中几善。几不善。几无记。答。

222　善二三种五　七应是无记

二在色当知　　一在无色地
善二者无想定灭尽定。三种五者得生老住无常。善中善不善中不善无记中无记。七应是无记者七无记无想天众生种类句味名命凡夫性所有。问。此中几欲界系。几色界系。几无色界系。答。二在色当知一在无色地。二在色当知者无想定及无想天是色界。一在无色地者灭尽定在无色界。

223　二界说于三　　谓余在三界
有漏无漏五　　其余定有漏
二界说于三者句味名亦在欲界亦在色界。非无色界离言语故。谓余在三界者众生种类命得凡夫性所有及四相通在三界。问。此中几有漏。几无漏。答。有漏无漏五。其余定有漏。五者得生老住无常。在有漏中有漏在无漏中无漏。其余定有漏者谓余一切是有漏。
问。此离圣法假名凡夫三界中无记。此云何舍云何断。答。

224　初无漏心中　　圣不成就舍
凡夫流诸界　　离欲时灭尽
初无漏心中圣不成就舍者第一无漏心中得圣法时得不成就舍。凡夫流诸界者流诸界时谓处所命终此处所舍。谓处所生彼处所得无记故。离欲时灭尽者谓地凡夫所有若此地离欲尔时得灭凡夫性。已说心不相应行。无为今当说。三无为法数缘灭非数缘及虚空。于中数缘灭者解脱诸烦恼。依于数缘灭有漏法离烦恼解脱。数缘力智力计校事有而无是名数缘灭。无挂碍之相是名曰虚空。谓不障碍色是虚空。

225　诸法众缘起　　亦从依与缘
不具以不生　　此灭非是明
一切有为法从众缘而生。无缘则不生。如眼识依眼依色依空依明依地依寂然。若此一切共和者便得生。若余不具便不得生。如眠时眼一切时生。尔时是余事不具眼识不得生。若彼眼识应当生而不生眼生已终不复更生离此缘故。是有未来不复当生。彼起具差违不和是非数缘灭。如是一切行尽当知。
已说无为。因今当说。问。有为法说是因。此中云何因为谁因。答。

226　前因相似增　　或俱依倚生
二因及一缘　　一向已生说
前因相似增者前生法后生相似因转增非濡。如濡善于自地濡善因及中因上因。中于中因及上因。上唯上因。行法时有住有增终不减以是故非为濡因。或俱依倚生者或因俱生如相应因及共有因。二因及一缘一向已生说者自然因已生当言。因非不生。前者后因。未生者无前后。若有者应渐渐生不从因。但不尔。是故不有。一切遍因亦如是及次第缘。问。谓此报者为是众生数为非众生数。答。

227 报是众生数

报者众生数法中说。非不众生数。所以者何。众生数者不共有。非众生数共有。是故非报。问。是果法云何。答。

有为解脱果

一切有为法性果所有由因缘故。无为解脱亦应说道果。问。有缘法云何行缘。答。

有缘者共俱

有缘法是相应。是共俱一缘中行不别。问。何处行。答。

行于他境界

他境界中行非自性。离自行及缘差别故。
问。心心数法为有处所为无处所。答。

228 无有住处所

所以者何。普因故。普因生心心数法。因二眼生一识。若有住处者应住一眼中一识故。若尔者第二眼不应见色而见。是故非一眼中住。如是一切尽知。若如是者以是故无住处。问。世尊说心解脱。云何心解脱。为过去为未来为现在。答。

生时而解脱

道生时解脱。所以者何。道生时诸烦恼灭。是故生时解脱。问。道生时断烦恼为不。答。

道灭时灭结 明慧之所说

道灭时断诸烦恼非生时。所以者何。道生时是未来。未来道者不能行事。以是无碍道灭时断烦恼。解脱道生时解税。
问。世尊说有爱无有爱。有爱几种。无有爱几种。答。

229 有爱有五种 无有独一相

有爱有五种。有爱名于生不生物若爱。是名有爱。此五种见苦断见习灭道断及思惟断。无有独一相者无有爱名已见断乐于断。是名无有爱。此一向思惟断。所以者何。从见爱思惟断。此是不转行相续中爱非爱见是故思惟断。问。世尊说三界断界无欲界灭界。此何相。答。

爱处余烦恼 灭尽是三界。

爱断是无欲界。处断是灭界。余烦恼断是断界。

问。十心欲界善秽污无记色界善秽污无记无色界善秽污无记及无漏心此心几秽污心中可得。几善心中。几无记心中。答。

230　秽污心得十　正觉之所说
　善心中得六　无记即无记

秽污心得十正觉之所说者秽污心中得一切十心。界及地来还时三界善秽污及无记此心一切得。退时得无漏。善心中得六者善心中得六心欲界善求学得及心口行亦变化心无记色界善变化心无记无色界善心及无漏。无记即无记者无记心唯得无记以劣故。
问。前已说道品十法。此中几根性所有。几非根。答。

231　道品有六法　当说是为根

此中六法根性所有信首五根及喜。余者非根所有。问。诸法为自性相应为他性。答。
问若此解脱当云何。答。

相应于诸法　是说谓为他

诸法他性相应不自性。非为自性于自性伴。
问。若此解妥当运何。答。

232　缘中解于缚　大仙人所说

诸烦恼于缘中愚。即彼不起愚缘中缚即于中解。不可以相应解相应。所以者何。以空故。问。若断即是解脱为异。答。如是若解脱者即是断。
问。颇断非解脱不。答。有。

或断已故缚　或见及思惟

苦智已生习智未生见苦所断烦恼断而见习所断烦恼缚。如是思惟所断一切种更互相缘故。问。见四真谛时云何得不坏净。答。

233　二解于三谛　四由见正道
　兴起清净信　修习于二世

二解于三谛者观苦习灭得于法不坏净。苦习灭智相应信是名不坏净。得是及圣戒。四由见正道兴起清净信者见道时具得四。问。几世修。答。
修习于二世。诸法修于二世现在者行修未来者得修。
问。心共回法云何。答。

234　一切心数法　说是心共行
　此相及余法　作亦应当知

一切心数法说是心共行者一切心数法说心共行心近故。此相者此心有四相生住老无常。亦心近故。及余法者余心数法相亦心共行。作亦应当知者无教戒如前说。

问。断法云何。答。

235 断诸有漏法

一切有漏法断杂恶故。问。知法云何。答。

知及诸无垢

有漏及无漏是一切法知一切智境界故。问。远法云何。答。

过去未来远

过去未来是说远不办事故。
问。近法云何。答。

谓余说于近

现在近办事故。无为近速得故。
问。定法云何。答。

236 无间无救业 及行诸无漏
慧者说是定

五无间业是定必至地狱故。无漏行亦是定必至解脱果故。余不定。
问。见处云何。答。

见处必有漏

一切有漏法见处五见处所故。问。若成就根是成就几根。答。

237 说有十九根 谓成就极多
少成就极八 晓了根所说

说有十九根谓成就极多者十九根成就极多如二形及具根者未离欲见谛。
少成就极八晓了根所说者成就八根如不具身根断善根及生无色中凡夫。
问。几种更乐。答。五种。

238 增有对无明 处中明更乐
圣道俱有二 能兴起成果

意识相应更乐是说增更乐。五识相应更乐是说有对更乐。秽污更乐是说无明更乐。无漏更乐是说明更乐。有漏非秽污更乐。是说非明非无明更乐。问。何等道得果。为无碍道为解脱道。答。圣道俱有二能兴起成果。二道俱得果。一者解缚。二者得解脱。此二道成果。
问。无著住何心取涅槃。答。

239 无著报心中 得无为涅槃

无著一切事无所作为无所求住。从报心中便取涅槃。
问。几有。答。

生有及死有 根本亦复中

生有者始生时阴是谓生有。死有者死时阴是谓死有。根本有者除生有及死有于其中间阴是谓根本有。中有者有所至阴是谓中有。
问。世尊说有厌有离欲。云何厌。云何离欲。答。

240　诸智在苦因　此忍修于厌
　　灭欲得无欲　说普在四中

诸智在苦因此忍修于厌者若智及忍缘苦习是说厌行厌处故。灭欲得无欲说普在四中者四谛中智及忍说无欲能断欲故。

# CHAPTER X. DISCOURSE[1]

> (241) When, having left restraint and non-restraint[2], one obtains them again, one does not bring about excellence because of this. May he who can decide this, answer!

Answer: Indeed! When, from formlessness, one is born in form[3].

> (242) [4]A formed clean and wholesome factor is obtained by all who have left evil when obtaining a noble fruition, though not developed.

Answer: Indeed! When, falling away, they obtain that which is past[5].

> (243) When a path arises, one has not yet renounced evil, but at the moment of deliverance one has renounced evil. Please decide and answer!

Answer: Indeed! It is namely a future development[6].

---

[1] *(dharma)kathā*: 论.
The Ms. XXVIII 2 adds: 有十偈, with 10 *gāthās*
For the explanation of these stanzas: see AH 868c-869ab, and MAH 963c-964c.
The Chinese 论 also implies the meaning 'conclusion'.

[2] *saṃvara* and *asaṃvara*.

[3] i.e. when, coming from the *ārūpyadhātu*, a *pṛthagjana* is born in the *rūpadhātu*.
Having left restraint and non-restraint, he obtains the *(dhyānaja) saṃvara* again. cf. MAH 963c.

[4] 颇: see chapter VI, note 238.

[5] This deals with the attainment of the *śrāmaṇyaphalas*. When, without perfecting one's faculties (*indriyasaṃcāra*), one falls back into and again obtains the noble path comprised within a fruition once obtained but extinguished, one merely obtains the past path, but does not develop it. See AH 869a and MAH 964a. Cf. *Kośa* VII 63.

[6] development: 修: Ms. XXVIII 6 and the 3 editions. This stanza deals with: *ānantaryamārga* (the last one in the *bhavāgra* being called *vajropamasamādhi*) and *vimuktimārga*.

(244) When afflictions of the shining ones[7] arise at the moment of concentration, the clean[8] first trance is obtained, falling away and receding.

Answer: Indeed! When the fruition of *arhatship* is developed, and when it is developed in a mixed manner[9].

(245) Several wholesome factors obtained in the path of the vision of the truths: these factors still have an object, but the noble do not see their object.

Answer: Indeed! Conventional knowledges developed in the realm of desire[10].

(246) The impure fruition of the wise is separate from clean qualities. Those who do not renounce, but who follow their desire also have that fruition.

Answer: Indeed! The magically transforming thought of the realm of desire[11].

(247) When, abiding in the immediate path, one accomplishes extinctions, the afflictions agree with it. It is not the case that they agree with pure vision.

---

7 *ābhāsvara*, gods of the second *dhyāna*. See stanza 177.

8 *śuddhaka*, i.e. *kuśala sāsrava*.

9 *vyavakīrṇa*, mixed. See stanza 170. There is a mixed development (*bhāvanā*) when, through the afflictions of the second *dhyāna*, one who has obtained the *arhattvaphala* falls away to the *śuddhaka* first *dhyāna*.

10 The *saṃvṛtijñāna* produced with *duḥkhe, samudaye* and *nirodhe'nvayajñana*, at the end of the intuitive realization (*abhisamayānta*) of *duḥkha, samudaya* and *nirodha*, does not take the object of the *anvayajñāna* (belonging to the 2 higher *dhātus*) as its object (belonging to the *kāmadhātu*). The *ārya* does not see the object of this *saṃvṛtijñāna*. See also stanza 133ab.

11 When an *ārya*, having renounced desire in the *kāmadhātu* but not yet in the first *dhyāna*, produces the *nirmāṇacitta* of the *kāmadhātu*, this *nirmāṇacittā* is an impure, *sāsrava,* fruition, because it is a fruition of that first *dhyāna*. In the second *dhyāna* the same can be said about the *nirmāṇacittas* in the *kāmadhātu* and in the first *dhyāna* etc.
About *nirmāṇacitta*: see stanza 175.

Answer: Indeed! When producing the superknowledges[12].

(248) The fetters are not undone. When purity [13] is obtained, one does not abandon the afflictions. They have (already) been destroyed by purity.

Answer: Indeed! When one is born in[14] the brahma-heaven, coming from among the shining ones[15].

(249) When a pure and clean stage, not obtained before, is obtained, one does not renounce desire, nor does one fall away, nor does one depend on the path of vision.

Answer: Indeed! When renunciation of desire for form is realized, one obtains the path of development in pure formlessness[16].

[833b] (250) When, not having obtained several factors yet, one obtains these factors, one does not reject it and one does not obtain it. May someone who knows this, answer!

Answer: Indeed! When the other pure qualities, not those which are obtained by the class of the first pure thought, are

---

[12] The Ms. XXVIII 11 reads: 兴诸通时.
When a *pṛthagjana* develops the *abhijñās*, the *ānantaryamārga*, not pure vision, extinguishes the obstructions to the *abhijñās*, the *kleśas* opposed to the *abhijñās*.

[13] 无: *a°;* 垢: *mala. vairāgya* seems to be meant.

[14] Ms. XXVIII 12: 生梵天上.

[15] When someone who has renounced desire in the *kāmadhātu*, is born in the first *dhyāna* (*brahma*-heaven), coming from the second *dhyāna* (*ābhāsvara* gods), he does not abandon afflictions of the *kāmadhātu*, because he has already abandoned them.

[16] Someone who has renounced desire in the *rūpadhātu* obtains, as the 16th. *citta*, i.e. *mārge'nvayajñāna* (*bhāvanāmārga*), is produced, the *anāgāmiphala*, and rising from an *anāsrava* concentration of the *rūpadhātu*, he for the first time obtains an *anāsrava* one of the *ārūpyadhātu*. At that moment there is no renunciation, *vairāgya*, because one has already renounced. There is no falling away, *parihāṇi*, and one does not rely on the *darśanamārga*.
See MAH 964b.

obtained[17], the state of a common man is obtained by none of those others[18].

Treatise on the Essence of Scholasticism. Vol. IV.

[17] MS. XXVIII 16 reads: 除 (not 余) 初无漏心 (i.e. *duḥkhe dharmakṣānti*, the first *anāsrava citta*).
品得…功德得 (not 舍)…
See also MAH 964b.

[18] The first *anāsrava citta* rejects *pṛthagjanatva*. The other pure thoughts neither obtain nor reject it, because it is already rejected.

**论品第十**

241 威仪不威仪 若离复获得
不由此致胜 能决定者答
答。有。从无色生色。

242 颇得圣果时 一切离诸恶
有为净善法 得已而不修
答。有。退时得过去。

243 道者兴起时 未远离诸恶
解脱时离恶 愿答已必定
答。有。谓当来修。

244 颇光曜烦恼 兴起于定时
清净初禅中 获得堕衰退
答。有。无著果修及熏修。

245 颇见谛道中 逮得诸善法
是法亦有缘 圣者不见缘
答。有。欲界中修行等智。

246 颇慧有漏果 远离净功德
不离从于意 此亦是彼果
答。有。欲界变化心。

247 颇住无碍道 成就于诸灭。
诸烦恼从彼 非如无漏见
答。有。兴诸通时。

248 颇结不解脱 无垢者获得
而不断烦恼 谓此无垢尽
答。有。从光曜中生梵天上。

249 颇无漏净地 未曾得已得
不离欲非退 不依于见道
答。有。离色欲取证时得无漏无色思惟道。

250 颇未得诸法 而逮得此法
不舍彼不得 若能知者答
答。有。除初无漏心品得余无漏功德得凡夫事余者一切不得。
阿毗昙心论卷第四。

# List of Sanskrit Terms
# (Vide Footnotes)

The numbers refer to the stanzas and to the prose which introduces or explains them.

# Chinese-Sanskrit-English Glossary

The Chinese terms are translations for —most probably— Gāndhārī. They are 'ancient' translations, i.e. before Kumārajīva (350-ca. 409), but after An Shigao (fl. ca. 148-170). The Sanskrit is based on the *Kośabhāṣya.* The English terms are hardly different from our 1975 edition. The *Encyclopaedia of Indian Philosophies*, ed. K. Potter, uses its own terminology.

| | | | |
|---|---|---|---|
| 1 | 一切入 | kṛtsnāyatana | all-basis |
| | 一切遍 | sarvatraga | universal |
| | 一向 | ekānta | only |
| | 一心 | cittaikāgratā | undivided attention |
| | 一种 | ekabījin | germinating one more time |
| | 上 | adhimātra | strong |
| | 上烦恼 | upakleśa | secondary affliction |
| | 下贱 | hīna | inferior |
| | 三十三(天) | trāyastriṃśa(deva) | the thirty-three (gods) |
| | 不信 | āśraddhya | disbelief |
| | 不共 | āveṇika | special |
| | 不动法 | akopyadharman | immovable one |
| | 不善 | akuśala | unwholesome |
| | 不坏净 | avetyaprasāda | perfect faith |
| | 不威仪亦非不威仪 | naivasaṃvaraṇāsaṃvara | neither-restraint-nor-non-restraint |
| | 不威仪戒 | asaṃvara | non-restraint |
| | 不放逸 | apramāda | heedfulness |
| | 不时解脱 | asamayavimukta | finally released |
| | 不热(天) | atapa(deva) | not distressed (god) |
| | 不烦(天) | Avṛha(deva) | not troubled (god) |
| | 不相应 | viprayukta | not associated |

| | | | |
|---|---|---|---|
| | 不与取 | adattādāna | taking what is not given |
| | 不虚言 | mṛṣāvādavirati | no false speech |
| | 不还果 | anāgāmiphala | fruition of one who does not return |
| | 世俗等智 | saṃvṛtijñāna | conventional knowledge |
| | 世第一法 | laukikāgradharma | the highest worldly factor |
| | 兩舌 | paiśūnya | slander |
| 2 | 中 | madhya | medium |
| | 中有 | antarābhava | intermediate existence |
| | 中间禅 | dhyānāntara | intermediate trance |
| 3 | 义辨 | arthapratisaṃvid | analytical knowledge of the meaning |
| 4 | 乘 | nairyāṇika | leading to escape |
| 6 | 事 | vastu | entity |
| 8 | 离欲 | vairāgya | renouncing desire; renunciation |
| 9 | 他化自在(天) | paranirmittavaśavartin | (gods) controlling (enjoyments) magically created by others |
| | 他心智 | paracittajñāna | knowledge of the thoughts of others |
| | | cetaḥparyāyajñāna | knowledge of the mental make-up of others |
| | 他心通智 | cetaḥparyāyajñāna | knowledge of the mental make-up of others |
| | 住 | sthiti | abiding |
| | 作意 | manaskāra | attention |
| | 使 | anuśaya | urge |
| | 依 | āśraya | basis |
| | 信 | śraddhā | faith |
| | 信解脱 | śraddhādhimukta | given to faith |
| | 修 | bhāvanā | development |
| | 修定 | samādhibhāvanā | developing of concentration |
| | 俱解脱 | ubhayatovimukta | twice-delivered |
| | 众生种类 | sattvasabhāgatā | likeness of beings |
| | 体 | vastu | entity |
| 10 | 光曜(天) | ābhāsvara(deva) | shining (god) |

| | | | |
|---|---|---|---|
| | 兜率陀(天) | tuṣita(deva) | tuṣita (god) |
| 11 | 入 | āyatana | basis; sphere |
| | 从信行 | śraddhānusārin | faith-follower |
| | 从法行 | dharmānusārin | law-follower |
| | 内净 | adhyātmasaṃprasāda | serenity |
| 12 | 共因 | sahabhūhetu | concomitant cause |
| 15 | 决定 | niścita | certain |
| | | niyata | fixed |
| | 净 | śauceya | purification |
| | | śuddhaka | clean |
| | | śubha | pure |
| | 净居 | śuddhāvāsa | pure abode |
| | 习 | samudaya | origination |
| 16 | 凡夫 | pṛthagjana | common man |
| | 凡夫性 | pṛthagjanatva | state of being a common man |
| | 凡愚 | pṛthagjana | common man |
| 18 | 利根 | tīkṣṇendriya | having keen faculties |
| | 前生 | pūrvajanman | former birth |
| 19 | 力 | bala | power |
| | 功德 | puṇya | merit |
| | | guṇa | quality |
| | 办事 | kāritra | activity |
| 21 | 化乐(天) | nirmāṇarati(deva) | (god) enjoying magical creations |
| | 化生 | upapāduka | apparitionally born |
| 26 | 卵生 | aṇḍaja | egg-born |
| 27 | 厌 | nirveda | disgust |
| 29 | 受 | upātta | appropriated |
| | | upādāna | grasping |
| | | vedanā | feeling |

| | | | |
|---|---|---|---|
| | 受戒 | upasaṃpanna | ordained |
| | 受福(天) | puṇyaprasava(deva) | (god) having increase of merit |
| | 受边见 | antagrāhadṛṣṭi | view of extremes |
| | 圣 | ārya | noble |
| | 圣种 | āryavaṃśa | noble attitude |
| | 变化心 | nirmāṇacitta | magically transforming thought |
| | 变異 | anyathātva | change |
| 30 | 口业 | vākkarman | verbal action |
| | 句 | pada | sentence |
| | 可见 | sanidarśana | visible |
| | 名 | nāman | word |
| | 名色 | nāmarūpa | name-and-form |
| | 吾我见 | ātmadṛṣṭi | view of self |
| | 味 | rasa | taste |
| | | āsvādana | relishing |
| | | vyañjana | syllable; distinctive mark |
| | 善 | kuśala | wholesome |
| | 善根 | kuśalamūla | wholesome root |
| | 善见(天) | sudṛśa(deva) | clearly-visible (god) |
| | 善现(天) | sudarśana(deva) | clear-visioned (god) |
| | 善趣 | sugati | wholesome course |
| | 喜 | saumanasya | gladness |
| | | prīti | joy |
| | | mudita | sympathetic joy |
| 31 | 四王(天) | caturmahārājika(deva) | （gods of）the four great kings |
| | 因 | hetu | cause |
| | 因缘 | hetupratyaya | condition as cause |
| 32 | 土 | pṛthivī | earth |
| | 地 | bhūmi | stage |

| | | | |
|---|---|---|---|
| | 地狱 | naraka | hell |
| | 垢 | mala | stain |
| | 境界 | viṣaya | range |
| | 增上缘 | adhipatipratyaya | condition as dominant factor |
| | 增更乐 | adhivacanasaṃsparśa | contact of designation |
| | 增益 | vivṛddhi saṃcāra | increase |
| | 坏 | vyaya | passing away |
| 33 | 声闻 | śrāvaka | disciple |
| 34 | 处 | sthāna | what can be |
| | | upasthāna | application |
| | | vastu | object |
| | | deśa | place |
| | 处中 | madhyastha | situated in the middle |
| 37 | 大 | mahābhūta | great element |
| | 大地 | mahābhūmika | of great extent |
| | 天耳 | divyaśrotra | heavenly ear |
| | 天眼 | divyacakṣus | heavenly eye |
| 38 | 如 | nyāya | right (conduct) |
| | 如意足 | ṛddhipāda | basis of psychic power |
| | 妄言 | mṛṣāvāda | false speech |
| | 威仪 | airyāpathika | relating to deportment |
| | 嫉 | irṣyā | envy |
| 39 | 学 | śaikṣa | one in training |
| 40 | 安隐 | praśrabdhi | peace |
| | 定 | niścita | certain |
| | | samādhi | concentration |
| | | samāpatti | attainment |
| | | niyata | fixed, destined |
| | 定中间 | sāmantaka | adjacent concentration |

| | | | |
|---|---|---|---|
| | 家家 | kulaṃkula | one (destined to be reborn) in several families |
| | 宿命 | pūrvanivāsa | former lives |
| 42 | 少光(天) | parīttābha(deva) | (god of) limited radiance |
| | 少净(天) | parīttaśubha(deva) | (god of) limited magnificence |
| 44 | 尽 | kṣaya | extinction |
| | 尽智 | kṣayajñāna | knowledge of extinction |
| 48 | 工巧伎术 | śailpasthānika | relating to craftsmanship |
| 49 | 已知根 | ājñendriya | faculty of understanding |
| 50 | 常见 | śāśvatadṛṣṭi | view of eternity |
| 59 | 形 | vyañjana | distinctive mark |
| 60 | 得 | prāpti | obtainment |
| | 得修 | pratilambhabhāvanā | development which means acquisition |
| 61 | 心 | citta | thought |
| | 心不相应行 | cittaviprayuktasaṃskāra | formation not associated with thought |
| | 心共行 | cittānuparivartin | companion of thought |
| | 心心数法 | cittacaitasikā dharmāḥ | factors which constitute thought and its concomitants |
| | 心数法 | caitasikā dharmāḥ | factors which constitute thought's concomitants |
| | 心解脱 | cetovimukti | emancipation of the mind |
| | 必升进 | prativedhanādharman | one who will penetrate |
| | 忍 | kṣānti | patient acceptance |
| | 念 | smṛti | mindfulness |
| | 念法 | cetanādharman | one who wants (to end his existence) |
| | 怨 | pratigha | hatred |
| | 思 | cint° | to reflect |
| | | cetanā | volition |
| | 思惟 | saṃkalpa | intention |
| | 思惟断 | bhāvanāheya | to be abandoned through development |
| | 思惟道 | bhāvanāmārga | path of development |
| | 恚 | dveṣa | hatred |

| | 息止 | nirodha | cessation |
|---|---|---|---|
| | | śamatha | appeasing |
| | 悦 | prāmodya | elation |
| | 悔 | kaukṛtya | remorse |
| | 恶 | pāpa | evil |
| | | doṣa | fault |
| | | sāvadya | faulty |
| | 恶口 | paruṣavacana | harsh words |
| | 恶道 | durgati | woeful course |
| | 悲 | karuṇā | compassion |
| | 意 | manas | mind |
| | 意思食 | manaḥsaṃcetanāhāra | the food of volition |
| | 意业 | manaskarman | mental action |
| | 意止 | smṛtyupasthāna | application of mindfulness |
| | 意解希望 | adhimuktimanasikāra | attention through resolve |
| | 意解脱 | cetovimukti | emancipation of mind |
| | 意识 | manovijñāna | mind-consciousness |
| | 愚痴 | moha | foolishness |
| | 想 | saṃjñā | perception |
| | 想智灭 | saṃjñāveditanirodha | cessation of perception and feeling |
| | 慈 | maitrī | friendliness |
| | 愧 | apatrāpya | moral dread |
| | 慢 | māna | conceit |
| | 悭 | mātsarya | stinginess |
| | 忧 | śoka | sorrow |
| | | daurmanasya | sadness |
| | 惭 | hrī | shame |
| | 慧 | prajñā | wisdom |
| | 慧解脱 | prajñāvimukta | emancipation of wisdom |

| | | | |
|---|---|---|---|
| | 懈怠 | kausīdya | indolence |
| | 愿智 | praṇidhijñāna | knowledge resulting from resolve |
| | 忆宿命智 | pūrvanivāsānusmṛtijñāna | knowledge which is recollection of the former lives |
| 62 | 戒 | saṃvara | restraint |
| | | śīla | morality |
| | 戒盗 | śīlavrataparāmarśa | attachment to mere rules and ritual |
| | 我 | ātman | self |
| 63 | 所依果 | niṣyandaphala | fruition which represents the natural result |
| | 所作因 | kāraṇahetu | cause which is the reason of being |
| 64 | 扼 | yoga | attachment |
| | 掉 | auddhatya | excitedness |
| | 揣食 | kavaḍīkārāhāra | solid food |
| | 择法 | dharmapravicaya | investigation of the factors |
| | 报因 | vipākahetu | cause of retribution |
| | 报心 | vipākacitta | thought which is retribution |
| | 报果 | vipākaphala | fruition of retribution |
| | 摄 | saṃgṛhīta | comprised |
| | 护 | upekṣā | evenmindedness |
| | 护法 | anurakṣaṇādharman | one who guards |
| 66 | 放逸 | pramāda | heedlessness |
| | 教 | vijñapti | information |
| | 数缘灭 | pratisaṃkhyānirodha | cessation as a result of careful consideration |
| 69 | 断 | uccheda | annihilation |
| | 断智 | prahāṇaparijñā | full overcoming comprehension |
| | 断界 | prahāṇadhātu | the element abandonment |
| | 断见 | ucchedadṛṣṭi | view of annihilation |
| 70 | 方便 | prayoga | application, preparation |
| | | vyāyāma | exertion |
| | 施 | dāna | giving |

| 71 | 无垢 | amala | stainless |
|---|---|---|---|
| | 无学 | aśaikṣa | one who has no more training to do |
| | 无常 | anitya | impermanent |
| | 无恚 | adveṣa | absence of hatred |
| | 无思想 | āsaṃjñika | absence of perception |
| | 无惭 | āhrīkya | shamelessness |
| | 无愧 | anapatrāpya | absence of moral dread |
| | 无想天 | asaṃjñideva | god without perception |
| | 无想定 | asaṃjñisamāpatti | attainment without perception |
| | 无想众生 | asaṃjñisattva | being without perception |
| | 无愚痴 | amoha | absence of foolishness |
| | 无我 | anātma(ka) | selfless(ness) |
| | 无教 | avijñapti | non-information |
| | 无所有处 | ākiṃcanyāyatana | sphere of nothingness |
| | 无所畏 | vaiśāradya | fearlessness |
| | 无明 | avidyā | ignorance |
| | 无明更乐 | avidyāsparśa | contact of ignorance |
| | 无间业 | ānantaryakarman | deadly sin |
| | 无有爱 | vibhavatṛṣṇā | craving for non-existence |
| | 无欲界 | virāgadhātu | the element renunciation |
| | 无热 | nirjvara | without feverishness |
| | 无为 | asaṃskṛta | unformed |
| | 无生智 | anutpādajñāna | knowledge of non-production |
| | 无挂碍 | asakta | unhindered |
| | 无挂碍(天) | anabhraka(deva) | unclouded (god) |
| | 无相定 | ānimittasamādhi | concentration of the signless |
| | 无知根 | ājñātāvīndriya | faculty of one who has fully understood |
| | 无碍道 | ānantaryamārga | immediate path |
| | 无色定 | ārūpyasamāpatti | formless attainment |

| | | | |
|---|---|---|---|
| | 无著 | arhat | one without attachment |
| | 无著果 | arhattvaphala | fruition of arhatship |
| | 无记 | avyākṛta | indeterminate |
| | 无贪 | alobha | absence of covetousness |
| | 无量 | apramāṇa | immeasurable |
| | 无量光(天) | apramāṇābha(deva) | (god of) unlimited radiance |
| | 无量净(天) | apramāṇaśubha (deva) | (god of) unlimited magnificence |
| | 无量空处 | ākāśānantyāyatana | sphere of unlimited space |
| | 无量识处 | vijñānānantyāyatana | sphere of consciousness |
| | 无愿定 | apraṇihitasamādhi | concentration of aimlessness |
| 72 | 暖 | uṣmagata | warmth |
| | 明更乐 | vidyāsparśa | contact of wisdom |
| | 是处非处力 | sthānāsthānabala | power of what can be and what cannot be |
| | 时解脱 | samayavimukta | temporarily released |
| | 智 | jñāna | knowledge |
| | 智力 | jñānabala | power of knowledge |
| | 普遍因 | sarvatragahetu | universal cause |
| 73 | 曲 | kauṭilya | crookedness |
| | 更乐 | sparśa | contact |
| | 更乐食 | sparśāhāra | food of contact |
| | 最胜 | jina | most excellent one |
| 74 | 有对 | sapratigha | with resistance |
| | 有对更乐 | pratighasaṃsparśa | contact with resistance |
| | 有爱 | bhavarāga | desire for existence |
| | | bhavatṛṣṇā | craving for existence |
| | 有漏 | sāsrava | impure |
| | 有为 | saṃskṛta | formed |
| 75 | 未来禅 | anāgamyadhyāna | pre-trance |

| | | | |
|---|---|---|---|
| | 未知忍 | anvayakṣānti | subsequent patient acceptance |
| | 未知智 | anvayajñāna | subsequent knowledge |
| | 未知根 | anājñātam ājñāsyāmīndriya | the faculty "I shall come to under-stand the not yet understood" |
| | 枝 | aṅga | member |
| | 果实(天) | bṛhatphala(deva) | (god) having great fruition |
| | 根 | indriya | faculty |
| | | mūla | root |
| | 根本 | maula° | fundamental |
| | 根本有 | pūrvakālabhava | existence properly speaking |
| | 梵天 | brahmadeva | brahma-god |
| | 梵富楼(天) | brahmapurohita (deva) | brahmapurohita (god) |
| | 梵行 | brahmacarya | pure conduct |
| | 梵身(天) | brahmakāyika(deva) | (god) of brahma's group |
| | 极微 | paramāṇu | molecule |
| | 极生生死七 | saptakṛtvobhavaparama | reborn seven times at the most |
| | 乐 | sukha | happiness; pleasant |
| | 乐居 | sukhavihāra | happy state |
| | （業）业 | karman | action |
| | （業）业道 | karmapatha | path of action |
| | 杀生 | prāṇātipāta | taking life |
| 76 | 次第緣 | samanantarapratyaya | condition as immediate antecedent |
| | 欲 | chandas | desire-to-do |
| | 欲爱 | kāmarāga | desire for sensuous pleasure |
| | 欲界 | kāmadhātu | realm of desire |
| | 软 | mṛdu | weak |
| 77 | 止 | śamatha | appeasing |
| | 正命 | samyagājīva | right livelihood |
| | 正志 | samyaksaṃkalpa | right intention |

| | | | |
|---|---|---|---|
| | 正断 | samyakprahāṇa | right rejection |
| | 正方便 | samyagvyāyāma | right exertion |
| | 正业 | samyakkarmānta | right action |
| | 正觉 | samyaksaṃbuddha | fully awakened one |
| | 正语 | samyagvāc | right speech |
| 78 | 死有 | maraṇabhava | existence at death |
| 85 | 沙门果 | śrāmaṇyaphala | fruition of *śramaṇaship* |
| | 没尽 | antardhāna | vanishing |
| | 法忍 | dharmakṣānti | patient acceptance of the law |
| | 法智 | dharmajñāna | knowledge of the law |
| | 法辨 | dharmapratisaṃvid | analytical knowledge of factors |
| | 流 | ogha | flood |
| | 满 | mauneya | *mauneya* (sageliness) |
| | 漏尽通智 | āsravakṣayābhijñā | superknowledge of the extinction of the outflows |
| | 浊 | kaṣāya | impurity |
| | 湿生 | saṃsvedaja | moisture-born |
| 86 | 炎摩(天) | yāma(deva) | yāma (gods) |
| | 灭 | nirodha | cessation |
| | 灭界 | nirodhadhātu | the element cessation |
| | 灭尽定 | nirodhasamāpatti | attainment of cessation |
| | 烦恼 | kleśa | affliction |
| | 熏 | vyavakīrṇa | mixed |
| 87 | 爱 | tṛṣṇā | craving |
| 94 | 猗 | praśrabdhi | repose |
| | 犹豫 | vicikitsā | doubt |
| 96 | 现法 | dṛṣṭadharma | the visible world |
| 100 | 生 | jāti | birth |
| | 生有 | upapattibhava | existence at birth |
| | 生死智 | cyutyupapādajñāna | knowledge of birth and death |

| 102 | 界 | dhātu | realm; element |
|---|---|---|---|
| | 畜生 | tiryagyoni | animal birth |
| 103 | 疑 | vicikitsā | doubt |
| 104 | 痛 | vedanā | feeling |
| | 痴 | moha | foolishness |
| 109 | 相 | lakṣaṇa | characteristic |
| | 相应 | saṃprayukta | associated |
| | 相应因 | saṃprayuktakahetu | associated cause |
| | 相续 | saṃtati | series |
| | 眠 | middha | sleepiness |
| | 睡 | styāna | sloth |
| | 瞋恚 | vyāpāda pratigha | hatred |
| 111 | 知足 | saṃtuṣṭi | contentment |
| 113 | 神通 | abhijñā | superknowledge |
| | 禅 | dhyāna | trance |
| 115 | 种 | bīja | seed |
| | | prakāra | kind |
| | 秽 | doṣa | uncleanliness |
| | 秽污 | kliṣṭa | defiled |
| 116 | 空 | ākāśa | space |
| | | śūnyatā | emptiness |
| 118 | 第一 | parama | best |
| | 第一有 | bhavāgra | the summit of existence |
| | 等住 | sthitākampya | one who abides unshakable |
| | 等智 | saṃvṛtijñāna | conventional knowledge |
| | 等谛 | saṃvṛtisatya | conventional truth |
| 119 | 精进 | vīrya | vigorous pursuit |
| | 粗 | sthūla | coarse |
| 120 | 细 | sūkṣma | subtle |

| | | | |
|---|---|---|---|
| | 细滑 | spraṣṭavya | tactile |
| | 结 | saṃyojana | fetter |
| | 绮语 | saṃbhinnapralāpa | frivolous talk |
| | 缘 | ālambana | object |
| | | pratyaya | condition |
| | 缘使 | ālambanato'nuśerate | developed by the object |
| | 缘缘 | ālambanapratyaya | condition as object |
| | 缘起 | pratītyasamutpāda | conditioned co-production |
| | 缠 | saṃyojana | fetter |
| 122 | 罢 | pratyākhyāna | refusal |
| 128 | 闻 | śruta | learning |
| 130 | 胎生 | jarāyuja | born from the womb |
| 132 | 自然因 | sabhāgahetu | similar cause |
| 139 | 色 | rūpa | form |
| | 色究竟(天) | akaniṣṭha(deva) | the highest (god) |
| 140 | 苦 | duḥkha | suffering; unpleasant |
| | 苦法忍 | duḥkhe dharmakṣānti | patient acceptance of the law in relation to suffering |
| 141 | 虚空 | ākāśa | space |
| 144 | 行 | saṃskāra | formation |
| | | ākāra | aspect |
| | | carita | conduct |
| | 行修 | niṣevaṇabhāvanā | development which involves practice |
| 147 | 见 | dṛṣṭi | view |
| | | darśana | vision |
| | 见到 | dṛṣṭiprāpta | one who has attained correct views |
| | 见处 | dṛṣṭisthāna | place of the views |
| | 见道 | darśanamārga | path of vision |
| | 见盗 | dṛṣṭiparāmarśa | evil adherence to wrong views |
| | 觉 | vitarka | adjusted thinking |

| | | | |
|---|---|---|---|
| | | bodhi | awakenment |
| | 观 | vicāra | discursive thinking |
| | | abhisamaya | intuitive realisation |
| | | vipaśyanā | insight |
| | 观察 | upanidhyāna | examining |
| 148 | 解脱 | adhimukti | resolve |
| | | visaṃyoga | disconnection |
| | | vimukti vimokṣa | deliverance |
| | 解脱果 | visaṃyogaphala | fruition of disconnection |
| | 解脱道 | vimuktimārga | path of deliverance |
| 149 | 说处 | kathāvastu | ground of discourse |
| | 诤 | raṇa | strife |
| | 谄伪 | śāṭhya | deceit |
| | 调 | auddhatya | excitedness |
| | 调御 | dama | self-discipline |
| | 谤 | apavadŎ | to deny |
| | 识 | vijñāna | consciousness |
| | 识住 | vijñānasthiti | abode of consciousness |
| | 识食 | vijñānāhāra | food of consciousness |
| 154 | 贪 | lobha abhidhyā | covetousness |
| | 贤 | ārya | noble |
| 156 | 趣 | gati | course |
| | 趣向 | pratipannaka | one who progresses |
| 158 | 身 | kāya | group, collection |
| | 身业 | kāyakarman | bodily action |
| | 身见 | satkāyadṛṣṭi | view of individuality |
| | 身证 | kāyasākṣin | bodily witness |
| 160 | 辨 | pratisaṃvid | analytical knowledge |
| | 辞辨 | niruktipratisaṃvid | analytical knowledge of expression |

| | | | |
|---|---|---|---|
| 162 | 近 | āsanna | near |
| | 迹 | pratipatti | track |
| | 退 | parihāṇi | falling away |
| | 退法 | parihāṇadharman | one who falls away |
| | 造色 | upādāyarūpa | derivative form |
| | 通 | abhijñā | superknowledge |
| | 进 | vīrya | vigorous pursuit |
| | 道 | gati | course |
| | | mārga | path |
| | | pratipad | path (of progress) |
| | 道品 | bodhipākṣika | contributing to awakenment |
| | 道路 | adhvan | time |
| | 遍净(天) | śubhakṛtsna(deva) | entirely magnificent (god) |
| | 远 | vidūra | far |
| | 边 | sāmantaka | adjacent |
| | 边见 | antagrāhadṛṣṭi | view of extremes |
| 163 | 邪行 | mithyācāra | wrong conduct |
| | 邪见 | mithyādṛṣṭi | wrong view |
| 167 | 金刚喻定 | vajropamasamādhi | diamond-like concentration |
| | 钝 | mṛdu | weak (dull) |
| 169 | 门 | paryāya | category |
| 170 | 除入 | abhibhvāyatana | sphere of mastery |
| | 阴 | skandha | aggregate |
| | 障 | āvaraṇa | obstruction |
| | 障碍 | āvṛ° | to obstruct |
| | 隐没 | nivṛta | obscure |
| 174 | 青 | nīla | blue |
| 175 | 非想非非想处 | naivasaṃjñānāsaṃjñāyatana | the sphere of neither-perception-nor-non-perception |
| | 非戒 | duḥśīla | immoral |

| | | | |
|---|---|---|---|
| | 非我 | anātmaka | selfless(ness) |
| | 非数缘灭 | apratisaṃkhyānirodha | cessation not as a result of careful consideration |
| | 非明非无明更乐 | naivavidyānāvidyāsparśa | contact of neither-wisdom-nor-ignorance |
| | 非梵行 | abrahmacarya | impure conduct |
| 181 | 顶 | mūrdhan | summit |
| | | prāntakoṭika | uppermost |
| | 颠倒 | viparyāsa | perversity |
| 184 | 食 | āhāra | food |
| | 饿鬼 | preta | hungry ghost |
| 186 | 香 | gandha | smell |

# Concordance

The stanzas of the ten chapters of Dharmaśreṣṭhin.

| | | AH | AH2 | MAH |
|---|---|---|---|---|
| I. Dhātu. | | | | |
| | 1 | 809a | 833c | 870a |
| | 2 | 809a | 833c | 870c |
| | 3 | 809a | 834a | 871a |
| | 4 | 809b | 834b | 871a |
| | 5 | 809b | 834b | 871a |
| | 6 | 809b | 834c | 871b |
| | 7 | 809c | 834c | 871c |
| | 8 | 809c | 835a | 871c |
| | 9 | 809c | 835a | 871c/872a |
| | 10 | 809c | 835b | 874b |
| | 11 | 810a | 835c | 875b |
| | 12 | 810a | 836a | 875c |
| | 13 | 810a | 836a | 875c |
| | 14 | 810b | 836b | 880b |
| II. Saṃskāra. | | | | |
| | 15 | 810b | 836bc | 880c |
| | 16 | 810b | 836c | 880c/881a |
| | 17 | 810c | 836c | 881a |
| | 18 | 810c | 836c | 881a |
| | 19 | 810c | 837a | 881a |
| | 20 | 810c/811a | 837a | 881c |
| | 21 | 811a | 837b | 882a |
| | 22 | 811a | 837c | 882a |
| | 23 | 811b | 837c | 882b |
| | 24 | 811b | 837c | 882b |
| | 25 | 811c | 838a | 883a |
| | 26 | 811c | 838b | 885a |
| | 27 | 811c | 838b | 885b |

| | | | | |
|---|---|---|---|---|
| | 28 | 812a | 838c | 885b |
| | 29 | 812a | 838c | 885b |
| | 30 | 812a | 838c | 885c |
| | 31 | 812a | 839a | 886b |
| | 32 | 812b | 839a | 887c |
| III. Karma. | | | | |
| | 33 | 812b | 839c | 888a |
| | 34 | 812b | 839c | 888b |
| | 35 | 812b | 840a | 888b |
| | 36 | 812c | 840a | 888c |
| | 37 | 812c | 840b | 888c |
| | 38 | 813a | 840b | 889a |
| | 39 | 813a | 840b | 889b |
| | 40 | 813a | 840c | 889b |
| | 41 | 813b | 840c | 889c |
| | 42 | 813b | 841a | 889c |
| | 43 | 813b | 841a | 889c |
| | 44 | 813b | – | 889c |
| | 45 | 813c | 841a | 890a |
| | 46 | 813c | 841ab | 890a |
| | 47 | 813c | 841b | 890a |
| | 48 | 813c | 841b | 890a |
| | 49 | 813c | 841c | 891b |
| | 50 | 814a | 841c | 892b (3) |
| | 51 | 814a | 841c | 892bc (3) |
| | 52 | 814a | 842a | 893a |
| | 53 | 814a | 842a | 893a |
| | 54 | 814b | 842b | 895c |
| | 55 | 814b | 842b | 896a |
| | 56 | 814b | 842c | 896a |
| | 57 | 814c | 842c | 896b |
| | 58 | 814c | 842c | 896b |
| | 59 | 814c | 843a | 896c |
| | 60 | 814c | 843a | 897a |
| | 61 | 815a | 843a | 897a |

| | | | |
|---|---|---|---|
| 62 | 815a | 843b | 898a |
| 63 | 815a | 843b | 898b |
| 64 | 815ab | 843c | 898b |

IV. Anuśaya.

| | | | |
|---|---|---|---|
| 65 | 815b | 843c | 899c |
| 66 | 815b | 844a | 899c |
| 67 | 815b | 844a | 900a |
| 68 | 815b | 844a | 900a |
| 69 | 815bc | 844b | 900a |
| 70 | 815c | 844b | 900ab |
| 71 | 815c | 844b | 900b |
| 72 | 815c | 844c | 900b |
| 73 | 815c | 844c | 900bc |
| 74 | 816a | 845a | 900c |
| 75 | 816a | 845b | 901a |
| 76 | 816a | 845c | 901b |
| 77 | 816b | 845c | 902a |
| 78 | 816b | 845c/846a | 902a |
| 79 | 816b | 846a | 902a |
| 80 | 816b | 846a | 902c |
| 81 | 816c | 846b | 903a |
| 82 | 816c | 846b | 903b |
| 83 | 816c | 846c | _ |
| 84 | 817a | 846c | _ |
| 85 | 817a | 846c | _ |
| 86 | 817a | 847a | 903b |
| 87 | 817a | 847a | 905a |
| 88 | 817a | 847a | 905a |
| 89 | 817b | 847b | 905b |
| 90 | 817b | 847b | 904a |
| 91 | 817b | 847b | 904b |
| 92 | 817b | 847c | 904c |
| 93 | 817c | 847c | 905b |
| 94 | 817c | 847c | 905c |
| 95 | 817c | 848a | 906a |

| | | | |
|---|---|---|---|
| 96 | 817c/818a | 848b | 907b |

V. Ārya.

| | | | |
|---|---|---|---|
| 97 | 818a | 848b | 908a |
| 98 | 818a | 848c | 908a |
| 99 | 818a | 848c | 908b |
| 100 | 818a | 848c | 909b |
| 101 | 818b | 849a | 909b |
| 102 | 818b | 849b | 909c |
| 103 | 818c | _ | 910a |
| 104 | 818c | 849c | 910ab |
| 105 | 818c | 894c | 910b |
| 106 | 819a | 894c | 910c |
| 107 | 819a | 850a | _ |
| 108 | 819a | 850a | 911a |
| 109 | 819a | 850a | 911ab |
| 110 | 819b | 850b | _ |
| 111 | 819b | 850b | 913a |
| 112 | 819b | 850c | 913b |
| 113 | 819b | 850c | 913bc |
| 114 | 819c | 850c | 913c |
| 115 | 819c | 851a | 914a |
| 116 | 819c/820a | 851a | 914a |
| 117 | 820a | 851b | 914c |
| 118 | 820a | 851b | 914c |
| 119 | 820a | 851b | 914c |
| 120 | 820a | 851c | 915b |
| 121 | 820ab | 851c | 915c |
| 122 | 820b | 852a | 916a |

VI. Jñāna.

| | | | |
|---|---|---|---|
| 123 | 820b | 852a | 916c |
| 124 | 820b | 852b | 916c |
| 125 | 820c | 852b | 916c |
| 126 | 820c | 852b | 917a |
| 127 | 820c | 852c | 918b |

| | | | |
|---|---|---|---|
| 128 | 820c/821a | 852c | 918b |
| 129 | 821a | 852c | 918bc |
| 130 | 821a | 852c/853a | 918c |
| 131 | 821a | 853a | _ |
| 132 | 821b | 853b | 918c |
| 133 | 821b | 853b | 919a |
| 134 | 821b | 853c | 919b |
| 135 | 821c | 853c | 919b |
| 136 | 821c | 853c | 919c |
| 137 | 821c | 854a | 919c |
| 138 | 822a | 854a | 919c |
| 139 | 822a | 854b | 920a |
| 140 | 822a | 854b | 920a |
| 141 | 822b | 854c | 920b |
| 142 | 822b | 854c | 920b |
| 143 | 822b | 855a | 920b |
| 144 | 822c | 855a | 920c |
| 145 | 822c | 855b | _ |
| 146 | 823a | 855b | 921a |
| 147 | 823a | 855c | _ |

VII. Samādhi.

| | | | |
|---|---|---|---|
| 148 | 823ab | 856a | 923c |
| 149 | 823b | 856a | 924a |
| 150 | 823b | 856a | 924a |
| 151 | 823b | 856b | 924b |
| 152 | 823c | 856b | 924c |
| 153 | 823c | 856c | 924c |
| 154 | 824a | 857a | 925a |
| 155 | 824a | 857a | 925b |
| 156 | 824a | 857a | 925b |
| 157 | 824b | 857b | _ |
| 158 | 824b | 857c | 927c |
| 159 | 824b | 857c | 928a |
| 160 | 824b | 857c | 928a |
| 161 | 824c | 857c | 928b |

| | | | |
|---|---|---|---|
| 162 | 824c | 858a | 928c |
| 163 | 824c | 858a | 928c |
| 164 | 825a | 858b | 929b |
| 165 | 825a | 858b | 929b |
| 166 | 825b | 858b | 929c |
| 167 | 825b | 858c | 929c |
| 168 | 825b | 858c | 930a |
| 169 | 825b | 859a | 930a |
| 170 | 825c | 859a | 930a |
| 171 | 825c | 859a | _ |
| 172 | 825c | 859b | _ |
| 173 | 826a | 859b | 930b |
| 174 | 826a | 859b | 930c |
| 175 | 826a | 859c | _ |

VIII. Sūtra.

| | | | |
|---|---|---|---|
| 176 | 826b | 860a | 931b |
| 177 | 826b | 860a | 934b |
| 178 | 826c | 860a | 934c |
| 179 | 826c | 860b | 935a |
| 180 | 826c | 860b | 935b |
| 181 | 827a | 860c | 935b |
| 182 | 827a | 860c | 936b |
| 183 | 827a | 861a | 936b |
| 184 | 827b | 861a | 936c |
| 185 | 827b | 861b | 936c |
| 186 | 827b | 861b | 937a |
| 187 | 827c | 861bc | 937a |
| 188 | 827c | 861c | 937a |
| 189 | 827c/828a | 862a | 937b |
| 190 | 828a | 862a | 937b |
| 191 | 828a | 862a | 937bc |
| 192 | 828a | 862b | 937c |
| 193 | 828b | 862b | 938a |
| 194 | 828b | 862c | 938b |
| 195 | 828b | 862c | 938c |

| | | | |
|---|---|---|---|
| 196 | 828b | 862c | 938c |
| 197 | 828c | 863a | 939a |
| 198 | 828c | 863a | 939a |
| 199 | 828c | 863b | 939a |
| 200 | 829a | 863b | 939b |
| 201 | 829a | 863c | 939c |
| 202 | 829a | 863c | 939c |
| 203 | 829b | 864a | 940a |
| 204 | 829b | 864a | 940ab |
| 205 | 829b | 864a | 940b |
| 206 | 829b | 864b | 940c |
| 207 | 829c | 864c | 940c |
| 208 | 829c | 864c | 940c |
| 209 | 829c | 864c | 941a |
| 210 | 830a | 865a | 941c |
| 211 | 830a | 865a | 941c |
| 212 | 830a | 865a | 942a |
| 213 | 830b | 865b | 942a |
| 214 | 830b | 865b | 942a |
| 215 | 830b | 865b | 942b |

IX. Prakīrṇaka.

| | | | |
|---|---|---|---|
| 216 | 830bc | 865c | 942b |
| 217 | 830c | 865c | 942bc |
| 218 | 830c | 865c | 942c |
| 219 | 830c | 865c | 942c |
| 220 | 830c | 866a | 942c |
| 221 | 830c | 866a | 943b |
| 222 | 831a | 866a | 943b |
| 223 | 831a | 866b | 943b |
| 224 | 831ab | 866b | 943c |
| 225 | 831b | 866bc | 944a |
| 226 | 831b | 866c | 944a |
| 227 | 831c | 866c/867a | 944b |
| 228 | 831c | 867a | 944b |
| 229 | 831c/832a | 867a | 944c |

| | | | |
|---|---|---|---|
| 230 | 832a | 867b | 945a |
| 231 | 832a | 867b | 945a |
| 232 | 832ab | 867c | 945a |
| 233 | 832b | 867c | 945b |
| 234 | 832b | 867c | 945b |
| 235 | 832b | 868a | 945b |
| 236 | 832b | 868a | 945c |
| 237 | 832c | 868b | 945c |
| 238 | 832c | 868b | 946a |
| 239 | 832c | 868b | 946b |
| 240 | 832c | 868c | 946a |

X.Kathā .

| | | | |
|---|---|---|---|
| 241 | 833a | 868c | 963c |
| 242 | 833a | 869a | 964a |
| 243 | 833a | 869a | 964a |
| 244 | 833a | 869a | 964a |
| 245 | 833a | 869a | 964a |
| 246 | 833a | 869a | 964a |
| 247 | 833a | 869ab | 964b |
| 248 | 833a | 869b | 964b |
| 249 | 833a | 869b | 964b |
| 250 | 833b | 869b | 964b |

# Bibliography


- *Taishō Shinshū Daizōkyō* 大正新修大藏經. Edited by J. Takakusu and K. Watanabe. Vol. XXVIII (Tōkyō 1925).
  No. 1550: 阿 毗 昙 心 论 *Epitanxinlun* (*Abhidharmahṛdaya*), by Dharmaśreṣṭhin.
  No. 1551: 阿 毗 昙 心 论 经 *Epitanxinlunjing* (*Abhidharmahṛdaya*), by Upaśānta.
  No. 1552: 杂 阿 毗 昙 心 论 *Zaepitanxinlun* (*Miśrakābhidharmahṛdaya*), by Dharmatrāta.
- Akanuma Chizen 赤沼 智善. 1967. *Indo Bukkyō Koyū Meishi Jiten* 印度佛教固有名词辞典. Kyōto Hōshōkan.
- Ch'en, Kenneth. 1964. *Buddhism in China*. Princeton: Princeton University Press.
- Chây, Thích Thiên. 1999. *The Literature of the Personalists of Early Buddhism*. Translated by Sarah Boin-Webb. Buddhist traditions 39. Delhi: Motilal Banarsidass Publishers.
- Demiéville, Paul. 1932. L'origine des sectes bouddhiques d'après Paramārtha. *Mélanges Chinois et Bouddhiques* 1: 15-64.
  -1961. Un fragment Sanskrit de l'abhidharma des sarvāstivādins. *J.A.* 249: 461-475.
- Dessein, Bart. 1998. *Saṃyuktābhidharmahṛdaya*. 3 Parts. Buddhist Tradition Series 33-35. Delhi: Motilal Banarsidass Publishers.
- Dhammajoti, Bhikkhu Kuala Lumpur. 1998. *Entrance into the Supreme Doctrine*. Kelaniya: University of Kelaniya.
- Frauwallner, Erich. 1963. Abhidharma-Studien. *WZKSO*, 7: 20-36.
  -1964. Abbhidharma-Studien. *WZKSO*, 8: 59-99.
  -1971. Abbhidharma-Studien. *WZKS*, 15: 69-121.
  -1971b. *Die Entstehung der buddhistischen Systeme*. Nachrichten der Akademie der Wissenschaften in

Göttingen. Philologisch-Historische Klasse, 6. Göttingen: Vandenhoeck and Ruprecht.
-1972. Abbhidharma-Studien. *WZKS*, 16: 95-152.
-1973. Abbhidharma-Studien. *WZKS*, 17: 97-121.

- Fussman, Gérard. 1994. Upāya-kauśalya. L' implantation du bouddhisme au Gandhāra. In *Bouddhisme et Cultures Locales. Quelques cas de réciproques adaptations*, ed. by Fukui Fumimasa and Gérard Fussman, 17-51. Études Thématiques EFEO 2. Paris.
- Fujieda, Akira. 1969. The Tunhuang Manuscripts (II) Dating of the Manuscripts and the Copying Offices. *Zinbun*, 10: 17-39.
- Giles, Lionel. 1957. *Descriptive Catalogue of the Chinese Manuscripts from Tunhuang in the British Museum*. London.
- Haloun, Gustav. 1937. Zur üe-tṣī-Frage. *ZDMG*, 91: 243-318.
- Hinüber, Oskar von. 1996. *A Handbook of Pāli Literature*. Indian Philology and South Asian Studies, Vol. 2. Berlin, New York: Walter de Gruyter.
- Hirakawa, Akira. 1993. *A History of Indian Buddhism. From Śākyamuni to Early Mahāyāna*. Translated by Paul Groner. Buddhist Tradition Series 19. Delhi: Motilal Banarsidass Publishers.
- Imanishi, Junkichi. 1969. *Das Pañcavastukam und die Pañcavastukavibhāṣā*. Nachrichten der Akademie der Wissenschaften in Göttingen: Vandenhoeck and Ruprecht.
- Kimura Taiken 木村泰贤. 1974. *Kimura Taiken Zenshū*. Vol. 4, Abidatsumaron no Kenkyū. 木村泰贤全集 4 阿毗达磨论の研究. Tōkyō: Daihōrinkaku.
- La Vallée Poussin , Louis de. 1971. *L'Abhidharmakośa de Vasubandhu*. 6 vols. Brussels: Institut Belge des Hautes Études Chinoises.

- Lalji 'Shravak'. 2001. Miśrakābhidharmahṛdayaśāstra: Fusion of Bahirdeśaka and Kāśmīra Abhidharma Traditions. *The Indian International Journal of Buddhist Studies*, 2: 71-84.
- Lamotte, Étienne. 1966. *Le traité de la grande vertu de sagesse de Nāgārjuna*. Tome I. Louvain: Institut Orientaliste.

  -1988. *History of Indian Buddhism*. Translated by S. Webb-Boin. Louvain: Institut Orientaliste.
- Li, Rongxi. 1996. *The Great Tang Dynasty Record of the Western Regions*. BDK English Tripiṭaka 79. Berkeley: Numata Center.
- Liebenthal, Walter. 1952. The Immortality of the Soul in Chinese Thought. *Monumenta Nipponica*, 8: 327-397.
- Lin, Li-kouang. 1949. *L'aide-mémoire de la vraie loi. Introduction au compendium de la loi*. Paris: Librairie d'Amérique et d'Orient.
- Litvinsky, B.A., ed. 1999. *History of Civilizations of Central Asia*. Vol. 3. Delhi: Motilal Banarsidass Publishers.
- Lü Cheng 吕澄. 1979a. *Zhongguo Foxue Yuanliu Lüejiang* 中国佛学源流略讲. Beijing: Zhonghua Shujü.

  -1979b. *Yindu Foxue Yuanliu Lüejiang* 印度佛学源流略讲. Shanghai: Renmin Chubanshe.
- Mochizuki Shinkō 望月信亨. 1961. *Mochizuki Bukkyō Daijiten* 望月佛教大辞典. 10 vols. Kyōto: Sekai Seiten Kankō Kyōkai.
- Oda Tokunō 识田得能. 2000. *Bukkyō Daijiten* 佛教大辞典. Tōkyō: Daizō Shuppansha.
- Ono Genmyō 小野玄妙 and Maruyama Takao 丸山孝雄. 2000. *Bussho Kaisetsu Daijiten* 佛书解说大辞典. Compact edition. Tōkyō: Daitō Shuppansha.
- Pelliot, Paul. 1930. Les stances d'introduction de l' Abhidharmahṛdayaśāstra. *J.A.*, 217: 267-273.

- Potter, Karl H., ed. 1996. *Encyclopedia of Indian Philosophies*. Vol. 7, *Abhidharma Buddhism to 150 A.D.* and Vol. 8, *Buddhist Philosophy from 100 to 350 A.D.* Delhi: Motilal Banarsidass Publishers.
- Ren Jiyu 任继愈, ed. 1985. *Zhongguo Fojiaoshi* 中国佛教史. Vol. 2. Beijing: Zhongguo Shehuikexue Chubanshe.
- Ryose, Wataru S. 1986. The Position of the Abhidharmahṛdaya in the Historical Development of Sārvastivāda Thought. *Abhidharma Research Institute Kiyō*, 5: 1-16.
- Shih, Robert. 1968. *Biographies des moines éminents.* Kao Seng Tchouan de Houei-kiao. Louvain: Institut Orientaliste.
- Stache-Rosen, Valentina. 1968. *Dogmatische Begriffsreihen im älteren Buddhismus II. Das Saṅgītisūtra und sein Kommentar Saṅgītiparyāya*. 2 vols. Berlin: AkademieVerlag.
- Tang Yongtong 汤用彤. 1938. *Han Wei Liang-Jin Nanbeichao Fojiaoshi* 汉魏两晋南北朝佛教史. Changsha: Commercial Press.
- Takakusu, Junjiro. 1904-1905. On the Abhidharma Literature of the Sarvāstivādins. *Journal of the Pali Text Society*, 5 (1897-1907): 67-146.
- Tsukamoto Zenryū 塚本善隆. 1968. *Chūgoku Bukkyō Tsūshi* 中国佛教通史. Tōkyō: Suzuki Gakujutsu Zaidan.
- Van Den Broeck, José. 1977. *La saveur de l'immortel.* Louvain: Institut Orientaliste.
- Watanabe Baiyū 渡边梅雄 and Mizuno Kōgen 水野弘元. 1976. *Kokuyaku Issai Kyō*. Vol. 20, *Bidonbu*. 国译一切经 20 毗昙部. Tōkyō: Daitō Shuppansha.
- Watanabe Baiyū 渡边梅雄, Mizuno Kōgen 水野弘元 and Ōishi Hidenori 大石秀典. 1976. *Kokuyaku Issai*

*Kyō*. Vol. 21, *Bidonbu*. 国译一切经 21 毗昙部. Tōkyō: Daitō Shuppansha.

- Willemen, Charles. 1978. *The Chinese Udānavarga: A Collection of Important Odes of the Law (Fa chi yao sung ching)*. Mélanges Chinois et Bouddhiques 19. Brussels: Institut Belge des Hautes Études Chinoises.
  -1988a. New Ideas about Sarvāstivāda Abhidharma. *The Indian Journal of Buddhist Studies*, 10: 82-94.
  -, Bart Dessein and Collet Cox. 1998b. *Sarvāstivāda Buddhist Scholasticism*. Handbuch der Orientalistik Abt. 2, Indien 11. Leiden: E.J. Brill.
  -1999-2000. The Indian Background of Buddhism in China. Some Facts and Remarks. *The Indian International Journal of Buddhist Studies*, 1: 45-49.
  -2001. Sarvāstivāda Developments in Northwestern India and in China. *The Indian International Journal of Buddhist Studies*, 2: 163-169.
  -2001b. Sarvāstivāda Dhyāna and Mahāyāna Prajñā. Observations about their Development in India and in China. *Asiatische Studien/Études Asiatiques*, 55: 529-534.
  -2004. *From where did Zen come? Dhyāna in the Early Buddhist Tradition.* Numata Lecture Series, Calgary.
- Wogihara Unrai 荻原云来, ed. 1959. *The Sanskrit-Chinese Dictionary of Buddhist Technical Terms, based on the Mahāvyutpatti*. Tōkyō: Sankibō.
  -1971. *Sphūṭārthā Abhidharmakośavyākhyā. The Work of Yaśomitra*. 2 vols. Tōkyō: Sankibō.
  -2001. *Bon-Wa Daijiten*. 梵和大词典. Tōkyō: Kōdansha.
- Yamada Ryūjō 山天龙成. 1959. *Daijō Bukkyō Seiritsuron Josetsu*. 大乘佛教成立论予说. Kyōto: Heirakuji Shoten.
- You Xia 游侠. 1982. Biography of Saṃghadeva in *Zhongguo Fojiao* 中国佛教. Vol. 2, compiled by Zhongguo Fojiao Xiehui. Beijing: Zhishi Chubanshe.

- Zürcher, Erik. 1972. *The Buddhist Conquest of China*. Sinica Leidensia 11. Leiden: E.J. Brill.